TRANSFER TO
MUNICH

TRANSFER TO
MUNICH

by

RAYMOND M. WEINSTEIN

Jordan & Simon Publishers
White Plains, New York

Published in the United States

Jordan & Simon Publishers
c/o R.M. Weinstein
2 Old Mamaroneck Road
Apartment 4C
White Plains, NY, 10605
914-258-8094
website: www.soldiersfieldnovel.com
e-mail: rayw@usca.edu

COVER DESIGN by Andria Mikkola and Michael St. John

COVER PHOTOGRAPH OF HENRY KASERNE, 1960
  by permission of Stephen A. Wilson

Books by the author

Soldiers' Field: A Novel of Postwar Germany

Assignment to Nuremberg

Dedicated to my six Weinstein grandchildren

MICHAEL, CLAIRE, MARY,

SOPHIE, EMMA, and ASHER

For the joy they bring to their Zeyde

RELATED PUBLICATIONS

2006   Weinstein, R. M., "Occupation G.I. Blues: Postwar Germany During and After Elvis Presley's Tour," *Journal of Popular Culture*, 39:126-149.

2007   Weinstein, R. M., "Foreword," in Peter Heigl, *Sergeant Elvis Presley in Grafenwöhr*, Amberg: Buch & Kunstverlag Oberpfalz, pp. 5-11.

2010   Weinstein, R.M., "Erinnerungen an Nürnberg 1959-1960: Ein Amerikanischer Soldat in Nachkreigsdeutschland," in Gerhard Jochem (Ed.), *Transit Nürnberg*, Volume 4, Nürnberg: Verlag Testimon, pp. 39-66.

2010   Weinstein, R.M., "Nuremberg 1959-1960 Remembered: An American Soldier in Postwar Germany, in Gerhard Jochem (Ed.), *Transit Nürnberg*, Volume 4, Nürnberg: Verlag Testimon, pp. 66-92.

TABLE OF CONTENTS

PAGE

PROLOGUE: THE COMPANY I KEEP

On January 18, 1960, at 0920 hours, I climbed onto a three-quarter-ton U.S. Army truck and sat next to the driver. On the floor in the back of the vehicle rested my duffel bag with Class A uniforms and fatigues, AWOL bag with toiletries and personal effects, and overseas bag with civilian clothes.

I left Merrell Barracks in Nuremberg, Germany that morning with orders in hand that read "Team 18, Area IV, 176th Signal Company (Repair)." I was being transferred to Munich to a team in a different area within the same company. The means of military transport that brought me to one Bavarian city ten months earlier was now carrying me to another.

The PFC driver from the Munich motor pool took Regensburger Strasse heading south in order to get on Autobahn 9. We passed on my right the back of the Tribüne along Zeppelinstrasse, the stately grandstand the Nazis built on Zeppelinfeld, their parade grounds. Despite Nuremberg being heavily bombed by the Allies at the end of the war, the white marble structure was not damaged. The Americans dynamited the huge swastika on top, renamed the grounds Soldiers' Field, painted the new name in six-foot-high black letters across the front of the Tribüne, and held our military parades there.

Before long we were rolling smoothly southeast down the Nazi-built motorway that extended from Berlin to Munich and ran through Leipzig and Nuremberg. The trip down one of Adolph Hitler's roads that connected major cities was an intermission in the life of a young soldier occupying the land of a former enemy. The two-hour drive with a stranger afforded a Jewish G.I. in a post-Nazi society time to think and talk about his life, his company, and his transfer.

The tour of duty in Germany was an enlightening experience for someone of my background, a boy from Brooklyn whose mother and her parents and siblings emigrated from Poland six years before Hitler and the Nazis came to power. Other relatives were left behind, never to be heard from again after war broke out

I was a Specialist 4, an E-4 in the Army, sporting a blue bird on my sleeve, one rank above the young black man beside me who had one yellow stripe. If I re-enlisted I could get Spec 5 and an umbrella over my bird but I had plans for higher education, not a military career. In my almost 31 months in the service, it was a struggle just to keep my rank and not get busted for doing something wrong or talking back to sergeants.

"All I want is to not get in trouble with the Army, remain a Spec Four, finish my enlistment, and be handed an honorable discharge in five months," I told the E-3 beside me on the road south.

My company was headquartered in Böblingen, a small town about nineteen kilometers southwest of Stuttgart. We had signal repairmen throughout West Germany divided into twenty-four teams in six areas of command. The job of the 176th was to fix, in garrison and in the field, the electrical and electronic equipment of units we were attached to, such as infantry, ordnance, and engineers. My MOS was radar repair, code 282.10, stamped on my record when I completed the 33-week course at Fort Monmouth, New Jersey that I enlisted for right after high school.

I arrived in Germany in late February 1959. After two weeks in Böblingen, I was assigned to Team 5 in Area II. I would be at Merrell Barracks, a former SS Kaserne in the southeastern part of Nuremberg, less than two kilometers from the infamous Nazi Party Rally Grounds. Here der Führer reviewed goose-stepping troops from the Wehrmacht and SS and spoke of global conflict and the final solution to the Jewish problem. My company made it possible for the son in a family that escaped Nazi persecution to behold every day from the window of his room remnants of Hitler's Third Reich that exterminated blood relatives on his mother's side who could not escape.

On Team 5, I worked in the repair shop but did not like sitting on a bench all day fixing broken parts, soldering copper wires, testing capacitors and resistors, and replacing electron tubes. But after a two-month stint I was offered the job as clerk in the Area Office by the master sergeant and warrant officer in charge. The company would not assign someone with a clerk's MOS. The team chief recommended me since he knew I was far from the best repairman in the shop. I took the job without hesitation as I much preferred to sit on a swivel chair behind a desk with pencil, paper, and typewriter. My bosses, I gathered, wanted someone to do their menial work for them.

I was Area II's first clerk, delegated to answer the telephone, type letters and reports, make graphic charts of equipment coming in and going out, and set up a filing system. This kind of work was fine with me as after my discharge I planned to enroll in college and major in something other than electrical engineering.

The driver and I chitchatted a while about the Army and Germany, nothing very important. But then he asked me, albeit in poor English, the most important question on my mind.

"Why is you being transferred to Munich?"

"Beats me," I answered quickly. "The warrant officer and master sergeant I worked for never told me. But I believe it was some sort of punishment though."

"Did you fucks up?"

"I suppose I did," I said, "in their eyes but not mine."

"What dids you do?"

"Nothing, I thought."

The driver looked at me with a bewildered expression.

"I did a good job in the office for seven months," I continued, "and they said so several times. But then they blamed me for a bad inspection rating by the Armored Cavalry unit we were attached to. They also didn't like it when I tried to help a teammate by asking them to make an exception to one of their decisions."

The driver nodded. "Yeah. The Army don't like to change no decision, that's for shit sure."

The young black man was correct, notwithstanding the fact that his grammar was not. If there was one thing I hated in the Army, it was the intransigence of higher authority, whether officer or enlisted rank, to admit to a mistake or reverse a decision even if it patently was wrong or misguided.

Looking out the window at the wearisome dullness of the Autobahn, I thought more about the transfer, but said nothing further.

It certainly was a coincidence that the sergeant and warrant officer in charge of Area IV in Munich needed a clerk too. My bosses readily accommodated them. Of course, they did not ask me whether or not I wanted a transfer. It seemed no Team 18 trooper offered to slide off the bench and clerk in the office. I was sure my fallout with the Nuremberg Duo did not make their decision to get rid of me more difficult. Someone within Area II on another team was simply brought in to replace me. It wasn't necessary for them to go through company headquarters and wait weeks for written orders as was the case with my re-assignment.

I had mixed feelings about my transfer to Munich. When I was informed about it, I was not happy. I liked the city of Nuremberg, its G.I. bars, and the Fräulein company I was involved with there. But in the past few months things changed for the worse. I broke up with my girlfriend, my roommate and best buddy moved off post to live with the Fräulein he planned to marry, and I was not crazy about my new roommate. The only consolation of the transfer was that, on the day I was to leave, my signal team was scheduled to bunk with our attachment unit in a different wing of the barracks and be under their strict supervision, something that was anathema to me.

Later I realized my being stationed in another city, and a bigger one at that, had an upside as well. The transfer, unwelcome as it may have been initially, represented a new start, an opportunity to meet another girlfriend and better barracks buddies for the remaining five months of my Army enlistment. Plus I liked the fact that I would be doing the same company job as clerk in the Area Office and not be glued to a workbench in a repair shop.

Also weighing on my mind during the 180-kilometer drive down a road paved during the Hitler era were two independent warnings I received a year earlier on the day I left home to sail for the Port of Bremerhaven. The admonitions directly affected the Fräulein company I would keep in Nuremberg and I feared now would do likewise in Munich.

"You be careful in Germany," my immigrant Yiddish-speaking mother who lost her grandparents, uncles, and cousins said to me in English. "Don't get friendly with the Germans. They're no good, all of them. They're all Nazis. They killed six million of our people."

Trying to tell my mother that the war has been over for almost fourteen years, and that not all Germans are bad, was to no avail.

Then, not fifteen minutes later, my boyhood friend from across the street, who three months earlier came home from the Army in Germany, also cautioned me when he walked me to the bus stop carrying my AWOL bag.

"Don't get married," he threw at me with a straight face. "Don't come back with a Nazi Schatzie."

But against my mother's and my friend's advice, and like any G.I. in Germany, I did get friendly with Germans and I did keep company with Fräuleins. First was Elsa, a bargirl who liked me very much but would not accept dollars or Marks from me as she did with other G.I.s and Germans. Then there was Karin, a nice German girl, whom I met through a German worker at the barracks, and our four-month affair might have led to marriage.

Interestingly, two Fräuleins I did not keep company with stirred my emotions and I could only imagine what lovemaking would be like with them. I was smitten with a blond, blue-eyed perfect-looking girl who worked in the barracks snack bar and tried to date her but to no avail. As my teammates later crudely pointed out to me, she was "color blind," keeping company with a trooper described as "black as shit" and called the "Ace of Spades" by whites. Marianne, a bargirl-friend of Elsa's, fit my image of a Fräulein I wanted to fit into, but I never could date her. She was always aloof toward me, but that didn't stop me from believing we could find romance to-gether someday.

In Nuremberg, my contacts with Elsa eventually fizzled out but my affair with Karin ended badly. I told the girl who never went with a G.I. before, who said she loved me and wanted to get married, that I couldn't marry her, or anyone else, at this stage of my life. I tried to explain that I planned to go to college and did not wish to re-enlist in the Army to support a wife like my roommate. The two reasons I gave her were true, and impersonal, not meant to hurt her feelings. Nevertheless, my unstated rejection of her as a G.I. Frau was per-sonal. I couldn't bring home to Mama a German girl or a Catholic one. Besides, I couldn't marry someone four years older than I was that I liked but did not love simply because we were intimate.

The nice German girl, however, took my nuptial refusal person-ally and responded in kind. She believed I should have told her I couldn't marry before she opened up to me so many times. She was right, of course, and I regretted not telling her sooner. In anger she voiced an offensive comment about her Germany and my religious group after I gave her the answer she did not want to hear.

"Is good what Hitler did to Juden," she said to my face, an opin-ion I did not want to hear. Any further contact with her, much less company I might keep, was thus impossible.

I was sure my Schatzie with sympathies of a Nazi would have refrained from saying that if I were not Jewish. My mother and neighborhood friend might very well have predicted such an outcome and shot back "I told you so."

The break-up with Karin motivated me to take the necessary steps to be the American college student I hurt the German girl for. I put female frolicking on hold and after work and on weekends I did a crash-course in studying for the College Boards. In early January at the area's main U.S. Kaserne, I took the all-important test.

Prior to leaving Nuremberg, I attended a five-day religious retreat at an Army Hotel in Berchtesgaden in the Bavarian Mountains, not far from the Berghof, Hitler's own retreat. I enjoyed the event for Jewish soldiers and airmen sponsored by the military very much. Rabbi Stark from Temple Emanuel in Manhattan, the guest speaker, invited attendees to give him the names and telephone numbers of people in the States they wished him to contact. I wrote my parents' name and number on a little piece of paper and slipped it to him.

The time in Berchtesgaden away from my company heightened my Jewishness and gave me a new perspective on the role of Jews in the world and the post-Nazi society I lived in for almost a year. It was on this trip that I decided to sign up for the annual tour of Israel arranged by Jewish chaplains in Europe each March, around the time of Purim and before Passover. The tour, scheduled to take off from Munich Airport, was destined to further strengthen my Yiddishkeit and prepare me mentally for another new start in my life, discharge from the service and enrollment in college.

As we approached our destination, I was still in limbo between the second largest city in Bavaria and the largest. I hoped I would get along well with my new 176th Signal bosses and not get into hot water with them, as well as my new teammates. Perhaps too I would find friends from the guys in my new attachment unit and in town.

I likewise looked forward to meeting and keeping company with another nice German girl, someone who did not hang out in G.I. bars or collect Gelt from Americans and Germans for feminine favors or harbor affinities for Nazi ideology. Most important, in the less than half year I had left in uniform, I longed to avoid conflicts with superiors, fist-fights with Army peers, and misunderstandings with locals, anything that could get me disciplined by the military or

I feared in the city I was headed to, where an unknown Hitler and his fringe Nazi Party got their start in 1923, there might be a repetition of the anti-Semitism I encountered in the city I just left where more than a decade later Chancellor *Hitler sounded warnings of war to the world when his official Nazi Party held foreboding annual rallies with marching soldaten and hundreds of thousands of spectators.*

On that transfer day in January 1960, I knew my remaining months in the Army would be affected by, and I would be judged by, the company I keep.

Today, reflecting back to that time, a former G.I.'s remembrance of soldiering in a post-Nazi Munich, as with his memories of a reconstituted Nuremberg, unlocked the portal to a seasoned young life sealed for more than five decades.

PART I

BEGINNING OF THE END

CHAPTER 1: MUNICH LANDING

The colored trooper that drove me to Munich was in the motor pool of the 24th Infantry Division, the unit I in the 176th Signal would be attached to, and did not have to ask anyone for directions to my new barracks. He exited Autobahn A9 at Ausfahrt 6 and continued south along Ingolstadtstrasse.

"You sees dat strasse on de right," the driver said, taking one hand off the wheel and pointing to a side street as we approached it.

"Yeah, so," I answered, not knowing why he was telling me this.

"Dat's where de Dew Drop Inn be. Ah meets mah schatzie at dat G.I. bar."

"Oh," I let out meekly.

I gathered the Dew Drop Inn was a Negerbar, most likely one of several in the Munich area serving the manly needs of non-white soldiers at various barracks who fraternized with an erstwhile enemy. I was sure Munich was no different than Nuremberg from whence I came, or other German cities, big and small, that had within their borders Kasernes taken over from the defeated Wehrmacht at the end of the war to house American troops of both races for the occupation.

One of the first things I learned as a greenhorn in West Germany ten months earlier was that a strict system of segregation existed off post. My teammates in Nuremberg took me and my roommate, the buddy I came over with, to town on our first night out to indoctrinate us into the local Kultur for G.I.s. We witnessed firsthand that white soldiers frequented certain bars and clubs, where the Fräuleins did not cross the color line, while our darker comrades sought female company in a different set of G.I. joints, where the locals, often older and less attractive, were willing to bed down with the Americans of African descent Uncle Sam deployed for the occupation. Like Coca-Cola and Campbell's soup, Jim Crow had been imported to Germany in 1945 soon after V-E Day.

"Ah might gets married with mah girlfriend," the young driver, who couldn't have been more than nineteen, added.

"Oh," I said again, thinking he must be from the South and in the seventh or eighth grade had dropped out of the segregated school he attended to pick cotton alongside his father and older brothers.

It was not uncommon for a handful of the dark-skinned troopers to hitch up with their lily-white maidens, notwithstanding the color disparity or age gap. In Nuremberg I often saw, on city streets or around the barracks or at holiday socials, black-and-white combos with hands clasped and occasionally touching lips, much to the consternation of both white troopers and Germans of all ages.

"What's it like in Munich?" I asked the driver, who obviously knew his place in the city.

I thought he might give me a head's up about the Army at his, and soon my, barracks or the city's unique history or places of cultural interest, but I was wrong.

"Plenty o' poontang alls around Munich," he noted unemotionally, "fo' you and fo' me."

Besides being wrong, I was surprised by this answer, a blithe reference to the most sensitive issue facing G.I.s in the postwar period, the off-post racial divide, and the local women who dally on one or the other side of the color line. Evidently, a young black American thought differently about a former foe than a young Jewish American.

"Yes," was all I could say to my driver. I did not wish to open a can of worms with either black or white invertebrates crawling out.

We turned left onto Kollwitzstrasse. Near the intersection on my left stood a two-legged sign with "U.S. Army" and "Henry Kaserne" printed on it with a long arrow pointing to the right. A tall and narrow metal tower with power lines was behind the sign. The main gate was a quarter-mile up the street. Automobiles and trucks going in the opposite direction were leaving Henry.

My new barracks was just south of Heidemannstrasse, on the north end of town. It was part of a trio of Army installations in proximity to one another—Warner, Will, and Henry—that Uncle Sam acquired in 1945. The base I would spend the rest of my time in the Army on was named for Robert T. Henry, a private posthumously awarded the Medal of Honor for single-handedly charging a German machine-gun nest and enabling his platoon buddies to destroy it and capture 70 prisoners. The poor boy from Greenville, Mississippi was killed on December 3, 1944. He and I thus had one out of three human conditions in common.

The truck driver handed a few papers to the soldier in green Class

A's standing by the small guardhouse at the gate. The guard sported a yellow braid on his right shoulder, had black boots on, and packed a pistol on his hip. He looked at the papers for a moment and waved us inside the confiscated Nazi compound.

Henry Kaserne was completed in 1938 under the name General-Wever-Kaserne, just in time for the Nazis to garrison their Flak units of the Wehrmacht there to later fight the anti-aircraft battles of the war. It was nothing like the Merrell Barracks I knew in Nuremberg that was constructed about the same time.

Henry was no single mammoth building in red brick, four stories high, dominating much of a relatively small camp site. The Kaserne had three long three-story stucco buildings with basements and small wings at the ends plus a number of smaller, at times attached structures for the motor pools, PX, repair shops, EM club, and movie theater. Each of the three main buildings housing troops from different companies had their own mess halls, orderly rooms, and day rooms.

Henry's front entrance was not a barrel-vaulted passageway on the ground floor of one building like at Merrell. To enter, personnel and motor vehicles had to pass under a free-standing stone arch with the name of the barracks in big black letters on the curved part and "U.S. Army" in smaller words above it. The seven-foot brick wall that surrounded the Kaserne with three feet of barbed wire atop it gave the now American barracks the look and feel of a Nazi concentration camp more than a German Army base.

The driver landed me and my three bags in front of the Orderly Room of the 24th Infantry Division, the first doorway of the first white stucco building to the left. The OR of my attachment unit was on the first floor, five steps up from the sidewalk.

Lifting my duffel bag with one hand, and holding my AWOL and overseas bags in the other, I slowly walked up the steps and through the doorway to my new outfit for the remaining five months in the Army.

In the Army unit I would spend the rest of my time in, I felt this was the "beginning of the end" for me. I recalled that expression being uttered by Winston Churchill in a documentary about World War II. The termination of the three-year enlistment I believed to be a mistake some months after I was sworn in could now be envisioned.

The words were first spoken by Churchill in 1942 after the British defeated the German and Italian armies in North Africa. El Alamein was an important step toward ultimate victory but the Prime Minister did not want the people in countries fighting Hitler and Mussolini to think the war would soon be over. The battlefield hero who fought on two continents in the Boer War and World War I was quoted as saying "Now this is not the end. It is not even the beginning of the end. But it is, perhaps, the end of the beginning." In 1944, after the successful Allied landing in Normandy, when the bloody beachhead in Europe was secure and Germany's ultimate surrender foreseeable, D-Day was taken as the beginning of the end.

As a peacetime soldier who also served on two continents, .Sir Winston's phrases of phases of war resonated with me. Halfway through my enlistment, when I received the news at Fort Ord that I would soon be shipping out to West Germany, this signaled a new episode in my life and was the "end of the beginning" of my Army days so to speak. In retrospect, the ten months of my assignment to Nuremberg that just ended could be termed a "middle period" in uniform. It was clear that my transfer to Munich represented the "beginning of the end" of service to Uncle Sam.

Like reading the final chapter of a book, I could see the end was coming, an honorable discharge, but I was not quite there yet. I was in a process occurring over time, playing the role of a soldier in the last act of a drama, readying myself for a final curtain call. At Henry Kaserne, I would await the denouement of my military career. The end of my middle period set in motion a transition to the conclusion I sought.

What I did not fully appreciate then was that, in general, the be-ginning of the end of *any* event or stage in life necessarily entailed being headed toward one of two paths, an upward trajectory to some-thing better, or a downward spiral to something worse. I did not know which path in Munich I would be on in the months ahead, or what I would encounter at the finish line.

Before approaching the company clerk standing behind a big desk, I stacked my three bags in a corner of the room near the door. I looked at the clock on the side wall. It was 1050 hours, almost time for chow.

"I'm Specialist Streiber," I said without saluting, "with the one-seven-six-signal repair company."

The Spec 4 looked up from the papers he was holding. He was in his Class A's, his rank shown on the green jacket hanging on a coat rack behind his desk.

"Oh, yes, we were expecting you." The clerk did not smile or exhibit a pleasant look. "You can report to Lieutenant Smith now."

Without turning his head or saying anything more, he pointed to an open door of a small room in the back of the OR to his right.

The second lieuy in charge of personnel sitting at a desk was as common and nondescript as his name. The young officer was white, clean-shaven, had hair cropped short, especially around the sides, with regular features and no distinguishing marks on his face, and could not be pegged as of Italian, German, Spanish, or any other ethnic origin. He did not look Jewish either.

"Specialist Streiber reporting for duty, sir," I uttered softly while standing at attention and saluting. I did not click my heels, raise my right arm upward, and cry Heil Hitler as any soldier at this Kaserne 15-20 years earlier would have done.

"At ease, soldier," he said, returning my salute.

I spread my legs a little, clasped my hands behind my back holding my fatigue cap, and waited for Mr. Nobody or Mr. Everybody to speak again.

"I understand you're with the one-seventy-six signal."

"Yes sir." I handed him the large brown envelope with my personnel file.

"They always fix our equipment right, and fast too," he said, taking my file. "Nice bunch of guys. Never give us any trouble."

"Yes sir," I repeated.

"What is your MOS?"

"Radar repair. I graduated from the course at Fort Monmouth a year and a half ago."

"You'll be on Team Eighteen, run by Sergeant McCarty. They work out of the shop near the motor pool. But the 24th doesn't have any radar equipment to fix."

"I'm supposed to be the clerk in the Area Office, sir."

"Oh," he let out in surprise.

"That's what I did in Nuremberg."

"Nobody told me."

"I worked on Team Five in the repair shop for two months," I began to explain, "but then a clerk was needed in the Area Office. The one-seven-sixth headquarters wouldn't send someone with a clerk's MOS so they offered me the job. I did it for eight months. That's why they transferred me here. Munich needs a clerk too."

"Oh," he said again.

After a momentary pause, the lieutenant called to the Spec 4 in the other room, then faced me.

"Streiber, you'll be bunking with your teammates on the top floor. Pick any room with an empty bunk. The Area Office is in the basement."

The Spec 4 came in and stood next to me. "Yes sir?" he questioned.

"Take Streiber upstairs to where the one-seventy-six sleeps," the gold-bar lieuy told his subordinate. "Let him put his bags near a bunk, then take him to Supply and get him squared away with sheets, blankets, and pillow. Also, show him where his Area Office is in the building and the shop next to the motor pool."

"Thank you, sir," I said, and saluted once more.

The lieutenant returned my salute and faced the Spec 4. "Take Streiber to the mess hall after that."

"Yes sir" the company clerk parroted again.

I picked up my bags and followed the 24th Infantry Division clerk whose rank was equal to mine.

The 24th's mess hall I would eat in every day was only part of the first floor of the building, a long rectangular room with tables and benches stacked close together. The kitchen was on the left as you walked in. Troopers picked up a tray, plates, and silverware and passed by an opening in the wall to get food dropped on their plates. The cooking facilities, a gas stove with grill and a number of large steaming pots, were visible behind the Germans on the serving line. No Americans were on KP duty here; they worked only as cooks. The mess was very different than the one at Merrell Barracks which was a building unto itself and served everyone on post, with the kitchen in a separate area from the serving line and some G.I.s dishing out food.

After chow that first day, it took the rest of the afternoon to get squared away in the barracks and meet the people I would be working under and with.

The only room I could take with an empty bunk was a large one that slept four. The bunk in the middle of the room near a window that faced the street outside the barracks was now mine. I flattened the mattress folded in an *S* shape and made my bed. My clothes, military and civilian, went into the empty double-locker against the wall. Socks, underwear, and toiletries went in the footlocker in front of my bunk, and secured both lockers with combination locks.

To get to the Area Office in the basement of our attachment building I walked around to the side and then down five steps. As you entered the Office, the first room was where I would work. It had a desk and typewriter and file cabinet but no telephone. Sergeant Ramirez had the next room, quite larger than mine, with a telephone. There was an open doorway between us and he could call out to me for one thing or another. Mr. Horner occupied the last room, larger still, and with a door to close for added privacy.

The Office was run by Mr. Horner, a CW2 like Mr. Barry in Nuremberg, and SFC Ramirez, one rank and stripe below Master Sergeant Bentley that I used to work under. Ramirez, an E-6 like McCarty under him, had previously been in charge of Team 21 in Straubing, part of Area II. As one of Barry's boys who did a bang-up job, Ramirez was transferred to Munich only weeks before I was, bumped up in title and responsibility, and promised a promotion.

The two people I worked for now, unlike the two Bs in Nuremberg, could not have been more different. John Horner was tall and thin, at least forty years old with deep wrinkles cut into his cheeks, an unsmiling Southerner of German background with a sour puss. He was unfriendly toward his troops, humorless, and colorless. Albert Ramirez, by contrast, was a Westerner, grew up in a barrio in New Mexico, was no more than thirty, of medium height in a very heavy-set rotund frame, a colorful and jovial character who appreciated a good joke as well as a hot tamale, and was amiable to those both below and above him in rank. His wife and kids did not come over to Germany and he was housed in a private room in the barracks.

My new bosses showed me around and explained the various tasks

I would do, not very different from those I did in Nuremberg. Then Ramirez took me to the shop and introduced me to Sergeant McCarty and my teammates. After some chit-chat with the team chief and signal crew, I was given the rest of the afternoon off and told to report for work the next day at 0800. All my new buddies in the shop, like those I left behind in Nuremberg, were white.

With three teammates snoozing in bunks near me, the relative privacy I enjoyed at Merrell with just one roommate was lacking. In my room was PFC Shepherd, an eighteen-year-old Iowa farm boy, tall and of medium-build, who recently came to Germany and had the most time left before he was to be shipped back to the States. He seemed a little naïve, judging from the questions he asked me about New York and definitions of words in English that I used. Spec 4 Monahan was the oldest, twenty-two, short and of slight physique, a South Boston Irish kid who would be going home four months after I left. His fatigue shirt seemed a size too big and was always coming out of his trousers. PFC Rogowski, in-between the other two in age, a big hulk of a guy about six two or three, was up for promotion and already purchased his bird patches to be sewn on his sleeves. I liked the Pennsylvania Polak the least because he was rude and impolite and voiced an anti-Semitic remark soon after I arrived.

"That PFC from the twenty-fourth on the second floor tried to Jew me down," he said to Monahan, with me standing right there in the room, when he explained his efforts to sell the unused small camera he bought in the PX in order to purchase a larger one. He spit that out whether he knew I was Jewish or not.

All three roommates, like other teammates in the shop, and team chief McCarty, completed courses at Fort Gordon, Georgia in radio or microwave repair. None of them were radar men or trained in one of Monmouth's other courses.

There was one guy in the shop that I especially did not like, Spec 5 Dickson. He thought he knew everything about electronic repair and bossed around the lower ranks by usurping McCarty's authority, a too-nice-of-a-sergeant to dress him down for this. Tricky Dick I called him out of his earshot because he was a classic Army brown-noser and always seemed to be scheming.

I went to the shop almost every day, to check on equipment awaiting repair and inventory the supply of parts. I hit it off fairly well with Sergeant McCarty and we often talked about non-military subjects. He was easy going, was not a stickler for Army regulations. Though two ranks above me, I felt comfortable around McCarty and he treated me almost as an equal.

Not so with Spec 5 Dickson, the next-ranking shop repairman. He was a son-of-bitch bastard if I ever met one. Always in a bad mood, he complained incessantly, and chewed out those just one or two ranks below him for any infraction of the rules.

"What the hell's wrong with you," I heard him say one day to one of the new guys fresh from Gordon. "Why didn't you sign out yesterday afternoon when you left the shop? I didn't know where you were."

"I was late for my dental appointment and I forgot," was all the young one-striper flushed with a red face could say.

Dickson's nasty disposition probably stemmed from his unbecoming physical appearance and need to compensate for it. Short, skinny, unattractive, and unmarried, I doubted whether Dickson had a Schatzie off post. He lived in the barracks in a private room a floor below us, was made head honcho over the rest of us squished into rooms on two floors, pulled rank, and seemed to like pushing people around.

By contrast, McCarty was almost six-feet tall and relatively slim, married, lived off post, and was not involved with what went on in the barracks. I frequently answered Dickson back and he did not take too kindly to my lip or the independence I displayed. I did not work in the shop and he had no control over my daily work activeties, but I was under him after hours and on weekends. McCarty stuck up for me when Dickson wanted to sanction me.

The guys who roomed in the barracks with me, and those who did not, would come to play important roles in the last months of my Army time.

For the next couple of weeks, I did exactly what I did in Nuremberg—type letters, make out reports, file papers, draw charts, and mind the store when my two bosses were away from their desks. I was assigned officially to Team 18, one of ten electronics repairmen, not counting McCarty, but unofficially I was the clerk of Area IV.

I soon learned that our signal repair team attached to the 24th Infantry Division was an extremely chicken-shit outfit headed by General Edwin A. Walker. His ass was in an office in Augsburg but his feet were often at Henry, Warner, and Will where he directed operations. In 1957, the two-star commander earned the ire of the white southerners he loved when, under orders from President Eisenhower, he put down the racial disturbances at Central High School in Little Rock, Arkansas. After being assigned to Germany in 1959, he irritated another group of Americans, this time his superiors in Washington, for instructing his troops on the dangers of communism and for claiming that certain government officials were communist sympathizers.

Thanks to the right-leaning Walker, we had wake up calls at 0530, bed check at midnight, alerts at 0200, inspections on Saturday mornings, and winter maneuvers that some of my teammates participated in. Since I functioned as a clerk and not a repairman, I escaped the unwanted extended excursions to the Hohenfels training area in the Oberpfalz district northeast of Munich. I was fortunate to not have to go on maneuvers in the field and be subjected to cold showers, mud marches, canned C-rations, and an occasional short-arm examination.

On January thirtieth, a Saturday, almost two weeks after landing in Munich, I celebrated my twentieth birthday, my third and last in the Army. I invited Shepherd, the roommate I liked the best, to join me for dinner at the Grand Hotel near the Hauptbahnhof, a U.S. Army-run facility.

CHAPTER 2: ON THE TOWN

The most disconcerting facet of the transfer to Munich forced on me was that it took much longer, at times the better part of an hour, to travel from Henry's gate to places of interest to me in town.

First I had to walk to Ingolstadtstrasse and pay twenty Pfennigs for the Blue Goose as it was called, a local bus with a wide blue stripe on its side, a means of transport that did not roll by every five minutes. At the last stop, Parzivalplatz, I had to wait to get the Strassenbahn. Most of the time the wait was not too discomforting, as it gave me the opportunity to relieve myself at the public urinal at the end of the streetcar line, a large round edifice crowded with males standing elbow-to-elbow. Whenever I utilized the Pissor, it seems I was defiling Parzival, a character in German mythology.

From this square north of downtown, I rode the Number 8 directly south along Leopoldstrasse, through the three-arched Siegestor in the middle of the street. The Siegestor was a Triumphal Arch, smaller than the famous one in Paris I scaled five months earlier, a Victory Gate meant as a reminder to peace. The streetcar passed within the larger center archway. The century-old monument sustained heavy damage during the war due to Allied bombing raids and was reconstructed afterwards but only partially restored. On top I could see the impressive statue of Bavaria with a quadriga, a chariot of the gods drawn by four lions in the Greco-Roman tradition.

The Number 8 that I frequently took ran past the University and Schwabing, the artist's district, and into the city's downtown area. If I were headed to McGraw Kaserne, the main post in the Munich area, where the Jewish services were held and the Main PX was located, I had to board yet another streetcar line.

In Nuremberg, it usually took only fifteen minutes to go the four stops from Merrell's gate to the Hauptbahnhof, even with walking to and waiting for the streetcar. The only time I had to take a bus and two streetcars was when I was gallivanting with Karin in her nearby town. In Munich I had to fritter away forty minutes or more every time I walked out the gate.

On February 5, 1960, I received a letter from home. I had given my parents my new address and APO number before I left Nuremberg. My father wrote to tell me that I got a letter from Brooklyn

College saying that my application was received. On the same piece of paper, my mother wrote that Rabbi Stark had telephoned. *Dovidl,* she scribbled, *the Rabbi said he saw you in Berchess somthing or other I couldnt make out he said you lookd good and was happy he must be an American the Rabbi I startd speaking to him in Yidish but he didnt understand so I had to go back to Inglish.*

Fifteen years after the war, Munich, the capital and largest city in Bavaria, had a population of one million. It was more than twice the size of Nuremberg, in terms of both people and land area. Munich too was bombed very heavily by the Allies, but a decade and a half after the last of the 71 air raids much of the rubble had been carted away and its pre-war population level restored. Old buildings still standing were reconstructed, notably the Hauptbahnhof and City Hall, and new ones put up in place of those completely destroyed. Henry Kaserne was hardly touched at all, as were, ironically, many structures the Nazis built. The Führerbau, Antiquities Museum, and Administration Building, to name a few, looked as good as new.

When I arrived in Munich I was not unaware of the fact that the name of this German city had a meaning all its own. The word Munich was synonymous with appeasement.

It was here on September 30, 1938 that the British Prime Minister and other leaders agreed to the annexation of the western part of Czechoslovakia, the Sudetenland, whose citizens spoke German, to the Third Reich in order to avoid war. The Führer promised he would have no more territorial demands, Neville Chamberlain took Herr Hitler at his word, flew back to England a happy man, and emerged from the airplane waving a signed piece of paper claiming this means "peace in our time."

But the famous Munich accord did not satisfy Old Adolph's appetite for a Greater Germany. On the contrary, it emboldened the habitual liar to cross borders and make more land grabs. Within a year, a war broke out that might have been averted had the Allies not appeased the Führer.

Both Hitler and the Nazis got their start in Munich. In 1913, Hitler moved to Munich to pursue a career as an artist and struggled to make a living by painting postcard scenes. When war was declared a year later, the joyful 25-year-old was photographed at a rally in the

Odeonsplatz, a large pedestrian square named for the Concert Hall on one flank. Photographs, appropriately it seems, show him singing along with the crowd that formed. Hitler promptly enlisted in the German Army and was assigned to an infantry regiment. The man who a quarter-century later would ignite World War II in Europe apparently loved soldiering, as he accepted dangerous duty and fought fiercely on the front lines.

But in 1918, three months before Armistice Day, the little corporal with the big mustache was awarded the Iron Cross, First Class, a rare medal for someone of his rank. The anti-Semite who took great pride in bearing his Cross, ironically, was recommended for it by his commander, a Leutnant who happened to be Jewish and who survived the next war only by fleeing to the United States. When there was all quiet on the Western Front, Hitler returned to Munich and joined the budding German Workers Party, later transforming it into the NSDAP, the *Na*tional So*zi*alistische Deutsche Arbeiter Partie, from which the acronym *Nazi* originates.

In Munich, political party gatherings often occurred in beer halls. Debates and rallies were held while dispirited ex-soldiers and unemployed workers guzzled frothy Steins. Hitler saw Germany's loss of the war as a betrayal by the central government and blamed Jewish capitalists.

On the evening of November 8, 1923, in the Bürgerbräukeller, the disillusioned former corporal staged a Putsch to take over the Bavarian government, as a first step in overthrowing the Weimar Republic and establishing Nazi leadership in Berlin. Hitler burst through the doors of the beer hall where 3,000 people gathered. Surrounding the building were 600 storm troopers with a mounted machine gun aimed at the doors. Throwback thugs the likes of Hermann Göring and Rudolf Hess were at their leader's side. Hitler fired a bullet into the ceiling and climbed up on a chair.

"The national revolution has broken out," the putschist head shouted. "Nobody is allowed to leave. A new government will be formed at once."

Bavarian officials were detained. Confusion and unrest lasted all night. The next morning Hitler and 2,000 loyal Nazis marched on downtown Munich toward the War Ministry building, but were stopped on the Odeonplatz by Bavarian police. There was no singing in front of the Concert Hall this time. Shots were fired on both sides, four policemen and fourteen Nazis were killed. Hitler was injured, went into hiding, and later arrested. The revolt was as flat as the last night's Bier.

Hitler was put on trial for treason in 1924. He used the forum to extol his motives and spread Nazi ideology. The press published every word he said, the presiding judges were impressed, and Hitler was sentenced to five years in a reasonably comfortable prison but only served eight months. The failed Putsch was a success, however, in the sense that it gave the nascent Nazi Party, virtually unknown outside of Munich, national exposure and a propaganda victory. And the time in confinement convinced a bitter man to disavow violent revolution to effect political change and employ only legal means in the future.

Hitler never forgot the importance of Munich for his Nazi Party and push for power. Around Königsplatz, a large square commissioned by King Ludwig I more than a century earlier, a number of government buildings were erected. Here the German dictator kept a working room and had offices for his staff, met with Chamberlain, and presided over Nazi ceremonies and Party rallies.

At one end of Königsplatz, two temples were erected to honor those killed in the Beer Hall Putsch. Hitler ordered their graves dug up, coffins placed in cast-iron sarcophagi, and the hapless heroes laid out in neat rows so that Germans can remember these sacred souls from here to eternity. But in 1947, the U.S. Army of Occupation made sure the Nazis who died for Hitler's lost cause would *not* be remembered. The poor putschists were dug up again, their profane bodies returned to war-weary bereaved families or dropped in unmarked graves, and the King's Square temples blown to kingdom come.

On Friday nights in February, I fell into the habit of going to Jewish services at McGraw Kaserne on the other side of town. Since it took a while to get there with the bus and two streetcars, Ramirez let me leave the Area Office about an hour early. This did not endear me to Dickson who expected me to hang around the barracks and take part in the traditional Friday night G.I. party, religion or no religion.

My three Christian roommates likewise were not too keen on my bugging out of this weekly chore, which meant more work for them, and did not understand or appreciate "church on Friday." But at this stage of my Army career I made no apologies for participating in my faith and could care less what they or Tricky Dick thought of me. I enjoyed the services, welcomed meeting Jewish G.I.s my age from other Munich posts and local Jewish families, military and civilian. The Oneg Shabbat after prayers substituted for my missed dinner chow at the mess hall. When I returned to my Kaserne later in the evening, to a fresh-smelling room and a clean latrine, I could cut my roommates' resentment with a bayonet knife.

On Saturday afternoons, I usually quit Henry after lunch and went south into town by myself. My roommates advised this newcomer to the barracks *not* to go north, not to seek the company of Fräuleins in the Dew Drop Inn, the Negerbar behind Warner Kaserne on a side street off Ingolstadstrasse pointed out to me by the Schwarzer the day he rolled me into town on a truck. They told me the bar was in effect off limits to white G.I.s. On this particular issue, I marched in cadence with the new company buddies I seldom agreed with.

I often went to Schwabing as it was the closest section of town of interest to an American soldier of my color and to young Germans. I breezed through the campus of Ludwig-Maximilians-Universität to get the feel of what it was like to be a college student. Königsplatz, with its huge open space, was within walking distance. I stood in the middle of the Platz and fed pigeons snippets of bread off the slice I pilfered from the mess hall. What once was used as a parade ground for goose-stepping Soldaten, to showcase Germany's military might, now was Munich's largest outdoor parking lot. This King's Square, which Hitler renamed Akropolis Germaniae, apparently typified the classical Greek architecture the would-be-king of Germany admired for his thousand-year Reich.

There was one building on the periphery of the Square that would have been of interest to me had I known its history. In 1937, in the former Institute of Archaeology, the Nazis disseminated their false-hoods about Jews and modern art. An ostentatious exhibit of so-called "degenerate art" occupied the entire second floor for four months. On display were paintings and sculptures and prints labeled by Goebbels as subversive or perverse, over 5,000 works, pieces of art blatantly confiscated from museums and collections throughout the Reich.

Only a few such pieces were crafted by Jewish hands, but that did not stop the pint-sized Minister of Propaganda from spreading the big lie that modernism and expressionism were part of a Jewish-Bolshevist conspiracy against German decency. Masterpieces by Henri Matisse, Marc Chagall, Pablo Picasso, Vincent Van Gogh, and scores of other discredited artists, were hung haphazardly, often with no frames, next to demeaning slogans painted on the walls. Aryan purity in art was what the Nazis sought. But how much revulsion of the banned pieces was actually instilled in the minds of the two million visitors remains an open question.

Walking around the Square, I could not help thinking about the estimated 2,500 Allied bombs that didn't go off, one-in-eight I heard someone at Henry say, and were buried beneath Munich streets. The EOD at the barracks, the Engineer Ordnance Demolition unit of the 24th Infantry, had the task of defusing the duds unearthed during the carting away of rubble and the digging for reconstruction. If a dud failed to defuse, the Army engineers then evacuated thousands of residents and detonated the 550-pound missile dropped from the sky. No soldier or civilian could decipher whether the World War II killer shell was built by American or British hands.

By late afternoon, I wound up at Harry's Bar on the west side of Leopoldstrasse, not far from the Siegestor and the University. I avoided the Cracker Box two blocks south on the other side of the street, as this G.I. bar had a reputation for frequent fights and raucous behavior. Harry's was more subdued and suited my taste better. It was a popular watering hole for both G.I.s and Germans, with a jukebox rather than a live band, and was less than halfway between Henry and the downtown area where the Hauptbahnhof was.

With a beer in hand, I took a chair at a table that faced the large windows abutting the street. This practice facilitated my checking out the Fräuleins who hopped in before they even turned the handle on the door. Many were young girls in their late teens, born during the war, some in their first or second year at the University. After more than a year in Germany, the possibility of dating, not to mention shtupping, a girl who was my age or a little younger was for me a new and welcome experience.

In Nuremberg I knew nothing of that. Karin was four years my senior, Elsa older still. The Fräuleins I coveted but never bedded, the Venus in the snack bar laying down with a Schwarzer and Marianne, Elsa's tough siren of a friend, I was sure had three-to-five on me. Before I was out and about in Munich, I was beginning to think there were no Mädels born in Bavaria after the war began.

Harry, the owner, often sat at a table with G.I.s. He was an affable fellow in his early forties with a fair command of English and liked to socialize with Americans. The trouble with Harry was that I did not know what to make of him at first. In appearance, he reminded me of people I knew back in Coney Island, the refugees who came over after the war. Short, somewhat heavy, and with a round face, he peered through his rimless eyeglasses with a persistent smile. Harry had a Jewish look about him but I dared not ask him directly if he was a Landsmann. It was only when I was at a table alone with him one day, and he by chance sported a short-sleeved shirt, that I saw the telltale number tattooed on his forearm and knew. I told him about myself, and my mother and her whole family coming from Poland. Coincidentally, Harry came from the same region.

"I too from Brest-Litovsk," the proprietor of the bar beamed about the province in Southeastern Poland. He seemed eager to talk to a fellow, albeit much younger, Jew. "No more Poland . . . now Russia."

Harry was right. Once Hitler took western Poland, Stalin grabbed the eastern part and did not hand it back to the Poles after the war.

I learned that Harry was in a Displaced Persons camp after the war and then immigrated to Israel. He did not like it there and a few years later came back to Germany.

"Too much work," he said. "Life hard. And always fight with Arab."

With the reparation money he received from the German government, Harry purchased the bar and catered to G.I.s.

"This good business," he stressed. "German not do. This not . . . not . . . ."

The native Yiddish speaker struggled to find the right word in English. "This not . . . respectable for German. Only Jew would do."

Harry was right again. In different countries Jews were marginal people and, citizens or not, tend to become involved of necessity in marginal businesses—money-lending, risky ventures, seedy commerce—activities few Gentiles would touch. Harry told me that his older brother, who had helped him survive in the Dachau concentration camp, owns a men's store nearby and sells only American-style clothing. With four U.S. Army posts in Munich, no doubt that was a good business too.

I enjoyed talking to Harry, often wound up at his bar on a Saturday afternoon or evening, and before long would meet an attractive Fräulein there.

CHAPTER 3: DON'T DROP INN

At Henry Kaserne, I did not go to the EM Club to drink, or pal around in Munich, with any of my roommates or teammates. I went to town by myself on weekends and frequently just took in the many sights, and downed beers at Harry's alone or with him at my table. Attendance at Jewish services at McGraw Kaserne, the main base in the Munich area, likewise was an unaccompanied trek as I did not know or meet any other Landsmann at Henry.

However, I did make a new friend at Henry who was in the 24th Infantry Division, Emmett Williams, a Schwarzer. I met the trooper and became friendly with him because I often went into the Orderly Room for one thing or another and found him interesting to talk to, much more so than anyone in my signal outfit. He seemed to like talking to me as well, we were on the same wavelength, and I surmised he was partial to associating with a white buddy.

My new friend was the Division clerk who handled passes, leaves, and reimbursements. I talked to the PFC about my planned trip to Israel in early March, how much leave time I had left in the Army, and payments I would receive for any of the 30-annual leave days I did not take when discharged at the end of June.

Emmett Williams was a very light-skinned black from St. Louis, Missouri. He was tall and thin and slicked his short kinky hair down with pomade, ostensibly to look more like the majority of soldiers in his outfit. I could not help noticing that his roommate and the other Schwarzers in the barracks he hung around with were much darker. His room was down the hall from mine and I liked being with him, but not when he was with his black buddies, who often laughed loudly and bantered in a manner stereotypical of their kind.

I gave Emmett my telephone number in Brooklyn and told him to call me when he gets out of the Army. He was scheduled to go back to the States a few months after my discharge. As he would be processing out at Fort Dix, New Jersey, I was sure he might spend a day or two in New York City and we could get together.

"Do you have a girlfriend?" I happened to ask Emmett one day when we were alone in his room.

He nodded his head.

"Is she white?" I asked again.

I was not at all apprehensive to talk about race with a Schwarzer I was friendly with, even though I already knew the answer to my question. There were no WACs at Henry, black or white, and I never saw an African woman, light or dark, in town.

"Yes," Emmett said, nodding again.

"Where did you meet her?"

"At the Dew Drop Inn."

"I heard about that G.I. bar from the driver who brought me here from Nuremberg. He met his girlfriend there too."

"That's where all the brothers on this side of town go."

I looked at Emmett but did not comment on his last remark. What could I say? I knew what he meant by *brothers*.

"You ever been to the Dew Drop?" Emmett then asked.

I shook my head. "My roommates told me not to go there. One said white soldiers call it the Don't Drop Inn."

Emmett laughed. "I know. Whites don't go there."

"What's it like in a bar I'm not supposed to drop in on?"

"See for yourself. I'm going there Saturday night. You can come with me if you like?"

I smiled and exhaled through my nose. "Would they let me in?"

My obvious reference to the Jim Crow pattern of off-post G.I. entertainment in Germany was not lost on my schwarzen friend. "Hell yeah," he quipped. "There's no law against a white guy coming in."

I remembered the embarrassing incident when I and my buddy from Fort Ord first came to Nuremberg. Our teammates took us to Mother Tucker's, a Negerbar, as a practical joke they played on every newcomer, and one of the MPs guarding the place immediately came over and ordered us to leave.

"What about the MPs in there?" Won't they kick me out?"

"Not if you're with me."

That made sense. In Nuremberg, our teammates waited outside Mom's, as they called the place, and told my buddy and me to go inside and get a table while they parked the car. Perhaps entering a Negerbar with a Schwarzer would not get me kicked out.

The reverse, however, was not true. I once asked a bar owner in Nuremberg what he would do if a black G.I. walked in, with or without a white buddy. There were no MPs to roust one or both but the owner told me he would ask the Schwarzer to leave saying the girls there won't dance with him, and the white soldiers might start a fight. The owner then gave him the name and location of a Negerbar where the girls *would* dance with him. Usually, the interloper was not offended by reference to Gerry Jim Crow and headed out the door to a G.I. joint where the Fräuleins desired his shaded anatomy. If he did not do an about face, white G.I.s often got physical with a comrade-in-arms who sought entertainment in the wrong company.

"All right, I'll go with you," I said.

Negerbars were not new to Germany in 1945 when the war ended. In the 1920s and early '30s, black-only establishments existed in Germany, Berlin especially, to accommodate the black entertainers and jazz musicians working in the cabarets. When the Nazis came to power, cabarets closed and the dark non-Aryans left or were forced out.

After the war, Negerbars appeared again, this time with a different clientele. Cities and towns with Wehrmacht Kasernes taken over by the U.S. Army and Air Force for the occupation suddenly saw garrisons of American troops roll in on deuce-and-a-half trucks. The military at that time was still segregated. All-black and all-white units descended on war-torn German communities ill-equipped to handle the large numbers of young men from both races vying for fraternization with local white women.

In occupied towns, it was inevitable that segregation emerged in off-post G.I. entertainment. It simply mirrored the on-post racial divide that already existed and what American troops were used to in the States and brought over with them. Although President Truman via executive order desegregated the military in 1948, the full integration of units in Germany was not achieved until 1956. But the racial mixing on the Kasernes that I observed less than three years later did not mean black and white G.I.s sought out each other's company once they walked out the gate.

The off-post segregation in the postwar years was indeed ironic as it contradicted Germany's new laws on equal rights. Black G.I.s, many of whom came from the South, felt a sense of freedom. They could eat in restaurants, sit in movie theaters, ride on busses, and wait at train stations without "colored only" signs relegating them to separate and unequal accommodations. Many rented apartments in town, were friendly toward Germans, and handed out Hershey bars to smiling children. The American military counted on troops, both black and white, to spread democracy to a people who experienced twelve years of an undemocratic regime, to support full integration in a society regardless of race, religion, or national origin.

White G.I.s, however, many of whom also hailed from the South, had different ideas on freedom and democracy. To them, freedom meant being free of competition from blacks, and democracy meant a right to associate with whites only in a public place. In their quest for female company, they wanted, even demanded via threat of boycott, certain German bars and clubs to cater only to white G.I.s and kick out any black who happened to mosey in.

Not surprisingly, the military itself supported off-post segregation. Top brass believed what went on in town was none of its business, it had no authority to order integration of German-owned G.I. joints, and voluntary separation averted unwanted fist-fights between white and black soldiers off base. White commanders from the North who supported integration did everything they could *not* to have a racial incident involving troops under them on their record, even if it involved denying equal rights to blacks. White commanders from the South needed no self-serving reason, other than their own prejudices, to discriminate, or undermine proposed integration ordered from above.

Germans too, despite any friendliness they had with black G.I.s, were not against keeping them apart and away from their young Fräuleins, as they historically harbored anti-foreign and racial biases reinforced during the Hitler years. Fräuleins of all ages who did fraternize with blacks, especially those that bore a Mishling child, were viewed as traitors to Germany and a pure Aryan race.

Perhaps the most important factor sustaining the presence of Negerbars was the tripartite stratification that sprung up among German women. In the first class were the so-called "nice German girls" in town, Fräuleins who often lived at home and would not, or were forbidden to, date any soldier, American or German, much less frequent disreputable G.I. joints. The bottom class contained females who were largely independent and willing to drink, dance, and go to bed with the black Americans in their midst. The sensibilities of Germans were very much offended by the actions of these transgressors, often labeled as prostitutes although some crossed the color line for love and not money. In the middle were Fräuleins who lived alone or with their families, worked on military bases or hung out in white-only bars, and fraternized solely with their white male cousins from the States. These in-between German women looked down on, and refused to associate with, their compatriots below them in status who romanced the descendants of African slaves. The second-classers, of course, would not be caught dead in a Negerbar.

American soldiers not only readily accepted the color-coded female stratification but welcomed it. White G.I.s stayed comfortably in their self-segregated front yard. They would not put their hands on a Fräulein once it was common knowledge she touched troopers of color. Black G.I.s preferred to stay in their fenced-in backyard, to do their cotton pickings in establishments they called their own, had control over, and knew the women there hankered for their hue. Segregation facilitated their search for sexual favors in a foreign land with no potential partners their own kind.

Negerbars were known for spontaneous violence and fights often occurred among the black buddies themselves. MPs were purposefully assigned there so they could put down disturbances quickly. The Polizei, who had no authority over American servicemen, went after Fräuleins instead. Germany's postwar police favored the racial dichotomy, since the Negerbars were known and confined to certain areas of the city, and enforcement of the country's anti-prostitution laws was not difficult. Third-class women in these forbidden places were subjected to routine round-ups and arrests. The second-classers, drinking and dancing in white-only bars, had nothing to fear from their own Polizei.

On Saturday February 13th, about 2100, I tagged along with Emmett to the Dew Drop Inn, his kind of bar. We were in civies and walked north about half a mile on Ingolstadtstrasse. None of his black buddies were by our side and I was thankful for that.

Emmett did not know it but before I was scheduled to leave Munich I really wanted to see what it was like on the dark side of town. My friend from the 24th Infantry was the only Schwarzer I knew personally at Henry, I was not planning to join his color club, and I was not disposed to enter a Negerbar on my own. Fording the white line in Germany, I surmised, would be a novel and interesting experience, something I could write about on essays for my college English and history classes in the next few years.

On my mind too when I was walking with Emmett to the Dew Drop were the encounters I had with the girl working in the snack bar in Nuremberg that I was enamored with. Would I lay eyes on a Fräulein as pretty and well-stacked as she in the Inn I was not supposed to be in? I wondered.

I practically went batty the first time I saw the girl in the snack bar almost a year earlier. I was immediately drawn to her almost perfect face and figure, a rosy-cheeked dream lover with unblemished skin and a seductive aura. I left my table and half-eaten food, went up to her, and tried to date her only to be told that she has a boyfriend.

"Maybe I see you again? she said politely after I apologized for bothering her.

I took that comment favorably, as a possibility of a future get-together should she be free. It never occurred to me her boyfriend was anyone other than a German or a white G.I. It was only minutes later when I left the snack bar after lunching with four teammates that they imparted the colorful news to me about the boyfriend, a soldier who in fact lived down the hall from us in the barracks and our different units shared the same latrine.

"She's fucking a nigger," one of my lunch mates happily informed me, while another eagerly described the horsy private part that hung on the dark American observed in the shower.

That unwelcome news was a direct blow to my ego, not to mention my normally liberal tendencies about race. I just could not believe the gorgeous girl I coveted preferred an oversized overdone buckaroo to an average white boy, one who was told he was comely.

In the months ahead I saw the colorblind girl that so captured my imagination three more times. First was in the snack bar when I took Karin to Merrell for dinner and a movie. I did not speak to Fräulein Perfekt this time but could not help looking over Karin's shoulder to gawk at that more beautiful face and figure. Then, at the Fourth of July picnic, my dream lover was with her schwarzen Liebling, and I got a clear picture of who she was spreading those lovely legs for or widening that kissable mouth to. With his broad nose, large nostrils, protruding lower lip, rabbit ears, curved cranium, and black skin with white blotches, he was no Sidney Poitier or Harry Belafonte. What Beauty saw in the Beast, other than the choice meat he was packing below the belt, I could not fathom.

The last time I eyed the girl I adored was also the last time I was with Karin. I left Karin's apartment and had stepped off the streetcar at the Merrell stop and was walking back to the barracks when I noticed she was coming toward me, apparently having just gotten off work. I felt a rush of adrenalin.

"Hello," I said softly, when Beauty was just a few feet in front of me. "Do you remember me?"

"Yes . . . I do," she answered, stopping to face me. "You ask me out. And I see you in snack bar with girl and at picnic."

I was pleased she remembered me and we spoke for a few minutes right there on the street less than a block from Merrell's main gate.

"Yes. That was my girlfriend," I said. "We just broke up"

"Oh. Why you break up?"

"She wanted to get married and I didn't."

"Why you not get married?" she asked, as if she thought every G.I. should marry his Schatzie.

"She wasn't as pretty as you. And she didn't have the great shape that you have."

"Dankeschön," she said with a smile.

After some more chitchat, I worked up the nerve to ask her if she still had a boyfriend. I wanted her to know I had not changed my mind about going out with her.

"Yes," she said simply and directly.

"Is he . . . ."

She cut me off. "Yes."

By not letting me complete my question, and with her one-word curt answer, she in effect readily indicated he was black. It was obvious that she assumed I was told the race of her lover boy or I saw them together at the picnic.

"Him I love," she added.

This time she was the bold one. What was it she loved, I asked myself, his blackness or his bigness? I doubted if Beauty looked behind the Beast's exterior and found an endearing heart and soul.

We talked a little more but I kept my eyes on that lovable puss and body. I revealed that I wished she was free and hoped she would go out with me.

"Dankeschön," she said once more, then looked at her watch and told me she had to go.

"Yes. I'm sorry I held you up. I enjoyed talking to you . . . and seeing you again." I may have lied to Karin several times, but I was not lying now to this Fräulein, or to myself.

She started to turn and walk away. "Auf Weidersehen."

"So long," I answered, as her back was toward me. The irony of my parting words, spoken so casually to the German girl who loved a black man, hit me later.

The last time I saw the Fräulein I fancied was certainly not the last time I thought of her.

As Emmett and I turned onto a side street and approached the Dew Drop, I could hear Rhythm-and-Blues music emanating from inside the bar. At the white-only establishments I frequented in two Bavarian cities I only heard the music, either by a band or on the juke-box, once I entered the bar. There was another difference between the two types of G.I. hangouts in Germany I could not help noticing on opening the door to the Inn. A musty odor redolent of an old building or stale food filled my nostrils. My olfactory sense never sniffed anything like that at Harry's in Munich or the Luitpold and Flying Dutchman in Nuremberg.

"Let's get a table," Emmett said. He walked toward a square one in the middle of the room that was empty.

I stayed close behind my first class private protector. "Okay."

A rosy-cheeked young waitress in a white apron with pockets came to our table. Emmett ordered two beers. My eyes shifted around the room filled with fifty or sixty coal-faced men and snow-faced women.

Some of the black troopers in the room were in uniform, but Emmett looked very different from those in civilian clothes. His dress was not as garish as that decked out on others, his pale skin and facial features contrasted favorably amid the darker African-looking servicemen. At a distance he could almost pass.

We sipped our beers and made small talk. Two MPs in helmet liners and sporting pistols stood in a corner, but neither came to us or told me to leave. Some black men at nearby tables glanced our way.

I could see their pairs of eyes fixed on Emmett and me, white balls shining in the darkened room. I was sure they were wondering what a white boy is doing here, and resented it, but none stood up and moved toward us.

"Is your girlfriend here," I asked Emmett.

He looked at his watch. "She should be here soon."

I did not see any Drop Inn Fräulein that appealed to me, even if I were so inclined to drop in a Fräulein who bedded with blacks. Certainly none looked anything like the colorblind girl working in the snack bar in Nuremberg I longed for. The deviant Damen around me were not of my age group, seemed to be in their late twenties and thirties, some even in their early forties. Most were a trifle plump, a few quite portly, all with heavy make-up, and had naturally blond or bleached hair in a poodle cut or just long and straight. Many wore tight-fitting slacks, smoked long cigarettes, and chewed gum vigorously.

About ten minutes later, Emmett, who had turned his head toward the door, raised his arm and waved to a Fräulein just coming in. She smiled when she saw him and came right to our table, maneuvering herself sideways around the two-color combos on the crowded dance floor like a combat soldier tip-toeing through a mine field.

My friend spoke first as she sat down opposite me and next to her off-white Schatzie. "Ingrid, this is my buddy David."

Emmett ordered a drink for his girlfriend without asking what she wanted, presumably her favorite spirit.

The Fräulein sitting across from me was not bad looking, possessed medium-sized tits, and displayed a fairly nice figure. Had I not seen her at the Dew Drop, I wouldn't have thought this postwar deutsche daughter was the type who dropped her panties for a G.I. across the great divide in her country. I could only think, like most of my comrades, that she preferred a grosse black Schwanz over moral approval by white Americans and Germans.

"Hello," I said, looking straight at her.

Ingrid peered at me, and then back-and-forth a few times between me and Emmett.

"Why you come here," she asked pointedly. "You not belong."

"Emmett invited me."

She looked at her boyfriend. "Why you ask him to come."

"He's my friend. I thought he might want to see what the Dew Drop is like"

"What he see?" the paleface paramour of pitchy putzes pitched at Emmett. "Fräulein not dance with him and G.I. might start fight."

"Some girl might dance with David," he shot back at Ingrid, "if she's not with a guy . . . ."

"Nein," Ingrid countered adamantly in her own language, cutting him off.

"And I don't think anyone would start a fight," Emmett went on.

"It doesn't matter," I said, trying to allay any disagreements between my friend who brought me to the Dew Drop and the girlfriend he met at this place. "I didn't come to dance or meet anyone." I looked fast around the room. "Besides, I don't see any girl I like."

"Oh, for you Fräulein here not good enough?" Ingrid evidently took my last comment personally.

"I didn't say that."

"What you say?"

"I meant," now trying to get Ingrid on my side, "if I saw a girl as pretty as you, I would ask her to dance."

Emmett turned toward me as Ingrid seemed more relaxed and sat back in her chair. "Why don't you ask someone to dance? Show Ingrid she's wrong."

I glanced around the room again. "Who do you suggest?"

Emmett nodded his head in the direction of a nearby a table. "See the three girls sitting over there. They're probably not with anyone or waiting for someone."

I focused on the trio of chalky crossovers. One was old enough to be my mother, another painted up like a clown. The third one at the table was the best of the lot, not too bad from what I could tell by her profile and chest.

"Okay. I'll give it a try."

Ingrid was still peering at me, now sipping her drink with a straw, as I got up and cautiously approached my possible dancing partner.

I extended my arm toward the bleached blonde with big-boobs. "Wilst du tanzen mit mir?" I asked politely. I wanted her to think I might be German, careful not to add Schatzie as most G.I.s say to a German girl they don't know just to insult them.

The Fräulein's face was easy to read. She naturally was surprised to see a white boy standing over her with his palm upwards. After staring at me and hesitating a moment, she looked to her two table-mates who were also taken aback, and then started to get up.

"Ja," she said, without smiling. "Danke."

We walked to the center of the floor and engaged arm-in-arm for a slow dance to a loud R & B tune. The slow dance appealed to me as I held her close and felt her well-endowed body part. She must like me, I thought. She thanked me for just asking her to twirl around.

She stared at me again. "You American? G.I.?"

My clothes and haircut ostensibly gave me away. "Yes."

"Why you come here? Why you not go to white bar?"

I could have asked this Fräulein the same two questions. She seemed about five years older than I am, did not look like a dog, and had a fair figure. No match for the girl in the snack bar in Nurem-berg, but touchable and acceptable.

"My friend invited me," I said instead, as I nodded over to Em-mett two tables away.

She turned her head, scanned several tables, but seemed puzzled.

"He's sitting next to the Fräulein looking at us."

"She look at us because I dance mit you?"

"Yes. She thought no Fräulein here would dance with me."

She unclutched her right hand from my left and tenderly touched my cheek. "I dance mit you because you look nice . . . have nice face."

Compared to the men around me she could be coupled with on the dance floor, with broad noses, wide nostrils, and thick lips, not to mention dark skin and kinky hair, I guess I did look pretty good to her. Perhaps she was AC/DC, got plugged in from both sides of the color line, and just happened to come in to the Dew Drop with two of her crossover friends for the same reason I came in.

"Danke," I said, appreciative of the compliment, but I dared not ask her what she was doing in a Negerbar.

"Why you come here?" she asked again. "Why you not go to white bar?"

"I wanted to see what it was like."

"What you see?"

"I see I don't belong here. But I'm happy to dance with you."

"Danke," she said, parroting a thank you for a compliment.

My next statement was going to be a tricky one, as I couldn't very well ask her outright, as some crass white G.I.s might put it, why she bunks with the boogies, or if she bunks with both types of barracks blood-buddies.

"Would you go out with me if I asked you?" were words that meekly came out of my mouth. I was not sure if I really meant what I said but I asked anyway to see what she would say.

"No," she answered immediately.

"Why not? Do you have a boyfriend?"

"No," she said again. "I go mit many G.I."

"Then why not? I thought you liked me."

"I like you, you look nice, but you not like I go mit black . . . and he pay much."

Here it was at last, the unvarnished reason she dropped in to the Dew Drop. She did not come simply to see what it was like. It was refreshing to meet a Fräulein who not only admits she crossed the color line but admits she does it for the money and not for love. I wondered how many goodly shafts of dark meat slipped between her legs in the last month alone. If she consented to date me, I would insist she pay *me*, for the damage to my reputation among my G.I. peers. And I would have to bring along a baseball bat, either to satisfy her or to protect myself if one of her paying patrons was offended by my encroachment into his territory and followed us to a hotel or her apartment.

"I understand," I told the conceded wide receiver. "I would not like." This postwar German girl knew her place in the stratification system and knew the mind of a white American boy.

We continued to dance but in silence. What else was there to say? She was a crossover cunt and a hooker to boot, but not real attracttive, not the kind of Fräulein I wanted to get involved with, much less pay to fall into bed with. The only action I sought with her was a freebee on top, to undo her bra and squeeze those tits.

The second song we were dancing to ended and we uncoupled. I walked her back to her table.

"Danke," I said. Her two tablemates looked at me but did not say anything.

Emmett and Ingrid were still sipping beers when I sat down. Neither asked what I talked about with the Fräulein while dancing, and I offered no information about her proclivities for dating black men with a fistful of dollars or Marks to fork over.

Suddenly I felt a tap on my left shoulder just as I took a swig of my beer again. I turned my head a little to look behind me when I heard a shrill voice.

"Motherfucker."

A tall monkey-face Schwarzer in uniform was standing over me with an angry look about him. I didn't have to ask the bury invader of my privacy why he came over to me or why he cursed me or what he was mad about.

"Get the fuck out, Whitey" he told me. "We don't want you here. Don't mess with our women."

From my sitting position, I peered at my ugly antagonist. The dark-skinned trooper breathed heavily through his mouth and I could smell his fowl breath. His body odor was no better.

Emmett stood up, while I remained sitting but looking up at the two contrasting black soldiers, one coal-faced and excited, the other light and calm, one in Class A's and smelly, the other in civies and deodorant-fresh..

"He's my buddy," Emmett informed the irritated stranger. "I invited him here. He leaves when I leave."

In his physique, Emmett did not look the pugilistic type, but yet he seemed ready to punch someone who *did* give the appearance of a prizefighter. I guess he took it as a personal affront that a guest of his in the Dew Drop would be forced to leave. I certainly did not want any friend of mine getting beaten up over me. It was best to stop any bloodshed before it started, even if I knew Emmett could knock the big bastard on his black ass.

"Why can't I be in here," I defiantly said as I stood up, positioned myself in front of Emmett, and stared down my American enemy. "There's no law against it. The woman danced with me willingly. I didn't force her. What's the big deal?"

Before the dark intruder could answer or make his next move, the white MP came over to us, nightstick in hand. "What seems to be the trouble?"

A year earlier on my first night out in Nuremberg, when the black MP in the Negerbar ordered me to leave, I skedaddled without argument. But I was not inclined to do so this time. I was now insouciant to black-white conflicts, the transfer to Munich soured me to the Army, I only had a few more months to my enlistment, and I was rejected by Fräuleins in both cities who preferred color and cock-size over comeliness.   .

"This guy called me a motherfucker and told me to leave," I said to the soldier cop, nodding to the G.I. in front of me. "My friend invited me," I added, turning my head and nodding to Emmett.

I deliberately uttered the offensive word that was used against me, knowing it would raise the ire of the black soldier ready to force me out of his domain. He clenched his fist and took a step closer, but I wasn't worried. The presence of the white MP was my protection.

"Germany is a free country," I continued in the same nasty tone of voice. "There's no law against my coming in to this bar. I don't have to leave unless I want to."

"That's true," the MP said. He looked back-and-forth among the three of us and toward Ingrid who just sat there with a look of 'I told you so'. "However, your being here is causing trouble already."

"Why? I didn't start a fight with anyone," I countered to the cop. "He came over to me and cursed me and told me to get the fuck out. He's the motherfucker, not me. You should order *him* out."

I knew I was daring and risky, using a word typically uttered by blacks, against a black who came after me. I thought monkey-face might explode, raise his fist, or pull a gun or knife, but he just stood there like a dummy.

"Go back to your table," the composed MP told the discombobulated G.I. hovering over me. "I'll take care of this."

The offended trooper opened his mouth as if to say something but did not. Instead, the blemished blackie did an about face and walked away. Emmett took this all in without saying anything. My Henry friend seemed relieved that I spoke up and interceded on his, and my, behalf.

The Army keeper of the peace then turned to me. "It would be best if you leave. I don't want to order you out, and I can't arrest you because you didn't do anything."

I was taken aback by the relative politeness and respect this white MP afforded me, compared to the gruff manner the black MP in Nuremberg exhibited in a similar situation. I knew it would be best if I just left. Even though my Negro nemesis hiked it back to his table, another annoyed Dew Drop Inn regular might come up behind me if I stayed.

"All right . . . I'll leave," I told the nice cop who did not have to club anyone with his nightstick.

The MP went to his post in the rear corner of the bar. I watched him as he repositioned himself, fiddled with his helmet liner, and put his nightstick in the holder loop on his wide belt I then turned to my friend and protector.

"Emmett, I'm going back to Henry. You don't have to leave too. Stay here with Ingrid. Thanks again for inviting me. It was an interesting experience."

"You sure that's what you want to do, David?"

"I'm sure."

I put my jacket on and started to leave, but turned to Ingrid. "Glad to have met you. You were right. I don't belong here. For me, this place is the Don't Drop Inn."

Ingrid laughed. I gathered she never heard that expression before. The third-class Fräulein probably never went out with a white G.I.

It was still Saturday the 13th when I got back to the barracks. The way the evening turned out, it could have been *Friday* the 13th.

I took from my wall locker the pen and paper pad I used for writing letters home. I scribbled some notes of my foray into the exotic and scary world of Negerbars. Who knows? One of the Dew Drop Schwarzers might have pulled a knife and slashed me. I described in detail the social atmosphere in such bars, my dance with a Fräulein who preferred partners of color with the color of money, the ugly black G.I. who accosted me, and the white MP whose job was to preserve order in a place where disorder frequently erupted.

I tried not to be too sarcastic, critical, or contemptuous of the black buddies from Henry, Warner, and Will Kasernes who drop in to the Dew Drop Inn to procure tabooed love with white females in the only venue for fraternization welcoming their sort on the north side of American-occupied Munich.

CHAPTER 4: DEFENDERS OF THE FAITH

On Friday night, February 19th, I went to Jewish services at Mc-Graw Kaserne as I usually did. When I touched the mezuzah on the sanctuary door frame and put my two fingers to my lips, little did I know that a defender of the faith I would meet there after the service would weeks later threaten my plans for the future. He would try to steer me on a path that was not an upward trajectory to the promising end of my Army days I desired, an honorable discharge, but rather a downward spiral to an ignominious end, a stretch in the stockade and a dishonorable discharge.

I picked up and placed atop my head a white yarmulke from the wooden box just inside the sanctuary. I passed by the rack of tallises neatly draped over ascending dowels since I knew that prayer shawls were worn on Saturdays, not Fridays.

The evening service had already begun when I took a seat in the rear. I picked up the prayer book lying in the middle of the chair, found the page the rabbi referred to, and alternatingly with the rabbi's reading of certain passages chanted other passages in Hebrew along with the rest of the congregation.

The room was filled with several different Jewish types connected with the military. There were young men in uniform, both officer and enlisted ranks. Like I, there were soldiers in civilian clothes, their military status apparent by their haircuts and/or American-style clothing. Sitting near me were older men in their late thirties and forties not in any kind of uniform, some with women and children at their side, civilian employees of the Army I gathered. A few men had women by their side that did not look Jewish. Other women in their late twenties or early thirties who looked Jewish were unaccompanied.

Two types I did not see at Jewish services on Munich's main Army base, types I did see in Nuremberg at the Palace of Justice, ironically the site of the Nazi War Crimes Trials, were German Jews who returned to the Fatherland after the war and concentration-camp survivors who after liberation chose not to go back to their home countries in Eastern Europe now under Soviet control. In Nuremberg, the Palace was centrally located and served the religious needs of all the city's Jews--soldiers on various smaller Kasernes, civilian

American Jews working in Germany, the returnees, and those not repatriated. Munich, a much larger city, must have had one or two synagogues that local Jews not linked to the U.S. Army attended.

With the conclusion of the service, everyone sauntered down the hall to the reception room for the Oneg Shabbat. Wine and refreshments were spread out on three rectangular tables covered with white tablecloths that ran halfway to the floor. Folding chairs were strewn about the room, but not enough for everyone to sit down on. Congregants took little white corrugated paper cups filled with red wine and held them up while the rabbi said the blessing in Hebrew.

A large braided challah rested on the middle table covered by a white cloth embroidered with a Star of David. The rabbi cut the Sabbath bread into small slices with a long cutting knife while he said the Hamotzi. People reached for challah and sponge cake, marble and yellow, to take with their coffee or tea. I put a few pieces of pickled herring and crackers on my paper plate and downed them with orange juice.

"David, David," a voice called out to me.

I turned and saw Leeann Armson, one of the women who came to services alone, walking toward me. I first met her two weeks earlier and got to know her somewhat. She was Jewish but was the wife of a warrant officer who was not. He was a helicopter pilot assigned to an airfield not far from my barracks on the other side of town. They had a nine-year-old daughter who was Jewish according to Jewish law. In the Halacha, it is written that a child is Jewish if the mother is, and it does not matter what religion, or race for that matter, the father is. Whether the little girl was being *raised* Jewish I had no idea and dared not ask. The Armsons lived on McGraw Kaserne, in the family housing section near the tennis courts. Mrs. Armson told me she came to services each week and was a member of Hadassah, the Jewish women's benevolent organization.

The lady defender of the faith about ten years my senior seemed to take a liking to me, as if I were a younger brother. She grew up in a small town in California, not far from where her husband was stationed after the war, where very few Jews lived. I gathered she liked talking to a Jewish boy who grew up in a city that had millions of Jews.

"Nice to see you again," she said when she stood near me.

"Nice to see you too, Mrs. Armson."

"Please call me Leeann. Mrs. Armson is my mother-in-law."

It felt funny calling an older married woman by her given name, but if that is what she preferred I was not going to argue about it.

"I shall be glad to . . . Leeann."

Leeann was beaming and seemed excited about something. "I just signed up for the tour of Israel next month. Are you going too?"

"Yes, I'm planning to. Weeks ago I wrote home and asked my parents to send me money from my bank account."

I had a joint account and sent home money each month to save for college, and now had over five hundred dollars. But ever since I attended the religious retreat in Berchtesgaden I was determined to visit Israel before I went home. It was worth it to me to withdraw almost half of it for perhaps a once-in-a-lifetime Jewish experience.

"Good. I'm glad to hear that."

"Is your husband and your daughter going?

"No. He can't get off work and she has school."

I did not say anything but I got the feeling these were not the real, or were not all of the, reasons. It could be that her husband wasn't going because he was a Gentile and not interested, and if the daughter wasn't being raised Jewish a trip to Israel may not mean much to her.

"Are other people from the congregation going?" I asked.

"Yes, a few. Others went last year. My friend is going and we'll share a hotel room." Leeann turned her head and nodded. "She's talking to the rabbi over there. Her husband is a captain . . . in Personnel."

The woman pointed out to me seemed the same age as Leeann, but was a little heavier and about the same height. A few minutes later she came over to Leeann and me, and Leeann introduced us.

"David. This is Doris Kaplan. Doris, this is David Streiber. He's at Henry Kaserne."

"Nice to meet you, Mrs. Kaplan," I said as we shook hands.

"Doris is a history teacher in the American High School next to the barracks," Leeann said. "And she teaches Hebrew to the Jewish kids in Sunday School."

"Where are you from, David," I was asked by this other defender of the faith. It was a typical question put to young soldiers at Jewish services, one that I had been asked many times by congregants in the States and in Germany.

Mrs. Kaplan did not ask me to call her by her first name and I did not take any liberties to be familiar with this female stranger. Like Leeann, she looked Jewish and judging by her last name her husband was too.

"I'm from New York . . . Brooklyn."

"So am I," she said. "Where in Brooklyn?"

"Coney Island."

"You must have gone to Abraham Lincoln High School."

"Yes I did," I said simply, not knowing where this question-and-answer deal was going.

"I'm from Flatbush. Went to James Madison High School . . . and Brooklyn College."

"Oh," was all I could say.

"Where in Coney Island," my inquisitor continued. "Sea Gate . . . Brighton Beach?"

Leeann just stood by, listening to her friend question me about my background. I was sure the small-town California girl had no knowledge of the different neighborhoods in New York. Evidently, the urbane central-Brooklyn girl did not know much about neighborhoods to the south in her own borough.

"No," I said emphatically, now somewhat annoyed by the questioning and misinformation. "My family lives in the *residential* section of Coney Island near the amusement area, *between* Sea Gate and Brighton Beach, what used to be called *West* Brighton Beach."

"Oh," was all the Flatbush woman could say, parroting me.

From the look on her face, I could tell she was surprised to learn I grew up in the "run down" part of Coney Island, what was fast becoming a slum, what Sea Gate and Brighton Beach residents sought to disassociate themselves from. Blacks and Puerto Ricans were moving into my neighborhood, Jews were moving to Long Island or better neighborhoods in Brooklyn, while many Italian homeowners remained in their little enclave near the subway terminal and refused to rent their basements to the darker-skinned newcomers.

Before long, after some more small talk and an avoidance of anything further about Coney Island, both women excused themselves and went off to talk to other people milling about in the reception room. I was not against talking to older, married, American-Jewish women, but as a twenty-year-old I was concerned more with meeting young, unmarried, German-Gentile women.

I was not alone for long, however. A man who seemed to be in his early forties came up to me. He held a coffee cup in one hand and a piece of cake on a napkin in the other.

"Hello. I'm Harold Berger." He put the cup on a nearby table and extended his hand to me.

I shook his hand.

"You're new here, aren't you?" he asked, turning slightly to pick up the cup.

"Yes."

"What's your name?"

"David . . . David Streiber."

"David, are you in the Army?"

"Yes," I said again.

"Where are you stationed?"

"I'm at Henry Kaserne . . . in a signal repair company."

"I've been to Henry. I know it well. And Warner and Will too."

Now it was my turn to ask questions. "Are *you* in the Army?"

"No . . . but I used to be. During the war I was a lieutenant in the Air Corps."

"Did you fly planes?" I thought he may have dropped bombs on Munich, and was responsible for some rubble that could still be seen on side streets around town.

"No. I worked in Admin."

I knew he meant he had some kind of administrative job. Since I was a clerk in the Army, we thus had a second thing in common.

"Harold, what did you do after the war?" He was a civilian and on a first-name basis with me, and not a warrant officer, so I had no reason to call him *Mr.* Berger.

"I went into business. And I joined the JWV."

The non-combat ex-G.I., ironically, associated himself with the Jewish War Veterans of America, a national organization dedicated to furthering the benefits and improving the lives of the many Jews who fought in foreign wars. Ostensibly, I myself could not join this group when I get out, since I would be classified as a peacetime enlistee and not a veteran, and was not eligible for receiving money for college under the G.I. Bill. Membership in the JWV was likely Harold's way of being a defender of the faith.

"What do you do here in Munich?" I asked.

Harold hesitated a bit before answering. "I'm in the import-export business. I set up a company here three years ago."

"Do you have to travel a lot?" I asked again matter-of-factly without thinking much about it.

Again he hesitated. "Yes. I often go to Berlin." But then Harold shifted the conversation back to me. "What do *you* do at Henry?"

I answered his questions simply and directly, never giving a second thought as to *who* this middle-age Jewish non-combat ex G.I. was and *why* he was asking me things about myself and my job.

"I'm a clerk in an office that oversees electronics repair shops."

Harold's face appeared to light up. He finished his cake and put his coffee cup down. "You don't fix equipment?"

"No. Last year I used to fix equipment in Nuremberg for a few months, but then I was given a clerk's job. I was transferred here a month ago to do the same kind of work."

"Do you know the pieces of equipment that are fixed?"

"Yes, of course, I went to radar school. I know the different names and nomenclatures. I type reports and make charts of pieces coming in, what work is to be done, how long repairs took, and what parts are on order for equipment awaiting repair."

Harold was silent for about ten seconds, looked at me intensely, and only said: "That's interesting."

The former World War II lieutenant must be batty, I thought. What I find dull, he finds interesting.

"Do you work on Saturday?" he asked.

I shook my head.

"You seem like a nice young fellow to talk to," he continued. "Maybe I can buy you lunch or dinner tomorrow? I know a good restaurant near the bahnhof."

The invitation of this stranger, a forty-something Jewish-American civilian working in Germany seemed harmless enough. I knew several such people in Nuremberg that I also met at services, even invited by one to dinner a few times with his family at his apartment.

"Dinner would be better."

"Good. Could you meet me about seven-forty-five in front of the main entrance to the bahnhof?"

I nodded my head. "Sure."

Harold smiled. "We can have dinner at eight."

"Okay. I'll be there."

Harold shook my hand again, then turned and went up to another young man in civies that was standing alone, a soldier judging from his short haircut. I did not think much of this at the time and did not think of Harold in a negative light. Indeed, in terms of age and war-time service, he reminded me of two of my uncles, one who was in the Army and the other the Navy.

The next day, when I walked out of Henry Kaserne, I planned to keep my dinner date. It certainly would be something different for a postwar soldier living in the barracks, a meal in a restaurant with, and paid for by, a World War II veteran. Harold reminded me somewhat of two of my uncles that fought during the war, one in the Army, the other in the Navy, who often told me bloody accounts of the damn Gerries and sneaky Japs. The evening would be a wel-come change from my customary forays into town on a weekend. I wondered what kind of war stories Harold, a G.I. who escaped combat duty, could tell me.

My plans to meet a middle-age male American at night afforded me time to hit Harry's Bar in the afternoon to try to meet a young fe-male German.

CHAPTER 5: QUARTER-JEWISH FRÄULEIN

It was at Harry's Bar that I met Erika, a university student, only nineteen. She came in that Saturday afternoon I was to meet Harold Berger, the man I met at Jewish services the night before, for dinner at eight.

Erika entered the bar with a friend about three o'clock. I was still sipping my beer. The two girls apparently knew Harry, as they said hello to him and spoke for almost a minute before sitting down at a table next to me. I noticed right away her most appealing qualities— a doll face and a hefty bosom. With her dark brown hair and five-foot two or three stature, she reminded me a little of Karin in Nuremberg. But Erika was prettier and sexier and that was enough to excite me into action. I wanted to kiss that adoring puss and get my hands and mouth on those big boobs.

"Wilst du tanzen mit mir?" I said in a familiar tone to the Fräulein I favored sitting a few feet away from me. I stood at the edge of her table, leaned over a bit, extended my hand, and looked straight at her. On the juke box, a slow song was playing. Two other couples were hoofing it up on the dance floor.

She smiled faintly, rose quickly, and took my hand. "Ja, bitte," she replied, two words I often heard in Germany.

I held Erika close to me, pushing in on her back so I could feel her chest against my body. She followed my steps very well, considering we learned to dance in two different countries an ocean apart.

"Was ist deiner namen?" I asked after a minute or so. I wanted to practice my German but still thought in English.

"You are American, no?"

"Yes."

"Soldier?"

"Yes. Is my German bad?" I asked.

"Your pronunciation is good but you spoke in a familiar voice when you don't know me. And you asked for my name incorrectly."

"I can see that your English is much better than my German."

"I study English at the University. And history too."

"What did I say wrong? I want to speak better German. I'll probably take it in college next year."

"You should use the formal *sie* with people you do not know, not *du*. Also, when asking a name, we say 'Wie heissen sie," like 'Who are you' in English."

"Why can't you say 'Was ist deiner namen' when asking for someone's name, like in English literally? Saying 'Who are you' can mean several things."

Erika was puzzled by my comment. "Like what it can mean?"

"Like what is your status or position in a company, or what is your relationship to someone," I gave as examples.

"I see, yes. But we just do not ask for a name in German."

"Okay," I said, as I held her a little closer. "Wie heissen sie?"

"Erika."

"Erika what?"

"Erika Kessler. Und vie heissen *sie*?"

"David . . . David Streiber."

"Streiber is German name."

"Yes I know."

"And David is Hebrew name . . . like King David in the Bible."

"Yes, I know," I said again.

The girl I was dancing with looked at me intensely, as if she were studying me. My hair wasn't blond and I didn't have blue eyes, but she probably wondered if I was of German background, and if not, what my ethnic identity was.

"You are German?" she asked first.

"No."

"Where your parents from? What country in Europe?"

Apparently, as a student of history, she knew that most Americans, whites at least, are of European origin.

"My mother was born in Poland, my father in the States. But his family came from Poland too."

"Your mother . . . what her name was before?"

"Neiman," I said. I knew she wanted to know my mother's maiden name. I pronounced it *Nay*man, as in German, not *Nee*man as in the American department store. .

"Neiman is German name. Why your parents have German name if from Poland?" she asked.

I answered her directly and truthfully, not worried about revealing my identity. "Because most Jews in Eastern Europe originally came from Germany."

Erika looked at me, staring for a few moments it seemed. She did not exhibit any surprise in learning that I was Jewish. Nine months earlier Karin did a double-take when I gave her the very same answer.

"The owner of the bar, Harry, is Jew also. He was in Dachau concentration camp."

"Yes, I know," I responded a third time. "He told me that himself when he sat down at my table. He's from Poland like my mother, from the same province even."

Erika hesitated before speaking again. We were still dancing to a slow tune and I was holding her close to me.

"My grandfather is Jew . . . but he married my grandmother who is Catholic. He let my grandmother raise my father Catholic."

"Oh," I eked out, somewhat astonished. Then I added, "Did your grandfather convert?"

"No, but he stopped going to synagogue."

"Oh," was all I could say again.

This was an unanticipated turn of events. I frequented Harry's Bar to meet a Fräulein I could establish a relationship and bed down with before going home in a few months, not expecting to run into a part-Jewish German girl, and one willing to talk about Jews and the war.

"I want to know more about Jews in Germany before the war and during the war," she said simply and directly.

"Didn't you learn about the Nazi period in school after the war or in your history class at the University?"

"No."

Her answer surprised me again. "Why not?"

The look on Erika's face changed somewhat, became more solemn. "We Germans don't like to talk about the war and Hitler and all those awful things that happened to Jews. My grandfather never spoke about it. What I know my grandmother told me . . . and Harry too said a little about the war."

"Well," I responded. "I'd like to hear about your grandfather."

"Some other time."

"And I can tell you what I learned about Germany and the war in *my* history class in high school, if you like."

"I like. Yes. But some other time," she repeated.

"I can also tell you what my mother told me about growing up in Poland during and after World War I, how Gentiles in her small town did not like Jews and made fun of them."

"Some other time," she said a third time. .

"Okay." Her one-quarter non-Aryan background intrigued me but there was no point pushing her to talk about it now. My mind, as well as my hand, was on her body and not her family.

The song on the juke box ended, but another slow one came on. We continued to dance and I held her as close to me as possible without alarming or offending her.

"Where are you a soldier?" she asked awkwardly, changing the subject. I knew she was asking where I was stationed in the Army.

"I'm at Henry Kaserne, on the north side of Munich. Near Warner and Will Kasernes."

"Yes, yes, I know it. Last year I went with soldier at Warner Kaserne. He first American I go with."

This last answer struck a nerve. I could only wonder *who* was the G.I. she went with, that is, what *racial* group he was in, not what his name was.

"Did you meet him at the Dew Drop Inn, a bar for American soldiers behind Warner?"

If she answered in the affirmative, then I knew she crossed the color line. If she answered in the negative, then I would be fairly certain she did not. A moment later, she said what I wanted to hear.

"No, I do not know such place. I met him at the University. He sat in one of my classes at night. We had coffee after. He speak good German."

It was a relief to hear that. The Fräulein I liked and wanted to get into bed with was not colorblind. We twirled around a bit and I felt at ease. But, I thought, is he a competitor for her affections?

"Do you still go with him?" I wanted to know.

"No. He went back to America," she said without a trace of emotion. "Five months ago."

For a second time in two minutes, I got the answer I wanted to hear.

So, she had had that romance in her life, a white G.I. had left for his sake. It hardly pained her now to think how poor a part she, his lover, had played in his life. He shtupped her, then took off, and she was just, like Natalie Wood in the 1956 Army movie with Tab Hunter, "the girl he left behind." Sounds like what I did to Karin in Nuremberg. The American boyfriend said auf Wiedersehen to Erika about the same time I walked out on Karin because of her unsavory comment about Hitler and the Jews.

Who knows? I thought. The German-speaking white G.I. in the barracks up the road from me may, like Karin, have harbored Nazi sentiments, and waved goodbye if Erika made a comment *he* did not like about Hitler and the Jews.

Trying to peg Erika was not easy. She obviously was not the nice German girl I thought I wanted to plug into, someone like Karin who never went with a G.I. before, since she frequents G.I. bars and has consorted with an American soldier. But I was sure my dancing partner was not a bad German girl either, not a hooker with a hand out for dollars or Marks, like the Fräulein I met in the Negerbar, and that was a relief.

The music stopped. "We sit down now," Erika said. "You can join us at our table if you like."

"Danke sehr," I responded quickly, hoping to impress the Fräulein with my German. "I will."

I picked up my half-finished beer, bottle and glass, and carried the two to the girls' table.

"My friend does not speak English much," Erika countered, as she introduced us.

I didn't catch the friend's name or look straight at her. She was not that pretty and I was too busy taking furtive glances at Erika's main upper-body part.

Erika spoke to her friend in their native tongue, telling her, from what I could make out, that I was an American soldier at Henry Kaserne. The friend nodded and looked at me several times. I listened to them talk, offered to buy them a drink but they declined and paid for one themselves, ordered another beer for myself, and occasionally said something to Erika. I could not sit there like a dummy all afternoon.

The two Fräuleins talking to each other in German most of the time gave me time to think about Erika and her Jewish grandfather. Did she want to know more about the Jews in Germany because she wanted to convert to Judaism? I wondered how Grosspapa survived

Nazi persecution? What did her Opa do after the war? Would Herr Kessler der Alte talk to me?

Later in the day I would get answers to my unspoken questions.

Erika and I danced twice more at different times but we didn't talk much. I thought she might ask me to twirl around with her friend but she didn't and I was grateful for that.

It was almost four-thirty when the two got up to leave.

"Can I walk you girls home?" I asked in English. I still had plenty of time before I was to meet Harold for dinner. And if Erika perhaps lived alone she might invite me up.

"If you want," Erika said.

"I want."

All three of us left together. I followed alongside the two girls but positioned myself next to Erika and not her friend. We walked north on Luitpoldstrasse, maneuvered around a number of parallel and perpendicular streets, and then made a left on Schellingstrasse.

The encounter in Munich that afternoon sitting at a table with two German girls in a bar, one who spoke English and the other who did not, one who turned me on and the other who did not, reminded me of what occurred New Year's Eve in Nuremberg. After 1960 was rung in, I left with the two girls I met, accompanying them home, but I was not invited into their apartment. I hoped this time around with Erika, a different scenario might unfold.

As we walked, my love interest started talking about her grandfather without any provocation on my part. She spoke in such personal terms to me, as if I were a long-time friend or boyfriend, but in English so her friend would not understand. I listened intensely and said nothing.

When we arrived at her apartment building on Schellingstrasse, it was apparent that Erika lived alone. Her friend continued on her way and I was invited upstairs. As events developed, the scenario with a pretty German girl in her apartment turned out to be different than that which occurred in Nuremberg New Year's Eve, but not the one I was savoring to play a part in.

Erika's apartment was small but comfortable enough for one person, what a university student on a budget could afford. She made some coffee, sat down on a chair across from me, and continued with the story of her grandfather. This was the "some other time" she referred to earlier. The quarter-Jewish Fräulein I liked obviously had some kind of affinity with her Opa's heritage and suffering.

It was soon clear to me, much to my consternation, that there was not going to be any intimate exchange between us on this day. But it *was* going to be a day of *knowledge* exchange, Erika telling me about her Jewish grandfather's life in Germany and I telling her about Jews in Germany from what teachers said and what I read in textbooks.

"My grandfather was Isidor Kessler," Erika said. "He was born in Berlin in 1889."

That year, when I heard it, rang a bell, for I knew it was the same year Adolph Hitler was born in Austria, Charlie Chaplin in England, and my maternal grandmother in Poland.

Isidor was an only child and, although his parents were not especially religious, he was enrolled in Hebrew School at age nine. He had his Bar Mitzvah on a Saturday four days after his 13th birthday in the synagogue on Oranienburger Strasse in the German capital. The family still cherishes the faded 1902 black-and-white picture of little Izzy, the smiling boy with a yarmulke atop his head, a talis around his neck, and a prayer book in his hands.

In 1914, when the Great War broke out, 25-year-old Isidor was drafted into the German Army to fight for his Aryan country. The irony of this was that big Izzy, unknowingly, could have fought side-by-side with the Little Corporal and fired across the trenches at the Little Tramp while my Bubba in a thatched-roof house nurtured Little Neimans, my mother one of them.

Erika's Jewish grandfather at the time of his conscription was a young lawyer and a newlywed with a baby on the way. Her father, Herr Kessler der Junge, was born in 1915 and quickly baptized under the name Christoph. Grossmutti did not want her child to have an obviously-Jewish given name.

Isidor's parents were not happy that their son was a soldier fighting for Germany on the front lines. They feared he could be killing fellow Jews from France and England without ever knowing if the dead soldiers were his kinsmen.

"Gott sei Dank," Erika's great-grandparents let out when their son came home to Berlin in one piece at the end of 1918.

The Kesslers pinched the discharged soldier a few times to make sure it was their Izzy. They put their fears behind them and prayed their son would resume his legal career and be successful at it.

And successful he was. Isidor Kessler passed his examinations and was admitted into the legal profession. In 1920, the 31-year-old German lawyer who could now practice was offered a job in a Munich law firm and moved there with his Catholic wife and five-year-old baptized boy. It was the first full year of the newly-formed Weimar Republic and much legal work had to be done, such as reforming the currency because of hyperinflation, dealing with para-military extremist groups on both the left and right, negotiating the terms of the Treaty of Versailles with the victors of the Great War, unifying tax policies, and instituting a railway system.

In the 1920s, Isidor advanced both in income and stature. He took on more lucrative cases, contributed to the development of renowned legal journals, and helped establish professional organizations. By that time in Germany, in large cities especially, about half the law-yers were Jewish or of Jewish origin. Some had renounced their faith while others had been baptized. But they never called them-selves "Jewish lawyers," for they were Germans first, Jews and lawyers second.

At the end of 1929, the relative success that Erika's unbaptized Zeyde experienced as a lawyer during the Weimar years came to an abrupt end. The stock market crash in the United States meant that American banks no longer could advance funds to Germany so repa-rations could be paid. Legal work he was doing dried up.

The onset of the Depression in the States hit Germany very hard. Unemployment throughout the land rose to extremely high levels and could not be stopped by conventional economic measures. In September 1930, the nascent Nazi Party entered the Reichstag with 19% of the popular vote, signaling political instability in the final two years and three months of the Weimar Republic.

Beginning in January 1933, with Hitler as Chancellor, Jews were to be ostracized from all areas of social life. His National Socialist Party made a distinction between "Jews" and "non-Jews," based on the *grandparents'* origin, one's current religious affiliation being of secondary importance. Non-Jewish lawyers, including partners in Izzy's own law firm, rejoiced. With much reduced competition, they stood to earn more money.

Middle-age Isidor Kessler didn't suffer as severely like other Jewish lawyers did during the first five years of the Nazi period. The new 1933 Law regarding admission to the legal profession required all Jews to apply for re-admission, unless they were admitted prior to 1914 or fought on the front lines in the Great War. Thus, Izzy was exempt from the new Law on the second ground and was allowed to continue practicing his profession.

"The exception for Frontkämpfer Jewish soldiers had been introduced by President Hindenburg," Erika told me, "but because of the large numbers of Jewish lawyers exempted from having to apply for re-admission, this was no safeguard against further discrimination."

Erika explained the discriminatory actions her grandfather and other Jews suffered. Partnerships had to be dissolved between Jewish and non-Jewish lawyers, legal aid cases were no longer given to Jewish lawyers, and Jewish lawyers were no longer consulted by the courts for their legal opinions.

Poor Izzy, classified as a Jew by birth but in a mixed marriage with a Christian son, struggled to make a living as a lawyer. But, on 30 November 1938, the Nazis, only one month following the British appeasement allowing Germany to annex the Sudetenland in Czechoslovakia, banned all Jewish lawyers from practicing law. From that day forward, very few Jewish lawyers were permitted to continue lawyering, and only under the title "Konsultent," to advise and represent Jewish clients only. Because Izzy was in a mixed marriage, and his non-Jewish Frau was alive, he was granted a privilege which provided some degree of protection against further persecution.

In 1939, after the outbreak of war, his income dropped to almost zero. The Jewish lawyer without non-Jewish clients had to survive on his wife's small inheritance. Any privilege he had been granted was now moot. In 1940 and '41, before mass deportations began in Germany, he tried to emigrate to America with his Jewish parents, planning to get his non-Jewish wife and child out later. Ironically, the Nazi regime eagerly provided passports to German Jews, as this meant their property could be seized and their citizenship revoked.

The United States, however, under the influence of a less-than-sympathetic president and a number of anti-Semitic State Department officials, refused to grant the three Kesslers, and tens of thousands of other European Jews, U.S. tourist visas, ostensibly, because the political refugees had "no return address." Similarly, Britain and most other countries refused asylum to Jews and obstructed Jewish immigration for various reasons of their own, all pretexts. Passports issued to stateless Jews without property proved to be no passport to freedom.

Erika's great-grandparents were soon taken from their apartment on Jüdenstrasse, formerly the Jewish district in medieval Berlin, and deported by truck and railway to Auschwitz in Poland. Nazi records captured after the war confirmed they both died at the infamous concentration camp in 1943. Their son remained in Munich with a useless passport until he too was transported to a concentration camp, Dachau, in a small town north of Munich.

Isidor survived the ordeal, perhaps because Dachau was not an extermination camp like the one his parents were sent to. Izzy could have shared one of the unheated barracks with Harry and his brother, as they all walked out of this hell-on-earth when the camp was liberated by American soldiers a week before Germany surrendered.

After the war, the grandfather, a clientless lawyer and a concentration-camp inmate for two years, returned home a disillusioned man in poor health. Son Christoph, a soldier in the Wehrmacht without an arm and half a leg missing from fighting on the Russian front, likewise returned home a disillusioned man in poor health. Grossmutti--after suffering through years of war, bombings, and food shortages in Germany--had the added burden of taking care of two unemployable men, a 56-year-old husband and a 30-year-old son.

Twelve years of Hitlerism and war during the Third Reich, plus family stress in postwar Germany, took their toll on the 65-year-old woman. Erika's story-telling grandmother died on June 27, 1957, the day I enlisted. We both entered a new world on the same day.

It was a little after seven when Erika and I stopped talking. Now I knew about her grandfather's life in Germany as a Jew and as a lawyer in the past four decades, a critical time in German history. I gave the girl I liked a guarded kiss on the lips, made a date to meet her at Harry's the following Saturday, and headed out the door to catch the Stassenbahn and keep the dinner date with Harold. .

CHAPTER 6: DINNER AT EIGHT

Harold was waiting for me at the Hauptbahnhof's front entrance when I stepped off the streetcar. It was ten minutes to eight. As I approached him, he reached out to shake my hand.

The World War II Jewish veteran was wearing a winter coat different from the one I had on. I was in a knee-length grey Loden coat with a hood folded in back that I bought in the PX at Merrell Barracks for twenty dollars. It was an English-style garment that the sergeant in *The Third Man* was wearing, who was shot and killed by Orson Welles at the end.

My coat had loose toggles on the front instead of buttons. That design was not very good at keeping the cold out, the main function of an overcoat. So I went to the German tailor at Merrell and had a long zipper put in to keep warm. I saw other G.I.'s in Nuremberg and Munich wear the same coat around the barracks, but I was the only one who had that zipper in front under the toggles. I felt good that I altered the coat to make it better and looked forward to wearing it next winter in New York, and in future winters.

By contrast, Harold, an Army man, was wearing a dark-blue armslength outer-garment with very large buttons that looked like a Navy pea coat. As sailors often do, he had the collar up but the neck was open. Wearing a dark grey hat with a wide brim, I thought he looked like someone trying to hide his face.

"The restaurant I know is just around the corner," Harold said. He put his hand on my shoulder and steered me to the left. "You'll like it."

I followed my dinner benefactor to the good restaurant he claimed he knew, but "just around the corner" was a misnomer. We had to walk the equivalent of nearly *three* city blocks, as the Hauptbahnhof rectangular building was quite large in length and width.

The Münchner Hofbräuhaus was a three-story old building on a corner street that looked pretty fancy from the outside. The well-lit restaurant was on the high-ceilinged ground floor. I glanced at the menu posted on the window near the door as I walked in. On the inside, the décor looked pretty fancy as well—small and large round tables covered with embroidered white tablecloths standing on varnished wide-strip hardwood floors.

Harold moved to a table for four that was not occupied and we sat down across from one another.

"They brew their own beer here," Harold noted. "It's very good. You should try it."

"Okay."

Harold raised his hand to motion for a waiter. "Zwei Bier, bitte."

A minute later, the waiter placed two menus in plastic on the table with two tall glasses of beer. I took a sip of the German restaurant's specialty right away.

"Not bad," I said.

We both looked at the menus while the waiter waited. Harold helped me discern some of the German words. I ordered the Wiener Schnitzel that came with pomme frites. Germans apparently use the French term for fried potatoes. Harold went for the Knackwurst and Sauerkraut. The dinner listings on the menu under "Schwein" were passed over by both Jewish boys. .

Harold spoke forcefully as he ate, something I preferred not to do. Every so often he would spit out a phrase or a sentence as he chewed his food. I uttered something only when my food went down and before I took another bite.

The former Army Air Corps lieutenant in administration and forty-something Jewish civilian running an import-export business in postwar Germany did not say much about himself, but he practically wanted to know my whole life story.

"I grew up in the Bronx," Harold revealed. "Graduated from City College in forty-one . . . majored in economics. When we entered the war, I enlisted and got a commission."

Harold never said anything about what he did before the war or after, whether he married and had children, or what he was doing now in Munich other than running a business. He did not say where he lived in town, if he had a Schatzie, what his connection to the military was, or how he came to know my Kaserne so well. Other than what little he told me the day before at synagogue and today at dinner, I just knew he went to Jewish services at McGraw Kaserne.

"Where did you grow up," I was asked as we both ate.

"I grew up in Brooklyn, in Coney Island, the opposite side of New York City from where you were. I only went to the Bronx a few times. My father took me to a baseball game at Yankee Stadium and in high school I ran track and I once went to Van Cortland Park for a relay race."

"I lived not far from Van Cortland."

"You were at one end of the subway line in New York and I was at the other end. For a dime, I traveled the whole length of the city."

"What high school did you go to?"

"I went to Lincoln High and graduated in fifty-seven. I joined the Army the next day. In January, I took the College Boards and applied to Brooklyn College."

"You're doing the right thing by going to college, David. When did you decide to do that?" he said as he chewed.

"When I was at Fort Monmouth," I answered after I swallowed. "Nine months after I enlisted for the 33-week course in radar repair." It was not necessary to mention New Jersey, as I was sure Harold knew where most stateside bases were located.

He sliced a bit of Knackwurst off, put the fork in his mouth, and then scooped up some sauerkraut. "Why did you join the Army? There was no war."

"I wanted to get away from home. I didn't like the apartment we lived in or the landlady. In my last year of high school, I lost interest in college. I also wanted to get my military service over with, and I thought I might want to make it a career so it was better to go in while I was young."

"I understand, but what made you decide to go to college while you were at Monmouth," he asked, still chewing his food.

"I had a chance meeting with the lieutenant in charge of the Army education program. He advised me to go to college when I get out and major in electrical engineering. He said the radar repair course will feed right into that."

Harold thought a moment. "Did you graduate?"

"Yes, I completed the course in the summer of fifty-eight, but I never got to work my MOS."

My dinner date seemed surprised. "How come?"

"Well, I was sent to Fort Ord after graduation with some of my classmates, and those in classes a week or two after mine. We were assigned to a signal battalion, but there was no electronic equipment of any kind to repair."

Harold laughed. "That's typical of the Army. So what did you do all day?”

“One buddy was made Battalion Mail Clerk. The rest of us just did bullshit details . . . like policing the barracks, picking up butts on the grass, and riding in trucks collecting garbage in cans around the fort. Occasional KP and guard duty too.”

“I see. How long did that go on?” Harold said as he swallowed another mouthful of wurst and kraut, then wiped his lips with the white linen napkin.

“For five months, until I received orders to go overseas. I used to bug out of details as often as I could, by sneaking away from the barracks and hiding out in the Service Club.”

“I guess you wanted to go overseas, to escape the monotony of details and to hopefully work your MOS.”

“Yes,” I said again, “but only to Germany. Half my buddies from Monmouth went to Korea. I was lucky to be on the Seventh Army list, in the group that was the other half.”

“Yes, you were lucky. Duty in Germany is much better than in Korea. Were you assigned to Nuremberg right away?”

“No. I first went to Böblingen . . . not far from Stuttgart.”

“I know where Böblingen is. What outfit were you in?”

“The One-seventy-sixth Signal Company Repair.”

“How come you didn’t stay in Böblingen?”

“Well, not many guys do. The one-seventy-sixth has electronics repair teams all over West Germany. First I was put on Team Five in Nuremberg, then transferred to Team Eighteen in Munich.”

“I see.”

“I was lucky to go to Nuremberg. I almost went to Fulda.”

“On the Czech border?” Harold said right away.

“Yes.”

“You were lucky a second time.”

“Yes. Somebody up there must like me,” I said facetiously.

“You said you never worked your MOS. How come you didn’t work it in Nuremberg? You were on an electronics repair team.”

“We didn’t have any radar equipment to fix when I first got there about a year ago. I worked in the shop for two months doing simple repairs, like replacing wires and soldering parts on headsets, telephones, and walkie-talkies. Other shop mates, more experienced repairmen, repaired radio transmitters and receivers, mobile devices on trucks, and power supply units."

"Well, at least you were working in electronics, doing job skills you could use when you get out."

Harold seemed awfully interested in the electronics work that I did in Germany. I wondered why. "To tell you the truth," I said, after I swallowed a piece of my Schnitzel, "I was bored. And it didn't much matter what I worked on as I'm planning to study something other than electrical engineering in college."

"Oh," Harold let out at this last comment. "But you said you only worked in the shop for two months. How come?"

"The Master Sergeant and Warrant Officer running the office in Nuremberg overseeing six teams in the area needed a clerk and they offered me the job."

I laughed a little, took another bite of veal and frites, chewed and swallowed, then continued. "The team sergeant recommended me because I was not a very good repairman in the shop. Taking the clerk's job got me off the bench."

"I guess you liked doing clerical work instead."

"As a matter of fact, I did. I liked sitting at a desk, typing letters, filing reports, and making color charts of repairs over time for different pieces of equipment."

"What about here in Munich?"

"I do the very same thing—clerical work. I was transferred since the team here also needed a clerk and I was experienced."

"You don't work in the shop?"

"No. But I go there almost every day to check on the supply of parts and the equipment repaired or awaiting repair."

"Does your team here have microwave equipment?"

"A few pieces. We're supposed to get more. The new men coming are from the microwave repair school at Fort Gordon."

"Oh," Harold said again.

"Why do you ask?"

"Well, I'm planning to add microwave ovens for use in kitchens to my list of items to export to Europe."

I looked at Harold but did not say anything.

"As you may know, a decade ago microwave ovens became commercially available in the States based on the radar technology developed during the war. That's why they're called 'radar-ranges'."

"I didn't know that."

"David," Harold said, clearing his throat and hesitating a moment. "Can you get me some Army technical manuals on microwave equipment?"

Again I looked at the man sitting across from me but did not say anything.

"I need them to decide which microwave ovens to export. Different models are made by Raytheon and Tappan. Right now they're very expensive but in the near future they should be affordable to the average household."

"I don't know."

"Does your company have microwave manuals?"

"Yes," I said. "We have those manuals in my office and also in the shop, but I don't know if I can get any for you."

"Well then maybe I can just look at them in your office on a Sunday or weekday at night. I have an ID that can get me on any Munich Kaserne."

So this is why Harold invited me to dinner, I thought. He wants something from me, something I probably shouldn't give him if I want to stay out of trouble with the Army.

"Isn't it against regulations for me to give a civilian a technical manual . . . or even let him look at it?"

"A *German* civilian, yes, but not an American," Harold answered with confidence.

In spite of a former G.I.'s assurance, I wasn't sure he was correct on that point. I paused before I spoke again. "I'll see what I can do," I told him, without clearly saying whether I would or would not give him what he was asking for.

Harold and I finished our meals without discussing anything of importance further, but what he asked me for was in the back of my mind. I left the restaurant at nine-thirty and caught the Strassenbahn back to Parzivalplatz and then the Blue Goose bus to Henry Kaserne.

CHAPTER 7: I SPY

"Don't do it," Sergeant Ramirez said to me Monday morning when I came to work and mentioned my encounter with Harold Berger and his apparently innocuous request.

All day Sunday I couldn't help thinking about what Harold asked me for at dinner on Saturday night. As an Army clerk overseeing electronic repair teams, I certainly could get my hands on technical manuals for microwave equipment but forking them over to an American civilian, one that I hardly knew, was another matter. My gut instinct as a soldier told me I shouldn't do it, but my Jewishness favored my accommodating a co-religionist.

I looked at my superior but did not respond.

"Better go see Counterintelligence at McGraw Kaserne and tell them about it," he told me. "You can take off this morning."

"Okay, Sarge. Thanks"

I left the Area Office soon after Ramirez said I could go. CWO Horner had not come in yet. I was in my fatigue uniform and black boots, and put on my field jacket and boxed cap. I did not go back to my room and change into my Class A's or civilian clothes. During working hours, it was not against Army regulations for G.I.s to travel around town outside the barracks gate in fatigues. On the bus and streetcar Germans looked at me askance, as an unwelcome occupier of their Fatherland, but that didn't bother me.

The HQ of the 66th Military Intelligence Group at McGraw Kaserne, Munich's counterintelligence unit, was housed in a long building located just inside the main entrance on the left, between the APO and the McGraw Theater. The back of the long building faced Peter Auzinger Strasse.

"Can I help you, soldier?" a sergeant sporting three stripes and one rocker asked me as I approached his desk near the front door.

"I need to speak to someone."

"About what?"

"About an American civilian who asked me to get some technical manuals for him," I answered.

The sergeant peered at me. "Who are you, soldier?

"I'm Spec Four Streiber," I said, although he could clearly see that from the nametag and rank on my field jacket.

"What outfit are you in?

"I'm the clerk in the office of the One-seventy-six Signal at Henry Kaserne. We oversee six electronic repair teams in the Munich Area Command."

"Wait here," I was told curtly.

The sergeant turned around and went into one of the rooms behind him. From where I was standing, I couldn't see who was in that office. He came back less than a minute later.

"Okay, Streiber, go to the office on your left and speak to Lieutenant Gibson."

The First Lieuy looked up from the papers on his desk when I came up to him. The one silver bar on his khaki shirt collar stood out to me. A brown nameplate spelling James J. Gibson rested in front of him. He was in Class A Greens. A jacket hanging on a rack behind him revealed his years of service and overseas tours of duty besides his officer rank.

I stood at attention and saluted. "Specialist Strreiber reporting, sir."

The O-2 saluted back and pointed to the wood chair beside his desk. "Have a seat, Streiber."

I sat down but before I could speak again he said: "I understand you're at Henry in the One-seventy-six Signal."

"Yes sir."

"What seems to be the problem? Why did you come to M-I-G?"

"Well sir, last Friday evening at Jewish services here at McGraw a man came up to me at the reception afterward and introduced himself. He said that he was in the Army during the war as an officer and . . . ."

The lieutenant interrupted me. "A *Jewish* man?"

"Yes," I said, without the 'sir.'

"What name did he give you?"

"Harold Berger."

I was not surprised by the questioning about Harold's name or religion. Perhaps his name was already on an M.I.G. watch list and just because he was at Jewish services did not necessarily mean he was Jewish. Non-Jews come to services with Jewish spouses or with friends. In Nuremberg I brought Karin with me several times.

"What was he doing in Munich?"

"He said he ran an import-export business . . . and travels to Berlin a lot."

The lieutenant pulled out his middle desk drawer, reached in, and took out what appeared to be a list of names. "What did you say his name was?"

"Harold Berger."

"How do you spell that?"

"B-E-R-G-E-R."

The lieutenant ran his index finger down the list of names, and stopped at one of them. "We know of him," he said. "We've been watching him for about a year now. He often travels to other cities in East Germany, not just Berlin, and to Moscow. But we don't know what he does there or who he meets."

I looked at the Lieuy, a little stunned by this revelation about Harold, but did not say anything.

"We checked him out. He *was* in the Army during the war. That part of his story is true. But for a long time now he has had leanings to the Left."

I listened but still did not speak.

"When did Berger ask you to get him technical manuals?"

"The next day, Saturday. He asked me to dinner."

"What kind of manuals?"

"Those related to microwave repair. He said he wants to export microwave ovens to Europe, radar-ranges they are called, based on radar technology developed during the war. I told him I graduated from the radar repair school at Fort Monmouth and that interested him."

The lieutenant leaned back on his chair, looked side-to-side, and thought for a moment. "Streiber," he said, focusing straight at me. "We can use someone like you."

I waited for the junior officer to speak again.

"I want you to meet with this Berger fellow again and try to get some information from him."

"Information?"

"Yes . . . like who he meets in East Germany and what does he do there."

"What about the manuals he wants me to get for him?"

"Stall him," the lieutenant emphasized. "Don't give him anything. Say you are working on it."

"You mean you want me to be a spy?"

"You would be a 'handler'," the lieutenant stressed, "that's what we call it. You would be *handling* a suspected spy, helping us get information about him so we can perhaps arrest him."

"I see." I should have said, notwithstanding the semantic differential, spy, handler, it's the same thing.

"How much time do you have left in Germany, Streiber?"

"My rotation date is six June."

"That's more than three months. You should be able to get some information for us by then."

"I don't know, sir. I don't like this sort of thing. If you want to arrest him, then arrest him, but I don't want to be involved. I just want to serve the time I have left to my enlistment and get an honorable discharge."

"Streiber. If you don't help us, we can charge *you* with consorting with a known spy and court martial you. You would get a *dishonorable* discharge and perhaps some time in the stockade too."

If the lieutenant was trying to scare me into becoming a handler, he was succeeding. It seemed I had no choice but to go along with what the M.I.G. officer was asking of me, or let him think I was going along with him, at least for the time being.

"Okay," I agreed, nodding my head.

"Go to Jewish services this Friday," the lieutenant told me. Talk to Berger if he is there. Go with him to dinner if he invites you. See what you can learn. Report to me next Monday."

"Okay," I said again.

Sergeant Ramirez came out of his room and into my little work space as soon as I got back to the Area Office. "How did you make out in Counterintelligence," he asked.

"I saw a first lieutenant there, James Gibson."

CWO Horner heard us talking, left his office, and stood in the open doorway between Ramirez' and my room. "I know Gibson. He's a good man."

"You told Gibson what you told me?" Ramirez wanted to know.

"Yes."

"What did the lieutenant say?" Horner asked.

I gathered Ramirez told Horner about my encounter with Harold Berger. "He wanted me *not* to give the American, a former officer during the war, any technical manuals, but instead wanted me to keep meeting with him to try to get information from him."

"Information about what?" they both asked at the same time.

"About the American's trips to East Germany and Russia."

"I see," Ramirez said.

Horner nodded his head. "Do what the lieutenant says, Streiber."

"I have to report back to M.I.G. next Monday, after I probably will see Berger again at Jewish services this Friday night."

"Do what the lieutenant says," Horner repeated.

"Yes sir."

I went back to my desk, sat down, and looked for something to do.

The next few days I tried to do my clerk's job as normal but my new job as unwilling spy or coerced handler occupied my thinking. I had a key to the front door and came back to the office in the evening after chow, when I knew Ramirez and Horner would not be there, and perused the technical manuals we had in a bookcase against the wall in Ramirez' office.

All the manuals were in Series 11, the ones for Signal equipment. I found a few dealing with microwave units with different nomenclatures and read through them. These units were new to me as I was familiar only with radar equipment.

I learned that the microwave oven was invented in 1945, accidentally as it were. An engineer with the military was researching uses for radar technology. He was standing in front of a magnetron and it melted the chocolate bar he had in his pocket. With a further test, he held near the magnetron a bag of corn kernels and they exploded into popcorn. Microwaves emitted from the radar equipment made the water molecules in food vibrate and heat up, causing the food to cook.

The first microwave ovens arrived in Britain in 1959, just a year earlier. I guess this is what Harold claimed he was interested in, exporting American-made ovens to Germany, East and West. But as an oven-exporter why he needed technical manuals for *repairing* microwave equipment was beyond me, that is, until I read about one particular unit with a three-digit nomenclature.

The AN/TRC-170 is an Army and Navy radio terminal set for air and ground transportable signals. Terminals use tropospheric scatter microwaves to provide a secure communications network between point-to-point nodes, facsimile circuits, and teletype channels. If Harold were a spy for East Germany and the Russians, such manuals would be of great use to our enemies, as they might be able to tap into our electronic signals. The U.S.'s communications networks would not be so secure anymore. It seemed to me that his claim of needing the manuals for deciding which microwave ovens to export was simply a pretext.

On Friday I went to Jewish services at McGraw Kaserne as usual. Ramirez and Horner were happy to let me out early from the Area Office so I could perhaps talk to Harold Berger before the service began and commence eliciting tidbits of information about his trips to the East that Counterintelligence was looking for.

I knew I had to tread lightly with Harold. I couldn't very well ask him outright who his contacts were in East Germany and what secrets he may be giving them. On the one hand I wanted to be a good soldier and do what my superiors in the Army expected of me, but on the other hand I did not relish being a spy or handler, especially toward a fellow Jew who served his country during the war and reminded me of my own uncles.

Would I have to *promise,* I wondered, that I would get Harold the manuals he asked for in exchange for information in all likelihood he would not want to reveal, to me or anyone else in the American military? Should I tell my new middle-age Jewish friend that Counterintelligence is on to him and he should be careful, after first getting *him* to promise he would not tell anyone I warned him?

I was conflicted about how to be in reality a spy, a counterspy, or euphemistically a handler.

CHAPTER 8: THE HANDLER

"Hello David, how are you?" Harold said, as he sat down next to me in a middle row at Jewish services.

It was February 26th, about ten minutes before the rabbi was to begin the evening service.

"Fine. And you?"

Harold ignored my perfunctory answer and question. He saw that all I held in my hands was a prayer book. I had no large manila envelope on the bench next to me that could have held the micro-wave technical manuals he asked me for. My spy-apparent wasted no time and minced no words.

"You didn't bring me anything," he snarled, more as a statement of fact than a question.

"No."

The American civilian I was supposed to handle looked at me with inquisitive eyes.

"I forgot all about it," I told Harold in a bald face lie, as I could think of nothing else all week. "I'm sorry."

This second untruth seemed to solidify my entrance into the role of reluctant handler. Lieutenant Gibson, Sergeant Ramirez, and Mr. Horner would have been proud of me.

"Can you get them for me next week?"

"I'll try," I replied in another falsehood, this time on two counts. I wasn't planning on coming to services next Friday night, as I would be packing and preparing to leave early Sunday morning for a trip to Israel, and, in any event, I wasn't planning on giving Harold any-thing, as per Lieutenant Gibson's admonition.

"Good." Harold sat back on the bench, seemingly satisfied for the moment, and picked up a prayer book in the cubby space in back of the bench in front of us.

At the Oneg Shabbat after the service, I noticed Harold going up to other young soldiers. I presumed he was asking them out to din-ner the next day, to pump them for information about their jobs and Army articles or resources they could get for him.

When I saw Harold was alone, I went up to him. Playing the role of a good handler and following M.I.G. orders, I began pumping him for information. He was holding a cup of coffee and biting into a piece of yellow sponge cake. I tried to ask innocuous questions so as not to arouse his suspicion.

"Harold, how much do you think you can sell the microwave ovens for in Europe?"

"I don't know yet. It depends."

"Depends on what?"

"What American manufacturers charge me and what the governments in each country say I could sell them for."

"Oh, did you meet with government officials in Berlin when you went there?" I deliberately refrained from saying Moscow because Harold never said he went there, only Lieutenant Gibson did.

Harold lifted his chin to loosen his shirt collar somewhat. He began to perspire a little. I could see he was uncomfortable with this line of questioning, especially by someone *he* previously questioned for information.

"Why do you ask?"

"No special reason . . . I was just curious," I said, falling deeper into my handler role and extending my untruthfulness.

"Yes, I met with a few officials."

I couldn't very well ask Harold outright what were the names of the German officials, which is what M.I.G. wanted to know, as such a brazen question would surely expose the secret part I was acting out for American officials.

"Did they agree to import your microwaves?" I asked instead, hoping he would reveal some names of his own accord.

"One did."

"Oh, that was nice," I retorted somewhat facetiously. "At least you got some business started."

"Yes," was all he could say.

Just then Leeann Armson came over to us. I sensed Harold was relieved that she interrupted us so he wouldn't have to answer any more of my questions.

"Hello, David, how are you?" Leeann said, exactly as Harold had said before the service, but with a smile.

"Fine. Thank you."

"And you Harold?" she added, turning her head to look at him.

Harold smiled back. "Fine. Thank you," he parroted me.

I faced Leeann. "I didn't know you knew Harold."

"I've known Harold for months. He had some business with my husband."

"Oh," I repeated, surprised at her comment. Could it be, I thought to myself, that Harold approached the Gentile warrant officer helicopter pilot for particular things from his unit too? "How does Harold know your husband?"

"Tom comes to services once in a while if he's off duty."

"Yes," Harold qualified, "and we met twice at the officers club for dinner."

All this was new to me, and very interesting, something I was sure M.I.G. would like to know. The officers club was off limits to me as an enlisted man but I didn't know a civilian former Army officer could go in and eat and drink and socialize with current officers. Harold must be pumping all sorts of military people during dinner engagements for information and materiel on behalf of his contacts in the East.

"Harold," Leeann said facing him, "a week from Sunday I'm going on a twelve-day tour of Israel. David may be coming too."

"Oh, how nice." Harold turned to look at me. "I've been there myself on business. You should go, David, you'll enjoy it."

"I'm planning to go," I countered.

"And you'll learn a lot about the Jewish people," Harold added.

"Yes," Leeann agreed.

"I have to run now. Hope to see you both next week." Harold looked at me again. "And don't forget what we talked about."

Harold turned and walked toward the door. Leeann looked around the room and spotted her friend, Mrs. Kaplan, talking with two other women. "See you next week, David. I have to talk to Doris now."

Leeann whisked away and I was left alone. I wondered if Harold had asked Leeann's husband for Army materiel, and if Tom had told his wife about it. Whether he did or not, I didn't want to ask Leeann about it.

A few minutes later, I went up to the rabbi who was sitting at a little desk with papers on it and collecting checks.

At Jewish services at McGraw Kaserne that last Friday in February, I signed up for the 12-day tour to Israel and paid the $259. My parents sent me a money order from the bank account opened for me after my Bar Mitzvah with the cash gifts I received. My account was more than double that with the money I had been sending home each month from Germany.

"Just endorse the money order," the rabbi advised me.

"Endorse it to who?"

"The Armed Forces Jewish Chaplains Association, the sponsors of the tour."

With the successful handling of my impending trip to Israel, I went back to the barracks. I could not fall asleep right away as my date with Erika the next day, and the possibility of an intimate encounter, occupied my mind.

On Saturday I arrived at Harry's Bar at 1350 hours, about ten minutes before I was supposed to meet Erika. I took a table and ordered a beer. Harry saw me and came over and we talked a bit, mainly about Komenets, the small town in the Brest-Litovsk region in Southeastern Poland that my mother came from. The bar owner came from a neighboring town.

"Komenets is Yiddish name of shtetl," Harry said. "Kamieniec is Polish name." He spelled them out for me.

My mother showed me her Polish passport once but I couldn't make out the names written in cursive. From what she told me, I knew that most shtetlach in Poland had two names and the two groups living there, Jews and Gentiles, had an almost equal population of from three to seven thousand. The two groups spoke different languages, practiced different religious rituals, espoused different political loyalties, and rarely interacted with one another.

"The Nazis took over the area in nineteen-forty-one, didn't they?" I knew the Germans bombarded their way into Brest-Litovsk during Operation Barbarossa, Hitler's attempt to defeat and occupy the Soviet Union, a failed strategy that contributed to Germany's downfall.

Harry put his hand to his head and shook it back-and-forth. "Yes, it very bad. Many Jew killed. Me and brother hide. Not three year later, Russia take back. Kill many German. Komenets now part of Ukraine."

Harry talked a little more about how he and his brother miraculously escaped Nazi persecution, first hiding out with a Gentile family and then surviving in the woods.

"I must go now. Talk to other people."

I watched the short man with the number tattooed on his forearm get up and walk briskly to another table. I thought of what would have become of me if my mother's family had not emigrated in 1927 and she married in Poland. Only her grandmother was left behind, and never heard from again after 1941.

Still sipping my beer, the round clock on the wall above the bar indicated it was a quarter-past two. Erika had not arrived yet. I kept glancing over to the door. Did she forget about our date? I wondered. Did something else turn up? I tried not to think what it would be like to experience love in the afternoon with this attractive and alluring one-quarter Jewish Fräulein.

It was close to 3 p.m. when I saw Erika walk through the door. She was with the friend she was with the previous Saturday. Right away I surmised the presence of this other German girl might put a damper on my romantic expectations for the afternoon, or the evening. How I would handle this delicate but awkward situation was foremost in my mind.

I kept looking at Erika as she and her friend went around to a few tables and said hello to people they knew, and to Harry, just as they did the week before. I tried to get Erika's attention but she did not look my way. Whether she *deliberately* did not want to see me, or had simply forgotten about our date, I could not tell.

When the two Fräuleins took a table, and ordered drinks, I went into action. I put my near-empty glass down and sauntered over to them. I was careful not to jump to conclusions or to say something I would later regret.

"Hello, Erika."

I stood over the girl I desired and peered at that adorable face but not those bulging boobs. I did not wish to sit down uninvited. She looked up at me.

"Hello," Erika said, without mentioning my name.

"I thought we had a date today about an hour ago."

"I said I see you here at Harry's. I come every Saturday."

I glanced over to her friend for a moment. "I thought we would spend the afternoon together and then perhaps go to dinner."

"You can come to my apartment later if you wish. You know where I live on Schellingstrasse." She turned her head toward her friend and then to me. "Other friends from the University also are coming."

Obviously, this was not the scenario I was expecting. I was stood up. This might be customary in Germany among Fräuleins, first making a date and then summarily breaking it.

"No thank you. It's okay. You spend the afternoon with your friends."

Erika seemed relieved. "Maybe I see you next Saturday?"

"I don't think so. Early next Sunday morning I leave for a tour of Israel for twelve days."

"Maybe I see you when you come back? You can tell me all about your trip."

I smiled at the Fräulein I desired but held back expressing any anger over the rejection. The lost opportunity for some intimacy that day hurt because I imagined Erika could be the new girlfriend I hankered for during my remaining three months in Germany.

I did not go back to my table or order another beer, but instead headed for the door to Harry's Bar and then back to the barracks.

It was clear to me that Erika did not forget about our date. I knew what was going through my mind but what was going through *hers?* At Henry that Saturday night and all day Sunday I wondered if I handled the situation right. Perhaps I should have expressed some anger or disappointment.

I surmised that Erika was not interested in a Jewish boy, in spite of her paternal grandfather's heritage. She was raised Catholic and may have thought in a serious relationship with me I would pressure her to convert. Or, she got burned once with an American soldier and was fearful of being abandoned again. Maybe she just did not want to leave Germany. If she assumed I as an American G.I. would not want to stay in Deutschland any longer than my rotation date, she was right.

On Monday morning I decided to telephone Lieutenant Gibson instead of trekking all the way to McGraw Kaserne and report to him directly. Ramirez I'm sure would have let me leave the office for that purpose but I just didn't want to go. I didn't have much to tell him and I wasn't going to reveal certain things.

"M-I-G, Lieutenant Gibson speaking sir."

"This is Specialist Streiber at Henry Kaserne, sir. I met you last Monday. "You told me report to you today about what transpired with the person who approached me." I did not want to mention the name Harold Berger over the telephone. The role of spy handler must be getting to me, I thought, as I exercised caution.

"Yes, but why didn't you come to see me at McGraw?"

"I can come if you want, sir, but I don't have much to tell. I figured I could do it just as well over the phone"

The Lieutenant sounded a trifle perturbed and hesitated a moment. "Okay, Streiber, what did you learn?"

"Nothing much, sir. I didn't give the man anything, like you said. I told him I forgot about it."

"How did he react?"

"He wasn't happy but simply asked me to get the manuals for him next week when I come to services."

"Did you handle him like I said, about his contacts with people in the East?"

"Yes sir. But I did it indirectly, so he wouldn't suspect anything. He just said he met with government officials in Berlin about importing microwave ovens, but didn't name anyone?"

"Anything else?"

"I saw him go up to and talk to other young soldiers at the reception after the service. But I didn't know what they talked about."

I held back telling the nosy M.I.G. Lieuey that I learned the suspected spy in his files had some contact with a warrant officer helicopter pilot stationed in Munich. I did not want to get Leeann's husband, a career soldier and someone I had never met, into trouble.

"Is that it, Streiber? Anything more to tell me?"

"No sir."

"Okay. Report to me next Monday, but come to McGraw."

"I won't be able to do that, sir. This Sunday I'm leaving for a twelve-day tour of Israel."

"Okay. See me when you come back," he said before hanging up.

The Lieutenant's words were almost exactly the same as Erika's two days earlier. I now have possible dates with two people when I return from the Holy Land, but I only looked forward to one.

After that telephone call, I told Ramirez I had to go to the headquarters of our attachment unit about my upcoming leave. He did not object to my taking off for a short time, but what I told him was a stretch of the truth. There was one more person I had to handle before I boarded the airplane on Sunday. Korba the Greek I wanted to talk to.

Nickolas Korba was the Mail Clerk at Division HQ of the 24th Infantry. Besides Emmett the Schwarzer, I was friendly with Nick too. Nick was born in Greece and came to the U.S. with his parents when he was ten. He was naturalized and spoke English with a noticeable accent. The Draft Board in Detroit, where many Greek-Americans live, called his number when he was twenty-one.

I got along well with this immigrant because my mother's whole family came from Europe, she and her siblings and my grandparents were naturalized, and she and the older siblings spoke with an accent.

Nick was working at his desk in his little office when I came in. He did not look up at me.

"Nick, on Sunday I'm leaving for a trip to Israel. Emmett got me a pass for twelve days of my accumulated leave. The tour makes a stopover in Athens for one night."

My foreign-born friend turned his head and looked up at me.

"We will have one day to see the sights before we board another plane to Tel Aviv."

"Give my regards to the Acropolis and Parthenon," Nick said with a smile. "I was there several times."

Nick," I said, now preparing myself for the main reason I approached him. "Where can I find some action in Athens at night?"

"Action?"

Korba the Greek learned standard English and apparently didn't know this idiomatic expression common in New York.

"Girls . . . prostitutes."

I was sure Athens, like every other European city I traveled to, has hookers, but I spoke no Greek and had no idea where to find them. Since I did not score with Erika, I was horny for some action. The female company I found in Paris and Venice months earlier came to mind.

"Oh," he let out when he understood my meaning. "There is one street in Athens where all the brothels are. Any taxi driver can take you there."

"What's the name of the street?"

Nick uttered the name, and it sounded like Solonos Otheos, but he did not write it down for me, either in Greek which I could not read, or in a Latin transliteration.

"Okay. Thanks."

Before I left Nick's office, I repeated Solonos Otheos several times in my head.

CHAPTER 9: ELVIS AND ME

On Wednesday March first I was in the shop when everyone was sitting around listening to the Armed Forces Network on the radio. The Army was holding a press conference, broadcast live from Weisbaden, for Elvis Presley who was about to depart from Germany. The most famous American soldier ever was going home.

The draftee's two years were up and he was to fly back to the States on a military transport the next day. The Army decided not to have a repeat performance of the mayhem that occurred on the *U.S.S. General Randall* seventeen months earlier, where hundreds of troops on the steamship besieged Elvis to sign autographs for girlfriends or sisters.

More than a hundred reporters and photographers were present at the press conference. .

"People were expecting me to mess up, to goof up in one way or another," Elvis said in response to a question about his being a regular soldier rather than an entertainer for the troops in a service club. "They thought I couldn't take it . . . and I was determined to go to any limits to prove otherwise, not only to the people who were wondering, but to myself."

At the gathering in Weisbaden too was not-quite fifteen-year-old Priscilla Beaulieu, stepdaughter of an Air Force captain, the girl Elvis met at one of the many parties held at the house in Bad Nauheim he rented for his family. Elvis' 3rd Armored Division commander presented the departing soldier with a certificate of merit for his outstanding leadership ability in a tank unit.

After the AFN radio broadcast, the guys in the shop returned to work at their benches and I went back to my desk in the Area Office. But that did not mean I would not think about the past two years of Elvis' and my Army career that occurred at the same time, or follow him to discharge in the days to come. .

Elvis and his military life were widely publicized in the media. I often read about his experiences stateside and in Germany at a Kaserne not too distant from mine. The *Stars and Stripes* and *Overseas Weekly* often included stories of American and German teenage girls' favorite G.I. in garrison and on field maneuvers. Photographs of Private, PFC, SP/4, and Sergeant Presley in fatigues or khaki or green dress uniforms—driving a jeep, standing in formation by the bar-racks, talking to other soldiers, coming out the hatch of a tank—were splashed across newspapers and magazines all over the world.

On March second, from what I read, Elvis arrived at Rhine-Main Air Force Base with Priscilla at his side. Where the two stayed the night before, or whether they stayed together, was never mentioned in the press. As she tried to kiss her tall and handsome buck sergeant boyfriend goodbye, MPs held her back. Priscilla was photographed waving to Elvis, and *Life* magazine published the picture with the caption "The Girl He Left Behind," title of a 1956 Hollywood movie about a reluctant draftee in Basic Training. The romantic comedy was set in Fort Ord, my Army base in California before I shipped out to Germany.

"Bye Bye Elvie" was cried out by crowds of teenage German girls waiting at Rhine-Main.

Elvis waved a final goodbye and boarded the airplane from the rear. He selected a seat in the back and sought to keep a low profile. Not long after taking off, news of the famous passenger on board spread like Blitz fire. Stewardesses joined the long line of female dependents of other G.I.s seeking the King of Rock 'n' Roll's signature. Other passengers on the overnight flight complained they could not get a cup of coffee or bottle of coke.

While en route to the States, the airplane stopped at Prestwick Airport in Scotland to refuel. While Elvis was above the clouds, I thought about his and my overlapping lives as U.S. soldiers.

Elvis Presley, for the two years that he served in the U.S. Army, had largely the same military experiences as I or any other G.I. The King of Rock 'n' Roll was drafted on March 24, 1958 in Memphis, Tennessee. Early that morning he bid farewell to his adoring fans, family members, and celebrity civilian life.

I was in radar school at Fort Monmouth, New Jersey at the time. His being in the Army as a regular soldier, media-wise, essentially began with the filming of his being given the famous G.I. haircut in a Fort Chaffee, Arkansas barber shop. As an enlistee myself in my ninth month in uniform, I followed the news accounts of the pre-inducted Elvis and draftee-scalped singer sans sideburns.

On January 8, 1957, Elvis' twenty-second birthday, the Memphis Draft Board assigned him a 1-A status, which meant that he was physically fit to be inducted into the Army. On December 16th of that year, Elvis received his draft notice and was scheduled to report for military duty on January 20, 1958. However, due to financial commitments at Paramount Studios and the planned filming of *King Creole*, the untrained actor was given a deferment. Had Elvis not been a world-famous entertainer, he would have received an extension anyway, since this was normal for a Draft Board to do and was not "special treatment" as many in the public thought.

It was no secret that Elvis did not want to be a soldier, not for one day and certainly not for two years. He hoped the Army would simply "not take him" because his presence in a barracks represented too much trouble, but the top brass felt that would signal special treatment for the 1-A man from Memphis and cause a public outcry. Instead, the Army offered Elvis assignment to the Special Services unit, like the offers to other well-known singers such as Vic Damone and Eddie Fisher during the Korean War. They said he could skip Basic Training, tour the world, visit Army bases, and sing for the soldiers to boost morale. But the 23-year-old singing sensetion, and his crafty manager, Colonel Parker, flatly refused.

"If the Army wants me to sing," Elvis reputedly was quoted as saying, "they shouldn't have drafted me."

Interestingly, the Air Force got involved too, telling the Army to draft Elvis and assign him to their branch of the military which had no draft. Air Force generals wanted to dress him in fancy colorful Class A's and have him travel around to various Recruiting Stations to speak to young men and entreat them to enlist. Elvis nixed that misguided offer as well.

"I don't want to be treated like a clown," he allegedly said.

So, the wealthy singer who did not wish to interrupt his career or sing for his supper had no choice but to raise his right hand, be sworn in, and step on the bus to Fort Chaffee like any other Memphis recruit.

I very much admired Elvis for turning down the Army's and the Air Force's offers of cushy jobs in the military for two years without having to play soldier or airman. It meant he would be, as were other draftees, assigned to the Infantry. Being in the Infantry and passing my days shooting rifles, firing advanced weaponry, or riding in a tank was a scenario I dreaded. And Special Services was out of the question as I couldn't sing to save my life. Instead, I enlisted for three years and had a choice of any Army school. Learning radar repair and being in the Signal Corps in a peacetime Army was more to my liking.

Private E-1 Elvis A. Presley took Basic Training at Fort Hood, Texas. He was in a tank battalion in the 3rd Armored Division, became a pistol sharpshooter, and liked the "rough and tumble" of the tank obstacle course. The King of Rock 'n' Roll got used to rocking and rolling inside a Patton tank rather than on a concert stage. Elvis rented a house near Hood for his mother, father, and grandmother. The lonely family-oriented soldier was allowed to live off post with them as they were his legal dependents.

In August 1958, the most important person in Elvis' life, his mother, took ill while he was in Advanced Infantry Training. The very overweight woman collapsed because of increased alcohol use and a deteriorating liver coupled with bad eating habits and prescripttion diet pills. She was rushed to a hospital and Elvis was granted emergency leave to be at her bedside with his father. Gladys Presley died from cirrhosis on August 14th, officially listed as a heart attack as the family refused an autopsy. The normally unhappy soldier went further into depression and before long began using prescription drugs himself to cope with the loss.

A month later, after completing AIT with a different group of guys, Elvis' unit was transferred to Friedberg, West Germany. He and his new Army buddies went by train to New York City and then to the Brooklyn Army Terminal where on September 22nd he embarked aboard the *USS General Randall* to Bremerhaven

Six months after Elvis' departure, I too headed to West Germany on a different ship but from the same Army Terminal that was not far from my home in Brooklyn. The only difference was that I was a lone transferee, while Elvis sailed to Germany with his whole company.

"Hey, look, there's Elvis," one of the transferees near me in the Terminal said just before we walked up the gangplank.

Elvis was photographed in his khaki uniform on the top deck of the *Randall* waving goodbye alongside some of the other 1,169 soldiers on board. An enlargement of the picture was later hung above the platform in front of the military transport ships for all Germany-bound troopers like I to behold.

Elvis arrived in Germany on October 1, 1958. MPs had to protect him from the crowd of adoring Fräuleins at the dock in Bremerhaven so the pop star who sold 50-million records worldwide could step on a train with his unit to Frankfurt, and then be transported by bus to Ray Barracks in nearby Friedberg. Elvis spent the first few nights in a foreign country bunking with his buddies in the barracks.

In Germany too Elvis was permitted to live off post with his dependent father and grandmother. They took rooms in two different hotels in Bad Nauheim, a resort bath town not far from Friedberg, along with some Memphis cronies Elvis brought over. However, all were kicked out by both establishments because of complaints by other guests of wild parties. The evicted off-post G.I. then rented a five-bedroom house at Goethestrasse 14 and lived there with his family and friends until he flew back to the States.

At Ray, the brass offered Elvis a way out of any further soldiering, the chance to join Special Services in Europe. Since the Army had the right to photograph and record Elvis' live performances at its own bases, parts of which could be sold to print media and television stations around the globe, the intransigent trooper again declined his superiors' efforts to exploit his fame and crooning ability.

Elvis was required to stand reveille at 0630 with the rest of his company. He rented a car and hired a chauffeur to shuttle him back-and-forth each day from Goethestrasse 14 and Ray to make sure he was not counted as AWOL. Elvis' barracks' buddies greatly respected him for soldiering with them as a regular G.I., a jeep driver and tank-unit teammate without the privileges the brass dangled in front of him. Private E-2 Presley was promoted to Private First Class while at Ray.

"Autogramme zwischen 19 Uhr 30 und 20 Uhr 30" was the sign posted by the Polizei in front of Elvis' rented house to avoid continuous crowds and round-the-clock pandemonium at Goethestrasse 14. Every evening at 7:30, Elvis took a few paces out the front door and for one hour happily gave autographs to his German fans.

At the end of November, less than two months after he walked down the *Randall* gangplank in Bremerhaven with duffel bag on his shoulder, Elvis went on maneuvers in Grafenwöhr, a training area in Bavaria not far from where I was later stationed in Munich. In magazines, I saw pictures of him in his temporary quarters, sitting on a foot locker playing a guitar with soldiers of different stripes watching him and smiling. Elvis is wearing his green fatigues, field jacket, and Daniel Boone cap with wool-lined earflaps tied atop his head and division crest on a raised flap in front. He was looking very sharp with his spit-shined black boots bloused above the laces. I had that same Army winter clothing that is worn in the field in my wall locker, but luckily never got to wear it. As a clerk, I never went out in the field.

Elvis' involvements with German and American women were widely covered in the press. In January 1959 he was photographed in his green Class A's sporting one yellow stripe on his sleeve with Vera Tschechowa, an 18-year-old German actress. Two months later, the PFC again was pictured with the attractive Fräulein in a bar in Munich while on 15-days of leave. Whether or not the two had a romantic relationship was never mentioned. Then there was the black-and-white image of Nancy Holloway busting out in a low-cut dress standing next to Elvis in a Paris nightclub.

There was one girlfriend that everyone knew about, 19-year-old Elisabeth Stephaniak, an American girl born in Germany, hired as the King's secretary because she knew German and could answer his flood of fan mail. They also dated and, for the convenience of doing work together, she too lived at Goethestrasse 14 with Elvis' Papa, Granny, and Memphis cronies.

"Who's the mystery girl," Elvis' barracks buddies would continually ask about another one of his lovers. There was much talk of an Elvis Schatzie in Friedberg, a local Fräulein the publicity-avoidant red-blooded young man was meeting in secret.

"Wer is das rätselhafte Mädchen?" Bad Nauheimer's likewise would wonder out loud in their language. The King, like other kings in history, was not known to be faithful to one intimate partner of the opposite sex at one time.

In April 1959, Elvis was photographed in uniform with his next promotion, as a Specialist 4, an E-4 with a blue bird on his sleeve. Somebody up there must have liked the rich and handsome singer/ guitarist as it did not take long for him to go one rung higher on the

Army's ladder of ranks. An unsmiling Elvis in an obvious "photo op" is seen doing some public relations work for the Army in Steinfürth, near Bad Nauheim, pretending to help relocate a German World War I memorial for its fallen heroes, men of the Reichswehr who undoubtedly killed American as well as British and French soldiers stuck in the trenches or entangled on barbed wire. The U.S. military in postwar Germany was not above using its most famous trooper to enhance good will toward a former enemy but current ally.

The most important person 24-year-old Elvis met while in the Army in Germany was 14-year-old Priscilla Beaulieu, who came to one of his famous parties on September 13, 1959 at the house in Bad Nauheim. The country boy with several attractive girlfriends was smitten with the beautiful American girl who looked two years older. They often were seen together in the remaining five-and-a-half months of Elvis' overseas tour of duty. From accounts told by relatives and friends, the King treated Priscilla like a queen.

In January 1960, less than two weeks after his birthday, Elvis was promoted to buck sergeant. With three yellow stripes on his fatigues and Class A's, he now had the position of tank commander. He must have been doing a bang-up job to reach the level of E-5 in a two-year stint. I was in the Army nine months longer than Elvis in a three-year enlistment and I was a grade below him as Spec 4. To get E-5, either as a Spec 5 or buck sergeant, I would have had to re-enlist, something I, like Elvis, had no desire to do.

Elvis' last weeks in Germany in 1960 were uneventful. He was preparing himself for civilian life and a resumption of his entertainment career as a singer and actor in movies. Hollywood producer Hal B. Wallis already had funding and a script for Elvis' first film after discharge, a musical-comedy about G.I.s in postwar Germany and their escapades with Fräuleins. Parts of the production underway were filmed at Ray Barracks with Elvis stand-ins and look-alikes.

Elvis departed Germany three months before my scheduled rotation date. I looked forward to the day when I too would be leaving this country on my way to a discharge, and then seeing the Hollywood film starring Elvis now being made dealing with the kind of women he just said auf Wiedersehen to. His arrival in the States, needless to say, was accompanied by much fanfare.

On March third, Elvis' airplane touched down at 7:42 a.m. at McGuire Air Force Base near Fort Dix in New Jersey to a waiting crowd and yet another Army press conference. Among those welcoming him home were Colonel Parker, Nancy Sinatra, her father's emissary for a television appearance, and RCA representatives with record contracts in tow. The crowd-weary soldier spent two days at Dix processing out of the Army, perhaps bunked in the same building as I had slept in or one not far from it during my basic training and overseas processing.

On March fifth, Elvis was handed an honorable discharge and a check for $109.54, his mustering-out pay.

"I don't need it," Elvis was heard saying, as he tried to hand the check back to the Paymaster.

"Better take it, Presley," the sergeant with six stripes on his sleeve said sternly. "If you owed the Army money, it's for damn sure they would collect."

By popular consensus, the 25-year-old millionaire from Memphis served his country well. Elvis turned down the Army's offer of a cushy singing job, toiled through infantry training, drove a tank near enemy lines amid Cold War tensions, earned his stripes up to an E-5 rank, and received commendations from superiors. The poor southern boy who made good reflected unsentimentally the American ideal that all young men, regardless of wealth or fame, should fulfill their military obligation and should do the time without special privilege. Fellow soldiers who served with Elvis stateside and overseas attested to his sympathy for others, unassuming character, respect for authority, and willingness to play the piano in the day room for his barracks buddies.

At Fort Dix on a cold and snowy wintry morning, a smiling Elvis, in pressed Class A's and with polished brass, saluting his fans and comrades, left the barracks for the last time. No one, military or civilian, thought his like in uniform would ever be seen again.

PART II

MID-EAST JOURNEY

CHAPTER 10: SOLONOS HO THEOS

The three of us left the hotel after ten. We walked to the nearest corner to look for a taxi and hailed one down as it approached us. None of us spoke any Greek. I knew only two words, the name of a street or district in Athens that the mail clerk in my attachment company at Henry Kaserne told me about, a draftee born and raised in Greece.

This hour of the night it was cool. Although it was not raining or even drizzling, I wore my beige raincoat, the one I lay on the ground in Zirndorf Woods that first time with Karin. I thought it would bring me luck the only evening I would be in Athens. My two companions, young soldiers on the tour with me that I just met, were following my lead. I was the one who was advised where men, foreign or domestic, go if they are looking for action in this ancient warring city.

It was Sunday, the sixth of March. That morning the first component of the tour group to Israel met in the U.S. and Allied Waiting Room at the Hauptbahnhof in Frankfurt before boarding the train to Munich. I was in the second set of tourists that assembled in Munich at the Swiss Hotel-Plan Office on Lenbachplatz. When I arrived, a bus loaded with the Frankfurt people was standing at the curb with its door open and driver behind the wheel.

I counted twenty-six persons that rode with me to the Munich airport. Seven were enlisted men in their early or mid-twenties, most from units in Germany but a few were stationed in France, all Jewish boys from different states who had volunteered or were drafted. Four had been to college and earned Bachelor's degrees, one even a Master's, two dropped out to enlist, and one, like I, was just a high school graduate. There were a number of Army officers in their late twenties—doctors, dentists, and lawyers—one accompanied by his wife and mother. We had several civilian American couples on the tour, one towing three pre-teen girls, husbands who worked for the military in West Germany. An elderly couple was with us too, the wife always speaking Deutsch to her husband and tugging at his arm. There were also two Jewish wives of officers going to the Holy Land without their husbands, one not Jewish. I knew one of the two from services at McGraw Kaserne, the only familiar face on the tour other than the local Jewish Chaplain and his wife who were the hosts. Rabbi Washer and the Mrs. from Nuremberg hosted the pilgrimage the previous year and were not on the bus.

That day, coincidentally, was the first anniversary of my arrival in Nuremberg on my first company assignment. I was so eager then to take in the culture of the Old World and tripping over myself to keep company with Fräuleins. It was a good year on balance. I had a meaningful relationship with a decent German girl for four months, although it ended badly, had hits and misses with homely and comely bargirls, and met but could not touch my dream lover. And there were memorable moments with a Parisian mademoiselle and a Venetian signorina. Now I was on the prowl for a Grecian goddess, a Mediterranean beauty the likes of which twenty-three centuries earlier Aléxandros ho Mégas might have favored.

We left Munich in a propeller airplane. The first stop on our itinerary was Athens for an overnight stay. Along the route, however, we refueled in Belgrade, Yugoslavia but were not allowed to leave the airport. That was the first time I ever set foot in a Communist country. Before we landed in Athens, I was sick as a dog, but not from having been behind the Iron Curtain. Severe thunder-storms caused the airplane to wobble up and down like a roller coaster, unsettling my delicate stomach. But by the time we arrived at our hotel, I felt much better. So much better in fact that I decided to head for town on my important mission, in spite of the late hour and the scheduled early morning call for a tour of the Acropolis.

The two friends I made were paired in another room. They knew I had the key to where to go for a good time in Athens and pleaded to come along with me. Alan Bachman from Newport News, Virginia was a college graduate, a bright boy with much knowledge of history but not women. Short in stature and pudgy, with irregular facial features, he did not possess a physical appearance most females would fall for. Marty Levine was from suburban Philadelphia and was no better. He had more under his belt than two years of college. Tall and meaty, with a barrel chest and pot belly, the poundage detracted from his looks as much as his big nose and mousy ears. I doubted whether either of my tag-along buddies had a steady Schatzie in Germany. They probably needed the action more than I did. Of the trio of Americans ready to deviate from the tour's planned activities and sights, I was the only one who did not deviate from the male norm in a woman's eye.

A taxi stopped and the three of us crammed into the back seat. I leaned forward to talk to the driver. He turned around and rattled off something in Greek that did not sound like any words in English, German, or French that I knew or could figure out.

"Solonos Otheos," I said to the driver, the words I was told to say but had no idea what they meant. All I knew is that this was where the brothels were. Every taxi driver would know that location.

The balding man about forty, with thick eyebrows and deep lines in his face, looked at me.

"Solonos Otheos," I repeated slowly, varying the syllable emphasis and pronunciation.

"Ahhh . . . Solonos *ho* Theos," he said rapidly, separating the *O* sound and adding an *h* to make a third word. He nodded and smiled. Turning away from me, he put the stick shift on the wheel in gear and took off.

We drove through a maze of winding narrow streets for five or six minutes. Athens looked nothing like Nuremberg but did resemble the Rome I visited in late December. The driver took us through a back alley and stopped short of a street corner, parking the left side of his taxi on the sidewalk. A lamppost provided the only light to see where we were going. He led us into an old brick house and up one flight of stairs. He knocked on an apartment. I heard voices inside. A Greek with a face like a mutt, more toward fifty than forty, taller and thinner than the driver, a lit cigarette hanging from his lips, opened the door. I could see five or six women. He recognized the driver and motioned us to come in. We stepped into a large room, with smaller rooms off to the side whose doors were open and single beds visible.

The first brothel I had ever been in was nothing like what I had seen in movies. There were no velvet sofas or cushioned chaises, no plush carpeting or thick patterned rugs, no Tiffany lamps, no polished antique bureaus, and no heavy damask drapes adorning this hole in the wall. All I saw were bare wood floors, stick chairs, and cheap curtains. The women were not young and pretty with heavy makeup, not decked out in fancy duds, no sparkling jewelry hung from their ear lobes or dangled around their neck. Only older hags and hardened maidens in their late twenties and thirties, in low cut bras, colored panties, and see-through negligées, were standing idly by in the middle of the room or sitting on stools or chairs positioned against the wall.

The two men talked to each other in Greek. The proprietor or manager of this establishment, called the Patron like in French, counterpart to the usual Madame, turned to us. He spoke some English. "You like," he said as he waved his hand around the room, gesturing to us to take our pick.

"I don't care for any of them," Marty whispered to me, shaking his head.

"Me neither," Alan agreed.

I was not crazy about any of the women either. "All right," I said, "let's go somewhere else. There must be plenty of other places." I walked toward the door and motioned the driver to leave with us.

The Patron sensed we were not interested and did not try to persuade us to stay. Surely this was not the first time there was no sale on his fleshy merchandise. The driver did not put up an argument as well. Why should he? It was his business to drag men around to different brothels, and the more places he takes them to the more money he makes.

A minute or so later we were in another apartment a block away, this one on the ground floor. We strode in behind the driver with high expectations. Again the two fuddy-duddies did not favor any girl and wanted to try yet a third place. I thought one girl was not bad looking and wanted to stay but did not wish to break up this three-pack of lovers-to-be. For young men who were not very attractive, they were awfully particular. I began to wonder whether they wanted to get laid or not.

By the time we hit No. 3, I could tell the driver was getting annoyed. Again my companions stood in the middle of the main room of the apartment and inspected the women on display, but were unable to make a choice. Suddenly, a girl about nineteen or twenty, wearing no top and stark naked but for high heels and panties, came up to me. She pushed her body against mine on one side and put her arm on my shoulder, fingers to my neck. Though not real pretty and a trifle plump, she was no Helen of Troy but was incredibly sexy to me. On the short side but taller than Karin, with full-size tits, shapely hips and legs, and a sensitive touch, I was in a quiver over this Solonos ho Theos pick that picked me.

"I don't know about you fellows," I said in a determined voice, "but I'm staying here." I reached into my wallet and gave Marty two dollars. "Here's my share of the cab. If you need more, I'll give you later."

The two irresolute Americans left with the driver. The Patron held out his hand and asked for five dollars. I gave it to him without hesitation. I had no drachmas anyway and did not know the rate of exchange. The girl was still hanging on me with one big boob rubbing against my chest. I was so hot for her I could have pulled off the only garment she was wearing and taken her right there on the floor. She led me into one of the smaller rooms, closed the door without locking it, and positioned herself on the bed. She had her knees up and legs spread as if she were readying herself for a doctor to do a pap smear. Sexier by the second she looked and I quickly undressed. A few times I glanced over to the door, half expecting her bulldog of a boss to break in, bite the rest of the money in my wallet, and bark me out of there before I had my piece of Athenian ass.

The girl spoke no English and I spoke no Greek but the young five-bucker caught my drift. I moved close to her on the bed, placed my hands of her knees, and ran them down along the outside of her thighs. Just as I was about to grab her panties by the waistband, she lifted up and I easily slipped them off. She looked good down there, not hairy, and I peered at her as she angled her knees toward her head. I touched her lightly at first but then worked two fingers in. She was moist and soft and the feel of her made me almost fully erect. I leaned forward to possibly try a little kiss, of the sort Karin stopped me from doing that night in the Pension, or brush up against her. But my olfactory organ was functioning well too. I detected a malodorous scent, not very foul but pungent enough to cause me to pull back. She must eat a lot of spicy moussaka and souvlaki, I thought. Or perhaps in her country's depressed postwar economy she cannot get her hands on feminine hygiene spray.

What she *could* get her hands on was me and that is what I desired. I stood up next to the bed, reached for her hand, and moved it to me. Without a smile or show of emotion, she fingered me around the head, then reached over with her other hand and cupped my balls. Both of these hand-to-private contacts raised my temperature even more. I had to take her hands away I was about to burst any moment. She was still in her ready position with knees up. I climbed on top of her, put my arms under her knees, and lifted her legs higher. I fit myself right in and in no time I shot off. To me this was not a premature act and I was not disheartened by its dispatch. I came inside of *her*, not in her hands or on the bed. The most important goal of the evening was achieved.

Without an exchange of words, I got dressed. The girl wiped around her middle with a small towel and put her panties back on. I wanted to thank her but did not know how to say it in Greek. Saying danke, merci, or grazie I knew would not do.

When I exited the little love room, I was surprised to see the taxi driver. He was sitting and talking to the Patron. "He take you friend to hotel," the Peloponnesian pimp said to me. "He come back for you. You want ride?"

Apparently the two peacetime soldiers surrendered, put their rifles down and took themselves out of action. "Yes," I said, nodding to the driver. "Thanks."

The driver stood up and started for the door. Then it dawned on me what I just said. I turned to look at the Greek who spoke my language.

"How do you say thank you?" I asked.

"Eycharisto," he said.

I looked over to the girl who satisfied my physical needs, now sitting next to her housemates. "I caristo," I pronounced with the rolled *r* as best I could.

She said something to me and her boss translated. "She say you have nice face. And you have nice . . . . " He ran his hands over his body as he struggled to find the word. "More nice than you friend. Again she want see you."

"I caristo," I repeated, nodding and smiling at the girl who stroked my ego too but still showed no emotion.

As I left with the driver, I thought how pleasing it would be to come back and act in another Greek play with this Aphrodite who aroused me so. If I ever did return, I hoped this goddess of love and sexuality would not beware of a non-Greek bearing a gift, a pharmaceutical product for her to spray down below. Perhaps next time there will be a more mature climax.

Later at the hotel I did not run into the two soldier boys who ran away from nighttime action.

A local guide joined the tour the following morning after breakfast. She was a short skinny woman with a pointed nose and big eyes, nothing like the statue of a Greek goddess or maiden. The thirty-something spoke English with a British accent and was very knowledgeable about Greek history and architecture.

As with almost any group of foreigners visiting Athens, we were taken to the Acropolis, a flat-topped rock about 500 feet above sea level. It was a citadel on the "edge of the city," as implied by the name, the site of beautiful temples and the spot where classical Greek civilization began. The most famous monument atop the Acropolis is the Parthenon, a tall rectangular building of great size with closely-spaced columns all around. I had slide film in my camera and was able to walk up to it and take several color pictures of the four sides at different angles. The guide told us that the origin of the Parthenon's name is from the Greek word for "maidens' apartments," since it was mainly a room for four young girls chosen to serve Athena, the protector of the city, each year. The name has also come to mean the "temple of the virgin goddess." The Parthenon perched high above Athens is a long way, both geographically and culturally, from Solonos ho Theos, as not too many virgins can be found on that lower-level street.

On the Acropolis, I also snapped good shots of the Erecthion, the building that contains the porch of the maidens. The statues of these young women seem to be holding up the structure, with the extended top piece resting on their heads. This is considered the most sacred site of the Acropolis, for it is here that Poseidon, god of the sea and storms, fought Athena, goddess of wisdom, strength, and justice. Athena won and that is how the city got its name.

Next we were taken to the Agora, or Greek Forum, located in the center of Athens, northwest of the Acropolis. It was an open space with a number of buildings that functioned as a meeting ground of Athenian citizens. The Agora was a public place for religious, political, judicial, social, and commercial activities. It contained private housing, the law courts, government buildings, an assembly, and temples. Colonnades enclosed the open space that had shops, statues, altars, trees, and fountains. I walked these ancient ruins where Socrates, Plato, and Aristotle once walked and talked, and developed their great ideas in philosophy, politics, and science. In the southwest corner of the Agora a prison once stood, where a disgraced Socrates committed suicide by drinking poison. Here too was the Dionysus Theater, the world's oldest stone stage setting, where the plays of Aeschylus, Sophocles, and Euripides were first performed. London's West End and New York's Broadway, capitals of the modern world's wild comedies and gay musicals, owe a debt of gratitude to this ancient Athens theater named for the god of wine, ritual madness, and ecstasy that inspired joyful festivals and celebration.

Before we went back to our hotel, I asked the guide what Solonos ho Theos meant. Her big eyes opened wider and she gave me a dirty look.

"It means 'Of Solon the God,'" she said. "He was a great man. They named streets for him in Athens. But one street is not so nice now."

"What did he do? What was he famous for?" I wanted to know.

"Solon lived in the sixth century B.C., before Socrates and Alexander. He was a poet and politician and founded democracy in Athens. He wrote laws and a constitution to reform Greek society and government. Solon tried to make less the conflict between rich and poor."

"I guess he was a hero," I said.

"Yes. One of the Seven Wise Men."

This ancient Greek was very wise indeed. Thomas Jefferson and Karl Marx must have read Solon and borrowed some of his ideas. Modern Greeks are smart too. They put brothels on a street named for the hero who equalized opportunities for men regardless of their wealth, status, or power. In 1960 Athens, Solon was the god of easy and cheap sex.

After lunch that day we were bussed to the airport for our flight to Tel Aviv.

CHAPTER 11: FROM DEUTSCHLAND TO PROMISED LAND

The two men were an unlikely pair. I caught a fleeting glimpse of them when I looked out the window of the airplane. They were walking along the red carpet laid out for them at the airport. One was white, the other black. One was short and rotund, the other tall and thin. One bald with a lengthy white fringe protruding from the sides and back, the other had a thick head of short kinky black hair. One the leader of a young democratic nation, an old man who for decades had fought the Arabs and the British for the right to form an independent state, the right for his people to live in peace and freedom in a reclaimed homeland after nineteen hundred years. The other, much younger, the dictator of a country ready to break away from British Colonial rule, a man who silenced political opponents by imprisoning them without a trial, who pushed through legislation that flagrantly restricted his people's individual freedom and human rights.

It was Day 2 on the tour's itinerary, the seventh of March, Monday evening. We had just landed at Lod Airport in Tel Aviv after the three-hour flight from Athens. This time there was no turbulence and I did not heave anything up. People on the ground crowded both sides of the runway, some snapping pictures, as the two men moved slowly. We were told we could not exit the airplane until David Ben-Gurion, Prime Minister of Israel, and Kwame Nkrumah, strongman from the African nation of Ghana, boarded their flights.

A military band played Hatikvah. We could hear Israel's haunting national anthem. I felt the hush that came over the airport. Ben-Gurion had a friendly and colorful sendoff, with Arab, Druze, and West African representatives in national dress. Where the black man was headed and for what purpose no one would say, but I knew where Ben-Gurion was going and why. Copies of the day's *Jerusalem Post*, the English-language newspaper, were available to us when we took off from Athens. The PM was scheduled to fly directly to Boston to receive an honorary Doctor of Laws degree from nearby Brandeis University and address the faculty. He would then travel to Washington to meet with President Dwight Eisenhower and

Secretary of State Christian Herter to discuss Mid-East issues.

After about twenty minutes we finally got off and were whisked to the terminal and through customs. Over an hour later, following a bus ride to the city, I was sitting in the dining room of a modest Tel Aviv hotel eating supper, forking through boiled chicken and mashed potatoes.

That night in Israel I went to sleep feeling good just being in the Holy Land. I was in the place God of heaven first promised to Abraham and his offspring in Genesis 24:7. I was one of the chosen people and this would be a great religious and personal experience for me. After living in a post-Nazi society for over a year, a Germany that in recent memory persecuted Jews inside and outside its borders, I was now in a country created in the aftermath of the Allied war victory and the Nazi's near total destruction of European Jewry. I would learn much about Jewish history and culture. But treading on ancient and contemporary sites and hearing our guide's discourses were not to be my sole sources of learning.

As I lie in my bed trying to fall asleep, it did not occur to me that the Deutschland I left behind the day before would follow me to the Promised Land.

When we arrived in Tel Aviv, I stepped into a nation only twelve years old. The state of Israel was established on May 14, 1948, the day before the British were scheduled to pull out.

With the defeat in World War I of the Ottoman Empire, which controlled the Middle East for centuries, Britain was given a mandate by the League of Nations to create "A Jewish National Home" in Palestine based on the 1917 Balfour Declaration. Palestine, the Roman name for the ancient kingdom of Israel, was to be administered by the British as a homeland for Jews who were without a home for almost two millennia. Arabs resented Jews from other countries coming in to take their land. Violence between the two soon broke out. Britain later halted Jewish immigration in an effort to appease the Arabs. After World War II, with great sympathy around the world for Jews because of the extermination of six million and the hundreds of thousands of survivors of Nazi death camps as displaced persons behind new barbed-wire fences, pressure mounted on Britain to permit Jewish immigration. In 1947, to settle the matter, the United Nations voted to partition Palestine into an Arab and a Jewish state. The Arabs flatly rejected partitioning, Jews heartily accepted the land cut, and bloody clashes erupted. Jews were outnumbered a hundred to one but toward the end of 1949, with poorly-trained Arab armies and political in-fighting among seven Arab nations, Israel won its War of Independence. After living in exile for so long and dispersed worldwide, the Jewish people now had a country to come back to. In 1950, Israel's legislature, the Knesset, passed the Law of Return which guaranteed the right of all Jews to become a citizen. The flood gates were open, Jews poured in from every corner of the world. This was the fulfillment of the prophecy in Deuteronomy 30:3-5, a miracle many said.

The partitioning of this ancient land was not simply along one of the globe's parallel latitude lines, an even slice across the middle for a North and South Palestine. Instead, the division of the country occurred according to existing Arab and Jewish areas of population. The resulting map of the two states resembled a salamander. Different-colored irregular patches depicted the separation of the two peoples, enemies since biblical times. Each state had three major sections linked by crossroads extending through the other's territory. Tel Aviv, Jerusalem, and Haifa, the Jewish state's three main cities, were in different sections. Jews got 56% of the land, most of which was in the Negev Desert, but almost an equal number of Arabs as Jews resided there. Palestinian Arabs were given 42%, with a minority of Jews to contend with inside their assigned borders. Jerusalem was a disconnected body within an Arab section under UN administration, sliced again for Jews and Arabs. A wall chart of partitioned Palestine, to any observer, clearly outlined trouble. To make matters worse, during the 1947-49 conflict, large numbers of Palestinian Arabs ran from their land and sought refuge in neighboring Arab nations, Jordan especially. Jews rushed in where Arabs feared to tread and were left with more territory than the UN initially allotted them. This infuriated the Arabs and set the stage for continuing battles.

The land now called Israel had three major geographic areas. The southern part was the Negev Desert, with the city of Beersheba at the top, Eilat at the bottom. The central region—Tel Aviv, Jerusalem, cities along the Mediterranean Coastal Plain, and the Judean Mountains—contained much of the country's population. The northern territory included the Haifa District, the Mount Carmel mountain range, and the hilly Galilee, both Upper and Lower.

With peace in the new state, albeit an uneasy one, hundreds of thousands of Jews the world over "made Aliyah," packed up their belongings and navigated their way to Eretz Yisroel by land, sea, and air. From 1949 to 1960, the Jewish population doubled, to more than one-and-a-quarter million. Some came from Christian/democratic nations in the West—the United States, Canada, England—for religious or Zionist reasons. Others gave up their property in North Africa and Asia Minor, Muslim/autocratic nations with a history of Jewish oppression, to be free in the Land of Israel. It was the concentration camp survivors from different countries mainly dwelling in Deutschland as DPs who perhaps appreciated immigration to the birthplace of the Jewish people the most. For them, Israel was truly the Promised Land. Men and women with numbers tattooed on their forearms can be found walking down the street in any city, digging in the fields of agricultural settlements, working in every occupation and profession.

Since the founding of Israel, tourism has been an important part of the economy. Jews and Christians the world over flock to the Holy Land every year to pace on soil Abraham, Moses, King David, Jesus, and the Disciples walked, to behold the mountain God handed down the ten commandments from, to stand before the hill on which Jesus was crucified. Muslims too make the journey so that they may pray on the spot where Muhammad, prophet and messenger of God, ascended to heaven. Jerusalem is always on the itinerary, as the quarter known as the Old City, until 1860 the *entire* city, is home to three holy sites: Temple Mount and its Western Wall for Jews, Church of the Holy Sepulcher for Christians, and Dome of the Rock mosque for Muslims.

In 1960, my tour group of Jews could not go everywhere or see everything in Jerusalem since it was a city sliced in two. Israel occupied the western part, Jordan controlled the eastern. Along the border several demilitarized zones were established. Walls and fences kept Jews and Arabs from co-mingling. The major checkpoint was the Mandelbaum Gate, named for the Jewish merchant whose house was on the Green Line that separated the warring parties. On one side of the Gate stood Israeli policemen, on the other we could see Jordanian legionnaires.

After the '48 war, the Old City was taken over by Jordan and Jewish residents summarily evicted. Jews were not permitted to ascend the Temple Mount. They could only see it from a distance. Arabs considered this part of East Jerusalem their Promised Land. It could be said that Arabs were Nazis in desert dress, as their barbed-wire fencing made Jews feel as though they were in a concentration camp. The Wall at the western side of the Mount, one of the most sacred sites in Judaism, is all that remains of the Second Temple built by Herod the Great. Dubbed the Wailing Wall, religious Jews no doubt would give much to be able to pray near it.

Another mount we as Jews could not scale was Mount Scopus, a UN demilitarized zone within Jordanian-occupied territory. A campus of Hebrew University and Hadassah Hospital are here for Jews, but the only access is by a mile-and-a-half narrow road that went through an Arab neighborhood. Sniper fire on passing vehicles is a common occurrence, not to mention the danger from road mines laid. Mount Scopus was where Roman Legions once camped, ground from which Titus in 70 A.D. launched the final siege of Jerusalem to suppress the Jewish revolt. This was still a contentious place in 1960. Barely two years earlier Jordanian troops fired on Israeli patrols, killing a UN officer and four policemen.

The Mount of Olives in East Jerusalem was likewise inaccessible to us. We could not visit the burial place of tens of thousands of Jews on top of a hill that once had a multitude of olive trees, nor could we walk on the ground where Jews expect the Messiah to return and bring about the resurrection of the dead. Christians, on the other hand, can go up this hillside overlooking the Old City that Jesus spent time on teaching and prophesying to disciples. Those wearing a cross are freely waved through by Arab guards and have the privilege of standing where Jesus wept over Jerusalem, came to the night of his betrayal, and following the crucifixion wandered forty days before ascending to heaven.

There were only two mounts we were allowed to rest our feet. On Mount Herzl in West Jerusalem tourists of all religious faiths can see the national cemetery of Israel, the final resting place for government leaders and fallen soldiers. And at the top of the hill there is the tomb of Theodor Hertzl, founder of modern Zionism, the man behind the dream of a Jewish homeland. Buried in Vienna in 1904, his remains and the coffins of his father and sister were brought to Israel in 1949, as he wished in his will. Onlookers cannot help but be moved by the unadorned black granite stone inscribed simply with the family name.

The more ancient Mount Zion, whose location has been in dispute for centuries, is a site both Jews and Christians have sought to step on. On this western hill extending south of the Old City, Jews are in awe when next to what is reputed to be King David's Tomb. Christians likewise feel something special when they grace the room the Last Supper presumably took place in, especially since it hardly resembles what is depicted in the Da Vinci painting. The importance of Mount Zion for Jews cannot be overstated, for this is where Abraham's binding of Isaac occurred and the two Temples stood.

A major institution and tourist attraction in Israel is the kibbutz. Before the British Mandate, Palestine was a harsh environment— swamps in the north, rocky hills in the center, a desert in the south. Early Jewish settlers were exposed to diseases such as malaria, typhus, and cholera. Their farms were often raided by Nomadic Bedouins, irrigated canals sabotaged, and crops burned. Collective farming was the only way individual settlements could be protected as well as raise the capital necessary to develop the land. Diaspora Jews gave generously to the Jewish National Fund so that land could be purchased from the Arabs and tools and equipment obtained. The first kibbutz, Degania, was established in 1909 in the north near the bottom of the Sea of Galilee. In the 1920s, other kibbutzim founded by Zionist youths from political movements on both the right *and* left dotted the landscape. With backbreaking work and tilling of the fields, a new type of society was created, one with democratic decision-making, equality for all, and without exploitation. The kibbutz ideals of returning to nature, reconstituting the desert, and living off the fruits of one's labor later became part of Jewish Palestine's credo. By 1939, there were 79 such communal farms with five percent of the Jewish population living on them. By 1950, eight percent of the Jews in the partitioned state were kibbutzniks.

The kibbutz movement in Israel was notable for its military service, not merely its economic activities or social ideals. Every kibbutz had rifles either paid for or manufactured. Its members drilled with them, practiced shooting, stood guard day and night. The location of settlements was chiefly influenced by the needs of local defense and the role they might play in the coming political struggle. In the 1930s, land was purchased, more often than not *reclaimed*, in remote parts of the country. Kibbutzim thus defined the borders of a future Jewish state by insuring that the defended outlying population areas would be incorporated into it. In the war with Arabs after partitioning, kibbutzniks fought bravely. Fighters at Russian-based Degania were instrumental in halting the Syrian tank advance into the Galilee by throwing homemade Molotov cocktails.

Twelve years after statehood, kibbutzim were known for far more than agricultural output. Tourists come there to view the beautiful surroundings, enjoy the guest accommodations, and sign up for the educational tours.

"Israel is in need of new immigrants," the government representative told his audience of mostly Americans eating breakfast on Tuesday morning, Day 3 of the tour. "Especially Jews from Western countries with good job skills and advanced schooling."

The man in his early thirties with dark hair and eyes was dressed in a white shirt and double-breasted suit jacket but wore no tie. His neck was wide open, with the shirt collar folded over the jacket collar, suggestive of both the informality of business attire and the hot climate in this Mediterranean country. The facial tan extended down to the hair on his chest. This Israeli Jew could have passed for Italian or Greek.

This was our first full day in Tel Aviv. We were in our hotel dining room, digging in to a very impressive meal, part of an official reception by the Israeli government. I sat at a table with my two taxi-mates to Solonos Ho Theos two days earlier, Alan Bachman and Marty Levine. Also sitting with us was Herbie Kramer from Chicago, my new roommate, a PFC my age stationed in France. We heard a speech about the new nation and Jews around the world returning after two thousand years as we downed scrambled eggs, fried potatoes, bagels, lox, pickled herring, a variety of cheeses, blintzes, and mixed fruit. I paid attention to what the spokesperson was saying, or rather *selling*, about the land flowing with milk and honey, some of which was on the table before me. Alan listened intently too but Marty was busy gobbling up food fit for Israel's ancient kings. Herbie whispered to us about the French girls he knew and seemed to care less about eating than connecting with a yaldah, any fresh and delicious local tart in a dress or skirt.

"Israel is changing economically," the Israeli continued in very good English but with an accent, "from a primarily agricultural nation to a more industrial one. And the Jews who are now making Aliyah are different too."

The official told us about Jewish immigration to his country. From 1882-1903 about 35,000 Jews entered Palestine. They came mainly from Russia to escape the pogroms unleashed after Czar Alexander II was assassinated. He called this the First Aliyah, the Zionists who established agricultural communities and small towns. The second wave of immigrants, some 40,000, also came from Russia, from 1904-1914, the period between the Russo-Japanese War and World War I. This rang a bell as I recalled my grandfather left Russian-occupied Poland in 1905 to escape the twenty-year conscription young Jewish men were consigned to by law. This group was more socialist minded and formed self-defense organizations to counter increasing Arab hostility.

"During the first war, Jewish immigration was effectively cut off," the young man said waving his hand in a sweeping gesture, "but picked up again in nineteen-nineteen."

For the next four years, in the wake of the war and the British Mandate, another 40,000 made their way to Palestine. Many in this Third Aliyah were pioneers, trained in agriculture. They drained marshes and cultivated the land. National institutions were created during this time—the labor federation, an elected assembly, and the Haganah, a Jewish paramilitary. The fourth wave, from 1924-1932 was even bigger, over 82,000, the result of strict immigration quotas to the United States and anti-Semitism rampant in Poland and Hungary. Rather than farmers, Jews from these countries, mainly middle-class families, settled in the growing towns and established small businesses and light industry.

"The Fifth Aliyah," the Israeli emissary noted, "should be of special interest to you here today." He glanced around the room at his audience of tourists who had come from Germany. "This flood of immigrants is closely associated with the rise of Hitler and the Nazis."

The elderly German couple sitting two tables away stirred in their chairs. Many others in the room put down their forks and listened now with both ears as the spokesman talked about the 60,000 German Jews—doctors, lawyers, professors, and other professionals— who from 1933-1939 fled Deutschland because of persecution and denial of rights, and who found refuge in the Promised Land. About 150,000 Jews from Eastern Europe also migrated in these years in a continuation of the previous wave and the Nazis' occupation of other countries.

Much to my surprise, I learned that Nazis and Jews were strange bedfellows. The unlikely confederates had collaborated with one another. In August 1933, not long after Hitler burned the Reichstag and encouraged anti-Semitic attacks on his own citizens, Nazi authorities approved a Transfer Agreement with the Zionist Federation of Germany. This facilitated the emigration of German Jews to Palestine and was a means for Hitler to rid the country of its purported Jewish problem. By law, Jews had to pay to leave Germany and could not take their assets with them. This deal-with-the-devil allowed Jews to convert their assets into Reichmarks and hand the cash over to the foreign ministry, which set up accounts for them to purchase German goods for export to Palestine. Palestinian merchants would buy the German exports and then transfer the proceeds to the Pfennigless Jewish immigrants in their new homeland. Large sums of money were brought into Palestine and this greatly aided economic growth and recovery from the worldwide Depression. With the onset of war in 1939, all immigration from Germany was halted and the continuation of the Agreement became impossible. Tragically, the British White Paper of the same year severely restricted all Jewish entry at a time when an open border was needed most.

After the war and before Israel's statehood, any Jew who ventured to enter the Promised Land was an illegal immigrant. Virtually all of the survivors of Nazi death camps—DPs in Germany, Austria, and Italy—who reached Palestine were smuggled in by ships and boats under cover of darkness. After statehood, the numbering or naming of waves ceased but immigration did not. More than half a million

Jews from around the world came to Israel in the first two years alone, many fleeing persecution in now Communist nations. After 1950, those coming in were very different from earlier waves of European immigrants, legal and illegal. Recently uprooted Jews left, escaped, or were expelled from *Arab* lands.

"Now, in nineteen sixty," the smooth-talking official said, "Israel is at a crossroads. Our economy is changing, industry is growing, and there is a need for engineers and scientists and technical people of all kind. People like yourselves, who may have graduated from college and who served in the American military." He stepped back a bit and caught his breath before he ended his talk. "I and the people of Israel ask you to consider making Aliyah . . . to think about bringing your talents and experience to a country of your ancestry, a Jewish state where you will be free to worship in your own faith and will have no fear of persecution by Gentiles."

When questions and comments were invited, a number of hands without forks went up. The elderly German woman was called on first.

"Ve made Aliyah in nineteen tirty-five, after Nürnberg law," she said, as she lowered her arm and placed her hand on her husband's. "Ve had to go vay from Hitler und ze Nazis. But ve come back to Chermany after ze war. Life too hard in Yisroel. Und ve miss old country. Ve here now yust to see friends und relatives."

This German couple could shake hands with Polish Harry in Munich, I thought, all émigrés from, and returnees to, a Deutschland that was far from a Promised Land for many Jews. This was not what the young man who hawked immigration to Israel wanted to hear, who happened to omit talking about *em*igration from his country. Since the war thousands of Jews—survivors, Sabras, and Aliyahs—left Israel for a presumed better life in Europe or America. For those who returned to Germany, which had either forced them out or forced them into concentration and/or DP camps, nostalgic or softer living among Gentiles in a former domicile apparently trumped being among fellow Jews in a struggling Jewish state.

Several young men on the tour asked questions indicating they might be interested in making Aliyah. The answers given, however, seemed to contradict what we were led to believe about Israel. Only Orthodox Judaism was recognized by the government, the idealistic representative told his audience. Conservative and Reform rabbis ordained in other countries did not have the legal right to head synagogues, perform marriages, or convert Gentiles. Continuing conflict with Arabs was downplayed, but I and perhaps others understood the ever-present danger to Jewish life and limb was a form of persecution not unlike that perpetrated throughout history by Romans, Crusaders, Cossacks, and Nazis. The Israeli government's benefits to new immigrants were talked about, the high taxes on income and consumer goods were not.

We were given much food for thought that first morning in Israel, from the Aliyah ambassador and the hotel.

CHAPTER 12: TOUR DE FORCE

Israel was a tower of strength, skill, and ingenuity in the Middle East, both militarily and economically. The tiny nation with a small population, outnumbered a hundred to one by enemies all around her, was victorious in the 1948 War of Independence with seven Arab nations. In the 1956 Sinai Campaign, the war over the Suez Canal fought against mighty Egypt armed with Soviet weapons, she achieved most of her objectives. Beginning in 1959, West Germany was a significant supplier of arms and military equipment to Israel. The biblical David was becoming Goliath, thanks in no small part to a former enemy.

Just eight decades earlier, on the eve of the great waves of migrations from Eastern and Central Europe, the country was a wasteland, neglected for centuries under Arab rule. The land was barren, arid, and sterile. Top soil had been blown away by the wind. It was the pioneer Jews who cleared rocks, irrigated the land, plowed the fields, cultivated plants, and literally made the desert bloom. Israel in 1960 was the leading producer and exporter of fruits and vegetables in the region.

The group from Deutschland, after digesting the big spiel about the Promised Land over breakfast in a Tel Aviv hotel, embarked on a sightseeing tour of the country. In the next nine days, group members would get to know firsthand what a great force in the world and their lives Israel was.

On our first full day in Tel Aviv, we were on our way to the city's neighbor to the south, the ancient port of Jaffa. Our guide was a Bombay-born Jew who spoke the King's English, an Indian lighter in skin tone than most of his Hindu countrymen, the bus driver a Yiddish-speaking survivor of Auschwitz who would not go back to his native Ukraine. The two men were postwar émigrés, one by choice, the other necessity. The driver carried a pistol in a leather holster on his hip and a rifle standing upright was always next to the steering wheel.

I leaned back in my seat and perused the printed itinerary handed out in Munich. The first page contained a map of Israel with numbers corresponding to various historical sites listed from north to south. On pages 2-4 there were descriptions of the daily activities and places to be visited. I studied the different sites and locations we would get to see in the days ahead. Sitting next to me on the bus was Herbie Kramer.

"Our first stop is Jaffa," I mentioned to him casually, looking at Day 3 on the itinerary.

Herbie turned his head from the window. "Yeah . . . and that was Jonah's *last* stop."

My tour buddy no doubt was referring to the biblical Jonah who set sail from Jaffa before being swallowed by the whale. He must have read that point in the tourist brochure all of us were given when we checked into the hotel.

Herbie was an interesting character but not the type I admired or wanted to emulate. He had no plans for college and was strictly working class in manner, speech, dress, and looks. A little shorter and thinner than I but with fairer and curlier hair, the young soldier was good-looking but anti-intellectual and crass. He wore those pointed featherweight shoes popular with Italians and he combed his crop as Hollywood's Tony Curtis did in his early films, sides pushed up to the top with a thick curl hanging over his forehead like a flaccid penis stretched across high testicles.

"Stanley Kramer, the Hollywood producer and director, is my uncle," Herbie mentioned to me and others in an effort to impress us, but offered no specifics of the familial tie.

The enlistee camped in a French town bragged about the many mademoiselles he was able to entré. Herbie believed he had to ball a girl in every country he visited. His boasts were often within earshot of the married women. In Israel a sexual encounter was likewise uppermost in his mind and most everyone on the tour knew it. One of the civilians told him there were no Jewish prostitutes in Israel, and advised him to stay clear of Arab women. The trooper one rank my junior kept insisting he could shoot into a Miriam or Esther, even if it meant shelling out some Israeli pounds. To Herbie, partitioned Palestine was just another American soldiers' field for plum pickings.

Jaffa was one of the sites given to the Tribe of Dan and was the port-of-entry for the cedars of Lebanon used in building King Solomon's Temple. The guide spoke about the many groups and leaders that occupied this port for three thousand years—Canaanites, Hebrew Kings, Alexander the Great, Arabs, Crusaders, Napoléon, to name a few, and lastly the British—a testament to the city's resilience. We visited Clock Square in the center of town. The way Herbie was eyeing the young females in shorts and skirts sauntering around us, the Square could have been called by another name, one without the *l*. We glided through Jaffa's Zodiac alleys, which led to the ancient wall and old seaport. I found my sign, Aquarius, in one of the alleys and touched it.

After lunch we spent the rest of the day sightseeing in Tel Aviv, a suburb of Jaffa carved out of desolate sand dunes on the Mediterranean coastline in 1909 by Jews fleeing the population swell in the largely Arab port town. Tel Aviv was now a sprawling metropolis, the largest city in Israel and the most modern and most secular. Its restaurants, bars, cafés, and shops were open for business, and its public transportation system not shut down, on Shabbat, from Friday at sundown and all day Saturday. We visited the Bialik House museum, the Town Council, and Museum of Art, then swung by the beach. Bathers out this time of year reminded me of Coney Island.

"Let's go to Dizengoff Square," Herbie said to me after dinner.

"Okay," I replied. I knew that place was one of the main modern sights to visit in Tel Aviv.

Herbie and I walked to Dizengoff Square in the evening. The circular plaza was a hub of six convergent streets. We sat on a bench opposite the fountain in the center. I was content to just take in the hustle and bustle of a big city at night. Herbie, with his head shifting from side to side as if he were viewing a tennis match, was poised to spring up at any moment and coil around any yaldah that caught his fancy.

"Why don't you go up to one of these girls and tell her you had a famous uncle in Hollywood who can get her into the movies," I said in jest to the hotshot sitting next to me.

"Maybe I'll do that."

Herbie seemed to take my comment seriously. We sat for a while longer, then went inside the four-story round building on the Square when there were fewer and fewer girl's passing by. We peered at colorful posters in Hebrew outside a movie theater and on kiosks, and browsed through department stores and shops. On more than the display merchandise was the lover-boy's sights.

The next day, Wednesday, we left Tel Aviv for Israel's capital. Our tour bus brought us to Jerusalem. It was 60 kilometers east and south along thin winding roads, high in the Judean Mountains. Looking out the window, I saw burned-out jeeps and tanks along the side of the road. Vegetation grew inside the rusted hulls.

"These are reminders of war," the guide noted. "Everything is left where it is. Military museums are not necessary in Israel."

We checked in to our hotel, ate lunch, and had free time the rest of the day. Walking around, I saw that Jerusalem was more traditional than Tel Aviv. Women wore plain dresses and scarves over their heads, the men outdated hats and double-breasted suits, often unbuttoned.

On Day 5 of the tour, March tenth, we had a full schedule. After breakfast, we were taken to the Knesset to see the workings of Israel's Parliament. Later we went to the Bezalel Academy of Art and Design, a school that attracted many teachers and students from Germany after the Nazis shut down the modernist Bauhaus schools in Weimar, Dessau, and Berlin. Both places interested me, but the next one we visited after lunch gave me a bit of a shock.

That Thursday afternoon I sat in the rear of the bus, preoccupied with changing the film in my camera. The guide was clueing us in about our next tour stop but I was not paying attention. For a moment or two I looked up. He was gesticulating with both arms, using sudden movements to supplement his accented English. Everyone around me seemed to be listening to the briefing but I was more concerned with loading a new roll of Kodak 36-exposure color film in my Retina IIIC. My mind was on securing the tab to the advancing spool, turning the tension mechanism, and firmly fitting the two lines of perforations on the film over the cogs on the sprocket wheel. The only thing I remember hearing the guide say was something about "going into the past."

The bus stopped. People in front of me formed a line to the door. When I got off and looked around, my listlessness quickly disappeared. I found myself standing in the middle of a narrow street paved with cobblestones. The curb was only a few feet past stone dwellings adjacent to one another. Above me were clotheslines that hung between houses on either side of the street. A blanket of darkness hung over the area even though it was only mid-afternoon. Everything around me was terribly decrepit.

The other members of the tour were dispersed and roamed about in pairs or groups of three. I walked alone, trailing the others, one hand on my camera so as not to have it continually banging against my chest. Oddly-dressed men were a short distance away. I peered at them, bewildered by their queerness, stunned by the fact that they were all garbed alike. They wore large black hats with wide brims, some trimmed with fur. Black frock coats, extending past their knees, fitted them tightly. Their bespectacled faces seemed dwarfed amid their unkempt black or graying beards. From ear to below the jaw line, they each sported two long curls, side locks of hair that dangled like wind chimes as they moved.

There was a strange atmosphere about this place that made me feel as though I were in another land and back in time. I saw the wo-man I knew from Friday night services at McGraw Kaserne, Leeann Armson, wife of a Gentile warrant officer. She was with another woman. They were standing in front of one of the shops. I hurriedly went up to her, still ignorant of my whereabouts.

"Where are we? Who are these people," I asked with a sense of urgency.

Leeann made a suggestive motion to me, indicating that I should lower my voice. "We're in Mea She'arim," she replied in a low tone, and then looked back into the open door.

"Meya *who*?"

"Shhhh," she motioned again with her index finger over her lips. "Weren't you listening when the guide told us?"

I shook my head.

"No wonder you look lost. This is Meya Shay arim." She pro-nounced it slowly in the Hebrew vernacular. "It means Hundred Gates."

"But who are these people?"

"They're the ultra-Orthodox Jews," my Munich acquaintance whispered, "the Chassidim."

I stood there agape, unable to move or speak for a few seconds. I did not know what caused the greater shock, not being forewarned on my first exposure to this extreme faction of Judaism or the fact that they were my own people. "Why are they all dressed like that?"

"Later ... later," Leeann said, impatient at the bombardment of questions. "I want to see this."

I stood behind the two women, able to peep over their shoulders. The door to the shop was wide open. Piles of feathers covered the planked floor. A middle-aged plump man was inside. He wore a black skullcap atop his balding pate. I watched him as he flattened his long beard by running his palm down on it, using his chest for support. His shirtsleeves were rolled to the elbows, suspenders prevented the loose-fitting trousers from falling below his protruding belly. The shopkeeper bent over and removed a chicken from one of the coops. He secured it under his left arm, grasped the head with his right hand and pulled the neck backwards to form a taut arc. Then, freeing his right hand by holding the head in his left, with one swift motion and before the bird could shriek, he took the razor from between his lips and deftly ran it through half the diameter of the neck. When I saw the gray mass ooze out after he squeezed the gash with his thumbs and forefingers, I looked away quickly. I did not care to see what else a shoched did to put fowl food on someone's table.

"Let's move on," I heard the other woman say, "or we'll fall too far behind the others."

We moved on. And I was moved by what I saw and what the other woman, a high school teacher married to a draftee dentist, explained along the way.

I was a time-traveler and student of Judaism that day. People in Mea She'arim, I learned, live much as their ancestors did in the shtetls of Eastern Europe. They do not read newspapers, listen to the radio, or watch television. They dress in styles of clothing reminiscent of the 18th and 19th centuries, garbs completely unsuitable for Israel's hot climate. Their life revolved around strict conformity to Jewish law, prayer, and the study of Hebrew texts. Men and boys grow side curls based on the biblical injunction against shaving next to one's ears. Women wear wigs and head-coverings, colored stockings, and long-sleeved dresses as a sign of modesty. Many of the children were clothed similarly as adults. Budding ear locks were visible on the beardless pre-pubescent boys. Mea She'arim was founded in 1873 by 100 Orthodox families who gated the entrances to their homes. On the Sabbath, these guardians of Judaism put up barricades to prevent the non-Orthodox—on foot or in automobiles—from entering their religious domain. To the dismay of many secular Israelis, the Chassidim are not Zionists. They oppose the modern state of Israel because it came about by violence and war instead of Messianic deliverance.

The tail end of our bus was sticking out from a side street. The guide and driver were leaning against it. Most of the tour members had already boarded. As we approached the bus, we were motioned to hop in quickly. I took my seat in the rear, turned around, and glanced out the back window. As we pulled away I got my last gander at this Jewish ghetto. The look-alike, animated figures grew smaller and smaller, disappearing into the distance.

We next hit the King David Hotel, the most luxurious in Israel, fit for modern presidents and heads of state the likes of an ancient Saul, David, or Solomon. Prior to Independence it was the headquarters of the British military. Pointed out to us was the side of the six-story building that was rebuilt after the bombing in 1946 by the Irgun, the Jewish Underground. So powerful was the blast that 91 people were killed. In erstwhile deluxe rooms and opulent offices of the hotel's collapsed southern wing, there was no fence or Green Line separating the flesh and blood of Jews from that of non-Jews.

Before a late dinner that second day in Jerusalem, we drove south to the edge of the city to Ramat Rachel, a kibbutz overlooking nearby Bethlehem and Rachel's Tomb. Founded by members of a labor brigade in 1926, there was a sculpture in the garden of the biblical matriarch protecting two children. This beloved wife of Jacob, mother of Joseph and Benjamin, was taken to personify the nation of Israel. The ideals of the kibbutz, Jews working for the common good and sharing equally, appealed to me at first. But to make Aliyah for a communal life, to toil in the soil and forgo individual rewards, to aspire to be no different from anyone else, meant abandoning my plans for college to better myself, to be more successful than those I knew back home and in the Army. This option for me was déjà vu. Six months earlier, I walked out on Karin rather than drive away from the path I paved for myself.

At a gift shop just before we came back to the hotel, I wanted to purchase two candlesticks and a Seder dish with three matzo trays for my parents. But I did not have enough cash, dollars or pounds, and traveler's checks were not accepted. Leeann loaned me twenty dollars.

"You can pay me tomorrow," she said nonchalantly. "There's no rush."

I loathed owing anyone anything and had never borrowed money before. Taking the twenty brought to mind the incident over the same amount soon after I arrived in Nuremberg the year before. I had loaned money to a teammate I hardly knew, he would not pay me on payday as promised in writing claiming he had to pay someone else, and I had to go with the defaulter to the Master Sergeant in the Area Office and wave the I.O.U. to settle the matter.

Soon as we arrived at the hotel, I made a dash for cash. I sprinted to the reception desk to convert traveler's checks into dollars, in lieu of following the crowd to the dining room. By the time I entered the eating area, everyone was sitting at tables, about to be served. I went straight to Leeann's table and handed her two ten-dollar bills, thanking her again. I was completely oblivious to waiters walking around the room with large silver trays resting on the palm of one hand filled with plates of food.

She smiled at me. "That's okay, David. You could have waited until tomorrow."

"No, no," I shot back, still breathing heavily. "I wanted to pay you right away."

I took several steps backwards, still facing Leeann and expressing my solemn appreciation, without looking behind me. All of a sudden I knocked into something and then heard a loud noise. I turned around and saw a waiter on his ass, face red as an apple, giving me a look like he wanted to kill me. A silver tray turned upside down was on the floor next to him. Shards of ivory-patterned plates, brown chicken legs, green peas, and white lumps of mashed potatoes were strewn all around the poor man.

"I'm sorry, I'm sorry," I pleaded, but the waiter said nothing, in Hebrew or English.

The accident was my fault and I knew it. Standing in the middle of the room, wallet in hand, everyone staring at me, was very embarrassing. Before I could lend a hand, the man I floored picked himself up, turned over the tray, and started collecting the now inedible food and broken China. Quietly I tiptoed to an empty chair at one of the tables. When another waiter set a plate down in front of me, I feared what was on it had come off the dining room floor and not from the kitchen. I ate in silence and avoided eye contact with my tour mates.

The next morning, in the dining room, I only walked forward and made sure I glanced to my right and left. I sat at a table with Herbie. He talked about his current beau, not the previous night's faux pas. Neither Leeann nor anyone else mentioned my sightless steps.

On Friday the eleventh, Day 6, we departed Jerusalem right after breakfast. Four successive stops were scheduled on our daily itinerary: Beersheba, Sodom, Masada, and the Dead Sea.

To get to the Dead Sea, we had to go south all the way around the West Bank, a large territory extending east to west from the Jordan River to Jerusalem, north to south from below Nazareth to above Beersheba. The West Bank belonged to Jordan and was off limits to Jews. The forced circumvention afforded our group the opportunity to tour three other interesting sites along the way.

Beersheba was the largest city in the Negev Desert. We traveled south for almost two hours to get there. Originally it was part of the Arab state after partitioning, but when the Arabs refused to accept the UN resolution for an independent Jewish state, the Egyptian Army moved in and set up a strategic base. Beersheba turned out not to be a good Egyptian soldiers' field for battle. In late '48, after bombing raids ordered by Ben-Gurion, the city was conquered by the superior Israeli Defense Forces. Egyptian soldiers were taken prisoner by the IDF, Arab residents fled on foot, Jewish settlers came in on wheels. The PM believed Israel's future lies in development of the Negev. By 1960, several thriving neighborhoods were created, a hospital opened its doors, and there was talk of starting a university.

"Beersheba was important in ancient times," our guide explained, sounding like he was reading from a prepared text. "It was located at the intersection of two international roads. This is where Abraham came and dug a well to water his flock, the Romans placed their defenses, and the Crusaders built a fortress."

I was impressed with the look and feel of this developing city but disappointed we could not visit the famous Bedouin flea market, not because there was a barbed-wire fence keeping Jews out but because it was closed on Fridays, the Muslim Sabbath. In this respect, Arabs are no different than Orthodox Jews. Praying to Allah takes precedence over handling money on God's commanded day of rest.

After lunch in Beersheba, we headed east to Sodom. Before we got there we came to Mount Sodom, a hill five-by-three miles along the southwestern rim of the Dead Sea. It consists almost entirely of salt. The chalk-like rock formations contain a series of shallow craters extending as far as the eye can see. Pointed out to us at the peak was a separate pillar that resembled a person, understandably labeled "Lot's Wife," the woman who disobeyed God and looked back at Sodom being destroyed. Near this pillar is the bumpy narrow road that descends into where the city of Sodom was believed to be, now a place for just Dead Sea industries and workers. The location of Gomorrah was probably on the other side of the Jordan River. Perhaps it is good that the two spots on earth famous for sin, vice, homosexuality, and deviant hetero-sexuality cannot be located exactly. Were it not for the fire and brimstone brought about by God's wrath, these cities near the partitioned border might very well have turned into an Israeli and Jordanian soldiers' field for fleshpot and bacchanalia to alleviate the pressures of war.

Masada, Herod's palace overlooking the Dead Sea, was erected three decades before Christ. It served as the hated king's refuge in the event of a revolt. We climbed the cliffs on the west edge, about 300 feet high, the easier and shorter of the two approaches. Many tour members were exhausted when we reached the top of the mountain, a flat and rhomboid-shaped walled fortress. The east edge is a sheer drop of over 1,300 feet to the sea below, enough to keep most Dead Sea attackers at bay. After Herod's death, a Roman garrison occupied Masada but in 66 A.D. a small group of Jewish rebels, with force of great skill and ingenuity, overtook it. When Jerusalem fell four years later, fleeing zealots and their families joined the rebels. For several years the fortress was a base from which to raid and harass the unloved occupiers of the Holy Land. The Romans constructed a rampart against the western approach to the stronghold and in 74 A.D. moved a battering ram up and breached the wall. The defenders of the faith chose not to be taken alive and nailed to a cross. The fortress was burned and nearly a thousand men, women, and children either committed suicide or agreed to be killed by zealots who drew lots.

The story of Masada moved me. Never mind its splendid view and elegant palace. The heroism of the Jewish people and their determination to be free in the land God promised to them I could not help but admire. In the 20th century, Jews hiding in the Warsaw Ghetto felt the same way as their first-century ancestors, choosing to fight the Nazis to the bitter end rather than be deported in boxcars to death camps.

Our final stop for the day was the Dead Sea, a salt lake with no marine life wedged between Jordan and the West Bank. One of the world's first health resorts, Kings David and Herod both came here. Minerals from the Dead Sea have been used to create cosmetics and herbal powders. Almost 1,400 feet below sea level, I stood at the lowest point on earth. With my loaded camera, a soldier on the tour shot a picture of me so I could later prove it.

We headed for Tel Aviv on the way back. We were scheduled to stay there for three nights. In Tel Aviv we would have Saturday free and not be restricted in terms of transportation and shopping. On Sunday we could see the Purim Parade or take the side trip to Eilat.

"Those two girls are looking at us," I whispered without pointing.

Herbie had his eyes in that direction too. He nodded slightly but did not say anything. Interest and excitement were written all over his face. We were on Dizengoff Street, near the Square, in front of a café we just came out of. The girls were not far away on the sidewalk, talking to each other and smiling, glancing over to us intermittently. They wore the olive drab uniform of the IDF with black berets. The two were in the Army of their country just as we were in ours.

It was Day 7, Saturday afternoon. The female soldiers Herbie and I saw on a Tel Aviv street were about eighteen or nineteen, suitable ages for us. In the Promised Land, in order to keep it that way for Jews, every man has to serve three years of active duty in the military and then reserve service of one month a year until age fifty-five. Women too were subject to the draft, but for two years, and were assigned to non-combat roles. Women who marry early and begin bearing children, Orthodox especially, were exempt from military duty.

Herbie started walking toward the girls. "Let's talk to them." He swaggered a little.

"Okay," I said, and followed closely.

The girls saw us coming and turned to face us. The color of their uniforms was not unlike that of the khaki shirts and OD jacket and trousers in my wall locker. One girl's jacket hung over her forearm, the other held it by the collar dangling from a shoulder. Berets atop their heads to one side did not conceal their short but full head of hair. Beige blouses tucked under knee-length brownish skirts revealed a good part of their upper and lower body. The girls had nice faces and sizable tits but were a little chunky, especially around the thighs and calves. The dark-haired Israelis were by no means fat but did not possess the strong, slender, and shapely figures of the two Aryan blonds I favored in Germany. To me they were good-looking enough to date in any country, but the fact that they were non-American Jewish girls peaked my interest and rendered them all the more attractive. Herbie, I was sure, was thinking only of what was beneath the skirt, not of the opportunity they posed for the cultural enhancement of an American boy their age.

"Hello, hello," the four of us said with awkward smiles.

This was Israel. We were all Jewish. People were friendly toward strangers, unless of course the strangers were, or were deemed to be, Arabs. I broke the ice, introduced myself and Herbie, and told the girls we were American soldiers stationed in Europe just visiting Israel. They spoke English very well, better than any Fräulein I had come to know, and conversed with us without hesitation or suspicion. They said they were on Sabbath pass. One was from Tel Aviv, the other Haifa. Both were Sabras, born in Israel of parents who emigrated before the war. Obviously they were not married, not with child, and not religious, perfect temporal partners for my buddy and me. This was their day off and they had to report back to their unit the next day, Sunday, the beginning of the work week in Israel. And this was our lucky day, running into two girls who had time on their hands and were not against fraternizing with foreign Jewish boys.

Herbie and I spent the rest of the afternoon and part of the evening with the girls. We treated them to coffee and cake, walked around the Square for a while, and later had dinner. They asked us all sorts of questions about ourselves, our Army, our lives in the States, our future plans. The one I paired with, Yael, I assumed was of Sephardic origin with the name Roubini, a variation of Rubin. I soon realized she was Ashkenazic, like I and most Israelis in 1960. Her parents came from Poland and Hungary, not North Africa or the Middle East. In Israel, European Jews often romanized their surnames or adopted Hebrew ones instead. No different than American Jews who chose to step into the melting pot by anglicizing family monikers from Schwartz to Black, Weissberg to Whitehill, Grünfeld to Greenfield. Yael seemed interested in me, kept asking if I liked Israel and would make Aliyah. She talked about the fundamental ideals of Israeli society, its promise of a homeland and decent life for Jews the world over, a life with dignity and justice and freedom, without want or persecution. Yael could have been Miss Herzl the way she spewed the Zionist Dream exposed to since childhood.

"Why don't you come with us to a party?" Yael said before we left the restaurant.

"Yes . . . I want you to come," the friend with Herbie added, looking at him.

Herbie and I gladly accepted the invitation. What else did we have to do? I was eager to meet Israeli people, not just visit historic sites. Herbie was hoping to fulfill his masculine objective in this country before the night was out. Earlier, when the girls went to the head, I told the horny soldier to stand at ease, not to count on any rapid firing. We were not in France or Germany, these were not bargirls or hookers. Herbie did not heed anything I said, likely gave a different interpretation to the words of the girl he sat opposite to.

The friendly females led us to an apartment blocks away. Seven or eight young people, men and women our age and a little older, were gathered in the small living room. Most were dressed in civilian clothes but all were in the military. We were told to put our jackets on the bed in the other room. I was struck by the informality of Israeli soldiers. Officers, sergeants, and lower-ranks fraternized and addressed each other by their first names, behavior taboo in the American Armed Forces. Yael's buddies befriended us too, seemingly more anxious to learn about my country than I was about theirs. One bombarded me with questions about working in the

States. He was getting out of the IDF soon and planned to leave Israel. The potential émigré had a five-digit tattoo on his forearm and the look of quiet desperation on his face. The image of a starving child in tattered clothes behind a barbed-wire fence, one I first formed of little Anna in my sixth-grade class, came to mind. Some country Israel, I thought. One citizen wants to forsake the Promised Land and live in exile in the Diaspora, while another beseeches someone in the Diaspora to end his exile and live in the Promised Land.

Somewhat later Herbie leaned over to me. "Go see if our jackets are still in the bedroom."

I was shocked by his call for a checkup on these people. "What are you worried about?" I immediately put to him, "The people here are all Jews."

"That's what I'm worried about," he hit back with a straight face.

Herbie was not kidding me. He truly believed these native Israelis and concentration camp survivors, fellow comrades in arms, might steal his farkockte jacket. He acted as if he was in an American Army barracks, where the lifting of articles lying around is commonplace, or back in his hometown, where Jews were known to be part of Al Capone's underworld. I gave a look in the bedroom just to satisfy Herbie's paranoia, but had no theft to report.

At the party I had a good time as I was not trying to make time with Yael. I knew the girls. were out for just a touch of amicable interaction with American boys, not fleeting amorous affairs with strange men. But Herbie had other ideas. He tried real hard to lure the girl he came with out of these safe waters, onto a lonely pier to put love in gear, to find a recess where they can undress. Like a character in one of his uncle's movies, I overheard him cast every hook in the book, throw every fine line, toss his tale for her tail, all to no avail. Before the girls left, the rejected romancer listened to me for a change. The American soldiers, not officers but yet gentlemen, discharged themselves from the apartment.

I was halfway out the door when Yael handed me a piece of paper she had scribbled on. The girl Herbie tried to bow out with made no such gesture to him.

"Are you going to Eilat?" Leeann asked me on Sunday morning during breakfast.

"No," I said. "I'm staying here to see the Purim Parade."

Leeann and others took the side trip for the day arranged by our tour host for an additional sum. They flew from Lod Airport down to Israel's southernmost city in the Negev at the northern tip of the Red Sea. Eilat was a busy port and a popular resort, vital to Israel's economy on both counts. The war that broke out in 1956 occurred because Egypt blockaded the port of Eilat, cutting off Israel's shipping trade and denying her passage through the Suez Canal.

From my Hebrew School days, I knew that Purim was a festive occasion—a day for eating, drinking, pageants, and merriment—not a high holiday like Passover or Yom Kippur. It is celebrated on Adar 14 on the Hebrew calendar, a date usually in March. People dress up in costumes or as clowns, wear colorful masks of all sizes, and dance in the street. On Purim there is a carnival atmosphere, a Jewish Mardi Gras. The origin of this festival is the Book of Esther, which recounts the deliverance in the 6th century B.C. of the Jewish people from a plot by Haman, an anti-Semite and wicked minister to the King of Persia, to kill all the Jews in the land. Esther is the King's beautiful and favorite wife, unbeknownst to him to be a Jewess, who would have been killed along with all of her people. She learns of the plot, reveals her tribal affiliation to the King, and begs him to spare her life and the lives of all her people. The King honors his wife's plea and orders Haman and his ten sons hanged instead.

As a child in the synagogue on Purim, when the biblical account was read, I got a big kick out of hissing, booing, stamping my feet, and rattling noisemakers along with the other congregants whenever Haman's name was mentioned. I loved to eat the traditional hamentaschen, Yiddish for "Haman's pockets," the triangular pastries filled with prunes or poppy seeds representative of the three-cornered hat that the ancient Persian Hitler wore.

Tel Aviv's Purim Parade was held in the afternoon on Allenby Street. A bunch of us on the tour went there together and found spaces to sit in the temporary bleachers placed along the main thoroughfare. I brought my camera and extra film. From way up high, I could not get close-ups of the floats that would soon be passing. I left the pack and maneuvered myself through the crowd. I squeezed into a small opening on the curb and sat down between two people. With no obstructions, I could get a clear shot of anything or anyone that rolled or walked by.

I was a real shutterbug that thirteenth of March. I snapped only color-slide pictures, getting virtually every float and assemblage of children or adults participating in the parade, using up two full rolls of film. There were floats depictive, often in caricature, of different countries. I observed a 20-foot Statue of Liberty, Buckingham Palace guards, a girl dressed as Cleopatra next to a replica of a pyramid, a gold-painted Buddha, African warriors carrying long spears. Teenagers wearing blue and white, the colors of Israel's flag, marched by blowing musical instruments. Branches of the military displayed their personnel and weapons. Children in Halloween dress and adults in gigantic cartoon-character costumes waved to the crowds on both sides of the street. Men rode by on horses in cowboy outfits and on camels in keffiyeh head coverings and ankle-length tunics. Many kibbutzim were represented in the gaiety, with members driving farm equipment and displaying placards with slogans of unity and equality.

Tel Aviv's annual Purim Parade dated back to 1912. Seeing it reminded me of its counterpart in New York, the Macy's Thanksgiving Day Parade down Fifth Avenue my father took me to see. In both cities, every year is different. Floats and themes and participants vary with the times. Tel Aviv parades once poked fun at Hitler and the Nazis. In 1935, automobiles disguised as Panzers moved slowly behind marchers in mock SS uniforms. In 1939, there was a float of a crocodile with an open mouth and big teeth, symbolizing Hitler's gobbling up of Austria and Czechoslovakia, and at the end of the parade it was set on fire on the beach. In 1960, I saw a procession of young Israelis marking twelve years of independence. The following year's parade should be a great commemoration, I thought. It will be Israel's Bar Mitzvah.

"Look . . . look . . . there he is," I heard one of the women on the tour bus say excitedly as she pointed out the window. "He's so handsome with those baby blue eyes."

It was Monday, Day 9, the beginning of our bus ride to the northern territory. After breakfast we started to leave Tel Aviv. We were on HaYarkon Street, ready to pass by the Dan Hotel, when the driver slowed down and came to a stop because of the crowd up ahead.

Paul Newman had just come out of the best hotel in town and onto the sidewalk when teenage girls formed a mob around him. They wanted to see the famous actor chosen to play Ari Ben Canaan, the leading character in the planned Hollywood movie *Exodus* based on the previous year's best-selling novel on the creation of the State of Israel. Newman's arrival at Lod Airport the night before was mentioned in that day's *Jerusalem Post*. The half-Jewish star told the press he would learn Hebrew for his role. Shooting was to begin in two weeks. I thought a couple of women on the bus were ready to bang on the door and force it open so they could jump off and get the heartthrob's autograph. Joanne Woodward, the distaff of Newman's own, was nowhere in sight.

Our first stop north was Netanya, less than halfway to Haifa. We had a beautiful view of the Mediterranean Sea during the twenty-mile drive along the Coastal Plain. We saw soldiers hitchhiking and being picked up, getting car rides by any stranger, a common practice in Israel. The city was named for Nathan Straus, owner of Macy's and well-known philanthropist. In 1928, the German Jew provided the funds for the establishment of a settlement on this ancient site. I enjoyed walking on the Promenade along the beach. Herbie walked with me but was not admiring the natural beauty of the sand and surf. Netanya absorbed many European immigrants in the '30s and '40s but was vulnerable to attacks due to its proximity to an Arab village.

Caesarea was next on our itinerary, an ancient port city, the midpoint between Tel Aviv and Haifa. Originally a Greek agricultural community, the Romans conquered it in 63 B.C., built an aqueduct, and made it the capital of Palestine. Herod later renamed the city in honor of Julius Caesar's nephew, the first Roman emperor, and put in a deep-sea harbor, amphitheater, and stadium. Caesarea was a pagan city, where Paul was imprisoned before being taken to Rome and Rabbi Akiva and other leaders of the Bar Kochba revolt were tried and executed. I got a lesson in medieval history by just walking around, a head start in my college career. The Crusaders conquered Caesarea and Louis IX later fortified it with high walls and a deep moat, parts of which were still standing. Much of what I saw was in ruins, the result of Arab sultans sacking the city for centuries.

We rolled into Haifa right after lunch, the largest city in Northern

Israel, third largest in the country. After dropping our bags at the hotel, we went to the main attraction, the Technion, the Israel Institute of Technology. The campus was modern and beautiful. Walking around, I got excited about going to college in six months. The university was founded in 1912 by German Jews for programs in the natural sciences, engineering, and architecture. A year later the "battle of the languages" began. The deutsch-jüdisch founders insisted on German being the language of instruction, but teachers and students struck, threatening a boycott if Hebrew was not used. The controversy over academic speech stressed the importance of establishing Hebrew as the official language of Israel in all spheres. Due to the strike and the world war, it was not until 1924 when classes were held . . . in Hebrew. Albert Einstein's visit to the Technion the previous year did not help the cause for his native tongue to be the appropriate language for science in Israel's first institution of higher learning. One can only wonder what the Jewish High Tech trustees would have done, had they won the battle for Deutsch, after Hitler came to power in Deutsch*land*.

Later in the day we toured this ancient city with a varied history, but now a mighty seaport and oil refining center. In Greek and Roman times Haifa was a fishing village, the Arabs conquered it in the 7th century A.D. and turned it into a trading port, Richard the Lionheart wrested control in 1191, Napoléon took over in 1799, and in the 1830s the city was governed by the Egyptian viceroy Muhammad Ali, a man who packed a powerful punch. Decades later German Christians came and set up a colony, and then Romanian Jews followed. In 1909 Haifa was central to the Bahá'í faith when a shrine on nearby Mount Carmel was built. Under British rule, Haifa became an industrial port and a railway was built but it remained largely an Arab city. With the arrival of survivors of the Buchenwald camp in 1945, nearly half the population was Jewish. In the ensuing war after the UN partition, control of Haifa, with its port and oil refineries, was critical. The Arab quarter was but a ghost town due to the exodus of its residents on orders from their leaders. I stood atop a low concrete wall on a hill overlooking the entire city— like an English, French, or Egyptian conqueror of yore—and had Herbie take a picture of me.

We spent the night at a very nice hotel in the former Arab quarter, a ghost town no longer.

"What's she doing?" I asked Leeann the next day, nodding toward another female member of the tour who stepped off the bus for a few minutes.

It was Tuesday, the fifteenth of March. This was not the first time the elderly woman had caught my attention. She was the mother of the Army dentist, visiting her son and daughter-in-law in Germany, and always had a sad look about here. Born in Poland, most of her family was lost after the Nazis invaded her country. For days, whenever we stopped, I watched her check bulletin boards at different places.

"She's looking for the names of people she knew in her town before the war," explained Leeann, putting down her copy of *Exodus*.

"Oh," I said.

"It's common practice in Israel for people searching for relatives and friends to put messages on bulletin boards or fences of empty lots."

"I see," I added. Now I knew why she was posting handwritten notes, in Yiddish and English, almost everywhere on the tour.

On our calendar for the next two days were the major points of interest in the north of Israel, the Upper and Lower Galilee. These two political regions differ greatly in geography. In the Upper Galilee the mountains are taller and the valleys deeper than those in the Lower Galilee. Our first stop after breakfast was Acre, an ancient city on Haifa Bay, up the coast from Haifa, one of the oldest continuously inhabited sites in Israel. Part Jewish, part Arab, Acre's origin dates back to the 16th century B.C. Its name means "cure" in Greek, as curative herbs that heal a soldier's wounds were found here.

From Acre we crossed eastward through the Upper Galilee to Safed, the highest city in Israel. The fresh, clean mountain air was quite an olfactory experience for a down-to-earth New Yorker. We got a breathtaking view of the Galilee's green mountains and snow-capped peaks. Safed was a picturesque and holy city that was wrapped in mysticism and mystery. For more than three centuries it has been the center of cabala. The Jewish quarter, with its ancient synagogues and winding cobblestone alleyways, and Chassidic-looking cabalists, was one of the highlights of the day.

After Acre, we drove north along the border, near the Syrian-controlled Golan Heights, to Kefar Blum, a village kibbutz in the northeast corner of the Galilee. There we would spend the night in its guest accommodations. The western section of the Golan rises to 1,700 feet and overlooks the Huleh Valley, Israel's richest agricultural area. Sadly, Syria uses the Heights as a military stronghold from which to snipe at Israeli civilians below. Children and adults in nearby kibbutzim sleep in bomb shelters. We too had to be very careful. The bus driver only took roads cleared by mine-sweeping vehicles.

Kefar Blum was a stone's throw from the Syrian and Lebanese borders. The kibbutz was founded in 1943 by young Labor Zionists from the United Kingdom, the Baltic countries, the United States, and South Africa. Its economy was based on cotton and dairy farming, fruit harvesting, and light industry, supplemented in recent years by tourism. We slept on bunk beds in double rooms and ate in the large communal dining hall. The long wooden tables and benches reminded me of a U.S. Army mess, stateside and overseas.

The kibbutz was named in honor of Léon Blum, the first Jewish and the first socialist Prime Minister of France. Plaques on the walls and the local guide told the story of his harrowing encounters with French and German authorities during the war. Blum was PM from 1936-37 and again briefly in 1938, and was a Deputy in the French parliament in 1940 when Germany defeated France and occupied the northern half of the divided country. He refused to leave France in spite of the danger to his freedom and life because of the two counts against him in the eyes of the Nazis. Instead, he fled to the south and, with many exiled Paris parliamentarians, opposed Marshal Pétain and his authoritarian, even Naziesque, Vichy government. In 1942 Blum and others were arrested and charged with treason, but the trial was an embarrassment to the Germans and halted. In 1943 Blum was deported to the Buchenwald concentration camp. Just before the camp was liberated in 1945, Blum was transferred to Dachau, a camp near my own Henry Kaserne. In the last weeks of the war, the Nazis ordered him executed but he was rescued in time by Allied troops. After the war, Blum returned to politics and was PM briefly in a transitional government that adopted many socialist reforms. He died in March 1950.

"As Jews and guests at Kefar Blum," I wanted tell my tour mates at dinner, "we could say kaddish for the kibbutz's namesake on this his tenth yahrzeit." But, I held back suggesting anything for the courageous French leader, as I feared another faux pas in a dining area.

Wednesday, March sixteenth, was our last full day of sightseeing on our tour de force. We left the kibbutz after a sumptuous and early breakfast and headed south to the Lower Galilee.

We hit Tiberias first, a Roman city named for the emperor Tiberius on the western shore of the Sea of Galilee, the largest fresh-water lake in Israel. In the time of Jesus, there was a string of settlements and villages along the lake and much of his ministry occurred here. Four of his apostles—Simon, Andrew, John, and James—were recruited from lakeshore communities. The Sermon on the Mount was given on a hill overlooking the Sea of Galilee, and this is where Jesus supposedly walked on water. Tiberias' hot springs, said to cure skin and other ailments, further guaranteed that this would be a holy place in Christianity. The city is venerated in Judaism as well. Herod's son made Tiberias, with its Jewish majority, the capital of his realm in Galilee. Following the expulsion in 135 A.D. of all Jews from Jerusalem in the south, many went north to Tiberias and it became a major Jewish center. Religious scholarship flourished with the writing of the Mishnah and parts of the Talmud.

Nazareth was our tour bus' next stop, driving south and west toward a distant Tel Aviv. This city called the "Arab capital of Israel," as any Christian knows, was the childhood home of Jesus and naturally is an important pilgrimage site for those making the sign of the cross. Throughout the town there were shrines commemorating biblical events, and Arabs selling religious articles and objects of questionable authenticity. I walked the crooked cobblestone streets as Jesus the Nazarene had two thousand years earlier, looked for a house that could have been his carpentry shop, wondered where Joseph and Mary might have lived, and speculated on the spot of the Annunciation. Before we left, I paid two Israeli pounds to ride a camel and got Herbie to take pictures of me on camelback. Bethlehem, the presumed birthplace of Jesus, was not next on our itinerary, as it was in the West Bank and off limits to us as Jews.

We stopped for a late lunch in Megiddo, a kibbutz southeast of Nazareth, on our way to Hadera. Mount Megiddo overlooking the valley where the kibbutz sits did not look like the end of the world. In the Bible it is known as Armageddon, the site of the final battle between the forces of good and evil.

Hadera is on the Mediterranean Coastal Plain, exactly halfway between Haifa and Tel Aviv. We pulled in late that afternoon. No ancient city like the three we saw earlier in the day, Hadera was founded in 1891 as a farming colony by Zionists from Lithuania and Latvia. The land purchased from a Christian was of low quality and mostly swamps. Hadera in the early years was a lonely outpost of just ten families and two guards. Land disputes and drainage problems were common. But Hadera symbolized the strength and possibilities of a young Palestine. We visited the Great Synagogue built in the late '30s with its impressive tower in front. After 1948, immigrants flocked to the city—Russians, other Eastern Europeans, and even Yemenite families. The first paper mill in Israel opened in Hadera in 1953, designed to meet all of the new country's paper needs. So modern was the city that if our bus broke down, we could have made it back to Tel Aviv in time for dinner by simply taxiing to the Jewish Bahnhof and jumping on Israel's main railway line that runs along the coast.

We made it to Tel Aviv after seven and drove straight to the hotel we stayed in previously.

"Where's Herbie Kramer" Leeann and another women said to me almost at once.

It was Day 12, Thursday morning, our tour's final day, time to leave the Promised Land and fly back to Deutschland. We had just finished breakfast, checked out of our rooms, and put our packed bags on the bus parked in front of the hotel. Everyone on the tour but Herbie was standing on the sidewalk ready to board. Our guide was visibly annoyed, running in and out of the hotel.

"I don't know," I answered. "He went out last night around ten and didn't come back."

I had no idea where Herbie was but I could certainly guess *why* he disappeared eleven hours earlier and *what* he was up to, or rather in to. Last night was his last chance to fulfill his self-proclaimed ambition for the Holy Land. The American soldier just would not take off from Israel if he did not first take off the panties of a local female, Jewish or not, working girl or not. Herbie knew we were to assemble at 9 a.m. to head out for the airport, but he was nowhere in sight.

"Where could he be in Tel Aviv?" I heard someone say as I looked around.

"I don't know," I repeated.

The guide started to motion people to get on the bus. The edgy Indian was quite determined to leave with or without the missing member of his party. Just then Herbie showed up carrying his travel bag. He came around from the other side of the bus, strutted up to everyone, and mixed in with the crowd. My roommate no more—with a broad smile on his face, a smirk one could say, and a twinkle in his eyes—became the center of attention. He was very relaxed despite others being in an agitated state, both nervous and excited about returning to whence they came a dozen days earlier.

Herbie stepped onto the bus but said nothing about where he had been, in spite of all the questions. He did not have to say a thing. His facial expression and composure gave him away. Everyone, women on the tour especially, read the young man's body language and knew that on our very last day in Israel he had accomplished his manly goal.

Later, on the first leg of our flight to Munich, Herbie talked to me of his own accord. "I went to HaYarkon Street last night," he revealed, "where the big hotels are. A taxi driver told me that's where the hookers hang out . . . Jewish and Arab."

I did not ask the American soldier in which camp he unloaded his liquid rounds and he offered no classified information. But I reasoned Herbie could have come to terms with a working girl idling on a velvet couch in one of the hotel lobbies, comments to the contrary by the civilian on the tour notwithstanding. If she were Jewish, she would be without babushka, if Arab, without hijab. An Orthodox or Muslim woman in traditional head covering would not entertain a man's propositions for a paid romantic encounter, in public or private.

Perhaps it was Herbie who did the working, with a different kind of girl on a different kind of couch. He might have picked up some starry-eyed seventeen- or eighteen-year-old in front of the Dan Hotel and plied his storytelling skills. A flash of a picture ID with his last name, a false claim that his famous uncle is producing the movie *Exodus*, and a fib that he was assigned to cast a girl for a bit part opposite Paul Newman, could have been a scene from his prevaricate playbook. If the young Israeli pickup this time was not a soldier, chances are she would not have shot down the tall tale.

CHAPTER 13: CHANGING TIMES

On my departure from Israel, as opposed to my arrival, the tables were turned, in my mind and on the ground. This time I was well aware that the Promised Land I just waved goodbye to *would* follow me to Deutschland.

The two-legged flight to Munich allowed me to reflect on what I saw and learned on the tour and the people I met. It also gave me a chance to read the articles I cut out from the *Jerusalem Post* that I picked up each morning at the desk of the hotels we stayed in. I was flying east to west, traveling across a time zone to return to a country I had mixed feelings about and would not be living in much longer. I turned my watch back one hour, and in less than three months I would be re-setting the time again when I crossed the Atlantic once more but in the opposite direction.

At Lod Airport and on the runway, unlike ten days earlier, I saw no crowd assembled and heard no national anthem played for any foreign or domestic dignitary. I half expected to see an American flag waving and hear the sounds of the Star-Spangled Banner based on a small item in the *Post*. Billy Graham was due to arrive in Israel on this day but no touchdown time was given for the famous evangelist. I also read the Israeli PM would not be coming home on this March seventeenth because he was still abroad. In another clipping, it stated David Ben-Gurion met Conrad Adenauer in New York on an unofficial visit. The leaders of two countries that were former enemies were in a tête-à-tête on the 35th floor of the Waldorf-Astoria Hotel. The two-hour meeting was characterized as a turning point in Israel-West German relations. Reparations were among the major topics discussed at the informelle Gespräche. The talks were described as trilingual, a lively mix of English, French, and German. Evidently Germans and Jews were now friends. The times they are a-changin'.

Israel in the east and Germany in the west actually had much in common, a basis for a solid partnership going forward. Both were new countries created as a result of the defeat of the Nazis in 1945. Both were nations carved out of larger geographic bodies of people. Both were modern societies struggling for world recognition. Both had political differences with neighboring states and were locked in armed, or potentially armed, conflict. Both were Western-oriented in values and ideology. Both were democratic dominions aligned with the U. S. of A. in the ongoing Cold War. Both signed a Reparations Agreement in 1952 via direct negotiations between Chancellor Adenauer and Prime Minister Ben Gurion. Both recognized that the Neue Deutschland has a moral obligation to compensate the victims of Nazi persecution and assist financially the tiny developing nation, a New Promised Land that took in the largest number of concentration camp survivors.

There were a number of items in the *Post* the past week relating to Germany. Ironically, I had to come to Israel and read an English-language newspaper to learn what Germans were doing about war crimes and ex-Nazis fifteen years after their defeat. Such stories routinely were not printed in the American press that I read in Germany, the military's *Stars and Stripes* or the private *Overseas Weekly*. I had no clue as to whether the German press published reports that reminded its readers of wartime events and atrocities committed in their name. And even if such news were printed, I could not read and understand them.

One *Post* article dealt with Alfred Rosenberg, the leading Nazi ideologist who was convicted and executed at the Palace of Justice in Nuremberg in 1946. The West Berlin Denazification Court ordered the confiscation of his Berlin property, valued at 29,000 DM, to be made available for payments to Nazi victims. The Court said Rosenberg was not merely following orders but was one of Hitler's trusted advisers. Ironically, it was this Russian-born high Nazi official with a Ph.D. from Moscow University who concocted the twisted racial theory of Nordic superiority over Jews, Gypsies, and his own Slavic people. Frau Rosenberg now living in Frankfurt had no comment.

In another article, it was reported that a West German court sentenced two former Nazi officials to prison for three-and-a-half and seven years, respectively, for the murder of three hundred Jews in the Ukraine in 1942. One said he had no alternative but to take part in the killings, although he deplored it, and could not have helped the victims. The prosecutor had demanded life sentences for both men. I also saved a small clipping about thirty West Berlin boys and girls who went on a nine-day tour of West German towns in order to raise funds to enable Israeli students to study in Germany.

The reconstructed Germany I was returning to did more than just replace the infrastructure destroyed during the war. By 1960, Germans were seeking redemption, replacing one mind-set with another. Collective amnesia for anything related to a swastika, an iron cross, the Gestapo, or the SS was giving way to collective guilt and individual responsibility for what Hitler wrought on the world. The postwar climate fostered judicial compassion for those who suffered under the Nazis, judicial retribution for those who committed murder of civilians, spousal indifference to a husband's complicity in crimes against humanity, an attempt at reconciliation by those too young to remember, and remorse by Hitler's willing executioners for bloodying their hands.

Countries occupied by the Nazis were likewise beginning to confront wartime events. In the Israeli paper I read Holland was taking measures to educate secondary school pupils about what occurred during the German occupation. They participated in a ceremony to commemorate the anniversary of the 1943 strike by Amsterdam workers against the first deportations of Jews. The mayor, an active member of the local resistance, recalled that the deportations caused his city to lose one-eighth of its population. I was sure these Dutch school children, like millions of others of all ages around the world by this time, learned about a teenage Jewish girl that lived with her family in the back of a building in Amsterdam for two years hiding from the Nazis, and kept a journal record of the ordeal. She was one of the 80,000 deportees and later died of typhus at the Bergen-Belsen camp just days before it was liberated. The diary of Anne Frank, found amid the debris in the secret annex at Prinsengracht 263 by the non-Jewish woman who protected the family, was given to her father who survived Auschwitz. It contained no final entry about the Nazis who, acting on a tip from an informer, busted into the ensconced living quarters and dragged everyone away.

"You should read *Exodus*," Leeann said to me during our refueling stop in Belgrade. She held the 626-page bestseller to her chest. A black bookmarker stuck out on top. "It tells the whole story of the Jews in Europe and the creation of the State of Israel."

Leeann seemed to take a liking to me during our trip, as if I were a younger brother. She readily loaned me money, did not reproach me when I knocked over the waiter, confided in me about herself and her family, and sat next to me on the bus when she was not with one of the other women. Her background in an American-born nuclear family and growing up in a small farming town in California with very few Jews was quite different from my upbringing within an immigrant extended family in New York, a city with over two million of our brethren. Leeann was searching for her Jewish identity, I could tell. She flipped through the pages of the Leon Uris book everywhere we stopped in Israel to check out references, questioned me about my experiences in a largely Jewish neighborhood and in Hebrew School, and talked about the problems of raising her nine-year-old daughter in her faith while on remote military posts with a less-than-enthusiastic Christian father. To the thirty-year-old alienated Army wife stationed near me in Munich, I was her coreligionist sociocultural opposite but someone she could relate to, have frequent contacts with, and learn from.

"When I get back to camp, I'll try to get the book from the library."

"I'll lend you my copy if they don't have it," Leeann promised.

"Okay." I wanted to read the book everyone was talking about.

She smiled a little and hesitated a moment. "When you get your pictures developed, you can come to dinner one night and show them to me and my husband."

"Okay," I said again, not to be impolite.

"I didn't take many pictures with my old Brownie."

Leeann was telling the truth about her lack of photographic success in Israel. She had a little rinky-dink camera that frequently locked up on her. Unlike with my Retina IIIC, she could not adjust her shots for light, range, movement, or depth. The married woman looked at me with a serious face after she invited me to her home. Her eyes were trying to tell me something.

Over the loudspeaker it was announced that we should start to board the airplane.

I was in high altitude again that day, cruising from one time zone to another. My thoughts also were in high gear, rambling from one female to another.

Tucked away in my wallet was the little piece of paper the young soldier I met in Tel Aviv handed me, with her name and address printed clearly in English. Yael obviously wanted me to write to her. What I might say to her and what would result from the long-distance, two-continent correspondence, I did not know but I was sure in time I would. Did this Israeli girl I saw only once just want me to make Aliyah, to help build her country? Or, did she have designs on me for marriage, not unlike the feelers Karin put out with strings attached to her body.

I could not walk down the aisle or take back to the States with me the German Catholic girl I liked but did not love. Could I, I asked myself, go under the canopy and step on the glass with the Israeli girl who can bear me Jewish children but who likewise did not fit the image of the type I favored? Why was I so fixated on a blond beauty with a knockout body? I was not yet in college but I knew all this ruminating was an academic exercise. At this time in my life I could not, and had no desire to, marry anyone, Jewish or non-Jewish, Aryan Goddess or Plain Jane. A good school is what I yearned to get into, not a good wife. Still, that plan could change as the thought of getting discharged in Germany and spending up to a year traveling in Europe or returning to Israel *before* going to college likewise appealed to me. A Deutschland DD-214, according to Army regulations, carried with it a ticket for a free trip by ship to the States good for twelve months.

Also tucked away in my wallet was the piece of paper Leeann handed to me with her Munich address and telephone number on it. Soon a twenty-year-old New York boy would be involved in a budding friendship with a married woman from rural California. In my remaining time in the Army, I would come to experience with Mrs. Armson my first relationship with an older gal, German or American, black or white, that was *not* sexual. Looking back on it today, I can only wonder what Elsa, Karin, or the Fort Ord WAC might have said about that kind of change.

On the final leg of the flight, I was going back to the future. I just left Israel, a land steeped in the past. The relics and ruins, churches and temples, King's palaces and Bedouin tents, ancient walls and medieval constructions, spots biblical figures moved on, sites holy to three different religions, salt pillars and hot springs, David's Tomb and Armageddon, etc., etc., etc., were all yesterday's venerations, packaged for and marketed to foreign tourists. The land I was headed to represented my tomorrows. I tried not to think of the Nazi Germany of the 1930s and '40s, with its crimes against humanity and mass killings of my people. The New Germany in 1960 was a changed place as well as a changed time. For some Jews it was home, for others a country to start life over in with a profitable business. For me, a Germany by any name held the key to my best laid plans. It is here that I hoped to stay out of trouble with superiors, keep my rank, not go to the stockade, and earn an honorable discharge. I wished to enroll in college with a clear mind and clean record. My sitting in a classroom or reading books, not signing re-enlistment papers or supporting a wife, is what I wanted to see in my crystal ball.

I thought about two people on the tour who affected my perceptions of myself. The eldest of the three pre-teen girls, skinny and owlish-looking with horned-rim glasses, the daughter of a civilian employee of the Army, paid me a compliment. She sat next to me on the bus one day and we talked about different subjects, Jews and the war especially.

"What college did you go to?" the little girl who seemed bright beyond her years asked me.

"I didn't go to college. I just finished high school."

She turned and looked at me, stunned. "You seem so smart. I was sure you went to college."

"Thank you," I said. "I'm planning to go to college in six months."

"Well, you talk like you've already been to college."

"Thank you," I repeated, pleased that I had such a persona, albeit in a pair of young eyes.

Also catching my attention was the soldier in the group that had the Master's degree. He was not an officer but was somewhat older than my E-3 and higher peers. I gathered he was drafted rather late, at twenty-five or so. I had limited contact with him and never got his name, but he often made comments about one thing or another that stuck with me. I thought of him as Mr. Brainy. He was about six foot, had narrow shoulders, and was heavy in the hips and thighs, not the athletic type like the young Israeli men in uniform I saw.

Balding, always seemed to be holding a pipe in one hand, and ready to bud in to other people's conversations, Brainy without a doubt was the pretentious type. He acted and spoke in a haughty manner, thought he knew everything, and did not hesitate to impart, or rather show off, his superior knowledge to others. He was exactly opposite to Herbie in every respect, in deportment and appearance and means of expression. Brainy had the education and sophistication I sought to acquire, but not the looks and unassuming character I admired. Herbie had the down-to-earth nature and outspokenness I sought to emulate, but lacked the wisdom and polish I respected.

We touched down in Munich late that afternoon. Even with moving my watch back one hour, I did not have enough time to make it to the mess hall at Henry Kaserne for dinner.

PART III

FINAL THREE MONTHS

CHAPTER 14: MEET THE ARMSONS

Sergeant Ramirez was all smiles when I came into the Area Office that Friday morning, the day after I returned from my 12-day leave. He stood in the open doorway between our two work spaces. Mr. Horner had not arrived yet. "How was your trip to Israel?" he put to me as if he were really interested.

"I had a nice time . . . and I learned a lot."

"Did you learn about the Bible?" he said jokingly.

"As a matter of fact, I did," I answered seriously. "I learned about people and events in the Old Testament and the New."

"Good," my boss responded mechanically as if he did not hear me. His mouth was half open and he was ready to say something else when I cut in.

"I may be going back."

"What do you mean?"

"I'm thinking of taking my discharge in Germany and spending some time in Israel before I go home," I explained. "I met a girl over there. She asked me to come back."

"How short are you?"

"I have seventy-nine days left in Munich until my rotation date, six June." I calculated that number by counting the days on the calendar in my wall locker just the night before. That date was twenty days before my discharge date, June twenty-sixth, the Army's way of allowing train time to get to Bemerhaven, ship time to cross the Atlantic, and processing-out time at Fort Dix. "If I want to get discharged here, I have to file my papers by six May."

"Good," he said again, without recognizing the implications of what I was saying, either to my personal or military life. "Say Streiber," Ramirez let out meekly, turning his head slightly, "lend me twenty dollars. I'll give it back on payday."

This was not the first time the sergeant asked me for money, and for the same amount too. He had a wife and three kids back in the States and much of his pay went directly to them. Soldiers of all ranks with families to support almost always needed extra cash toward the end of the month. He first tapped me in late January, only three days after I arrived in Munich to work for him, and I did not say no. I knew Ramirez was good for it. He probably was too embarrassed to ask Mr. Horner, his boss, for a loan. The following pay-day he paid me back, unlike the Spec 4 I disliked in Nuremberg. I was hit again for a twenty in mid-February and gladly shelled it out. I didn't mind handing my boss two sawbucks each month when he asked, as it rendered him, in some measure, obligated to me. In the coming seventy-nine days, I might need a favor.

"Sure thing, Sarge." I reached into my back pocket for my wallet, took out one of the three twenties, and gave it to the only NCO over me I ever liked in the Army. I still had enough for the rest of the month.

"Thanks. My promotion should be coming through soon. I may not need to borrow again."

"That's okay," I said. "I'm glad to help."

I wondered who accommodated his financial needs before he came to Munich, who the Shylock was on his Straubing team. As with my two previous loans to a superior, I did not ask for a receipt or IOU.

Ramirez quickly slipped the bill into the front pocket of his trou-sers, as if to hide it. He turned and went across the room to his desk and picked up some papers. "You came back just in time, Streiber." He handed me the papers. "Mr. Horner needs you to type up this court martial."

The following Friday night I went to Jewish services at McGraw Kaserne. I skipped a week deliberately. I did not wish to meet Har-old Berger so soon after I returned from Israel and tell him that I had no technical manuals to give him. And I was tied of trying to garner information from him about his trips to the East and the handler role Lieutenant Gibson forced on me. During the past seven days, Ra-mirez and Horner did not ask me what I was doing with M.I.G., and that was a relief to me. I also checked in with Gibson and told him I have no news for him about the spy he was tracking.

Fortunately for me, I didn't see Harold at services that Friday night, March 25th. I guess he skipped a week too. But I did see Leeann and a few other people I recognized from the tour group. Our smiling faces attested to the fact that we were all happy to see each other again. We schmoozed about Israel as if we were part of some exclusive club.

After the Oneg Shabbat, Leeann invited me to her apartment for another round of coffee and cake. We walked together to the V-shaped two-level building in the south-west corner of the barracks, the family housing section near the tennis courts. I told her about my future plans. She spoke about her husband, a World War II veteran and a chief warrant officer.

CW3 Thomas C. Armson was assigned to the 110th Transportation Company at Schleissheim Army Airfield in Oberschleissheim, about thirteen kilometers north of downtown Munich. On the way to work every day he drove right past me at Henry Kaserne. The airfield, straight north of Henry, was constructed by the Royal Bavarian Flying Corps during the World War I period. The Nazis later used it for military purposes. The Dachau concentration camp was nearby and some of its prisoners were kept in a satellite camp at Oberschleissheim utilized mainly for the production of armaments. Immediately after the war the airfield was turned into a medium bomber base for the Army of Occupation, and contained an ordnance depot and scrap metal yard. In 1956 it became a base for helicopters and the flying sections of artillery units. Mr. Armson piloted the Sikorsky H-34 and H-37 for air rescue missions in Bavaria, mainly the high mountain area, and VIP transportation service. In the eastern part of the Schleissheim airfield, there was a monitoring station for Radio Free Europe.

The Armsons lived in an upstairs two-bedroom apartment. It was modest and comfortable, not fancy but nicely furnished. When we arrived, it was almost nine o'clock. Her husband was home. He was sitting in a lounge chair reading a newspaper, babysitting for the daughter fast asleep in the smaller bedroom. If he were a commissioned officer, they would be living in a duplex in Perlacher Forest, the fancier housing complex near the American High School. Like a gentleman he stood up and faced us.

I was initially struck by the man's appearance compared to his wife's. Leeann was not ugly but she was not what men would call very attractive either, rather average looking with frizzy blondish hair. She possessed a slim five-foot-five figure but one that was not shapely in a sexy way. To me she had a pleasant enough face and body frame but there was one detracting attribute about her, a slightly gawky gait that took away from a woman's desired feminine gracefulness. By contrast, Mr. Armson was quite a handsome man, with smooth facial features, unblemished skin, and a full head of dark hair combed with a part on the side in perfect style. The six-footer with eyes, nose, mouth, and jaw set just right also had an appealing medium build. He was neither bulging with ungainly bicep and chest muscles nor hampered by a double chin or spare tire around the middle.

Leeann introduced me. "David, this is my husband Tom." She extended her hand in his direction.

"Hello, sir," I said, shaking hands with the man I knew should be addressed that way. "Nice to meet you."

Leeann did not say it in words but I think she wanted me to call her husband by his first name, as if I were part of the family, or his equal or Army buddy. However, even though this was a social occasion and we were both in civilian clothes and off duty, as an E-4 enlisted man I observed military decorum. Mr. Armson, Leeann mentioned earlier, was called "Arms" by most of his military peers and high NCO friends at the airfield, but it would have been inappropriate for me to do so.

Tom was reserved and unemotional and did not say very much. He did not make small talk by asking me about my rank or outfit, or the trip to Israel with his wife, and did not reveal anything about himself. He was fifteen or sixteen years older than I and must have looked at me as some lost kid the wife dragged in. I got the feeling the gentle Gentile had been through this before, his loquacious Jewish partner picking up and bringing home a young Jewish soldier for discourse and companionship that was perhaps lacking in their marriage, something he had been unable or unwilling to render. My presence did not seem to bother Tom, he just was not enthusiastic about it. If the Mrs. brought home a soldier his or her age, I'm sure that would have evoked a bit of a concern and/or husbandly reaction.

Leeann went into the kitchen to make coffee and tea. She then put down on the dining-area table an uncut apple pie, a batch of cookies, and a half-eaten chocolate cake. The Mistress of the house chatted away between bites and sips while the Master remained silent.

"Would you like to see our family album?" Leeann asked after we finished eating and drinking. She started to remove the spent dishes, cups, silverware, and plates from the table.

"Yes . . . okay." What else could I say to the hospitable Jewish hostess I traveled all over the Promised Land with?

Tom was still tight-lipped when Leeann came out of the bedroom carrying a large brown picture album six inches thick. She moved to my side of the table and sat down next to me. She flipped page after page, explaining the history of the places in the photographs taken of her and her brother as teenagers, and those of her husband in the Army and daughter as a child. The ones that caught my attention the most, and the stories behind them, were pictures of Tom in uniform on different bases and locations. In kaleidoscope fashion, almost like a still-frame documentary with sound added, Leeann's continual talking and turning of pages detailed and depicted the last days of World War II, the postwar peace, the Korean War, and the current Cold War period. Most of these shots did not look like they were snapped with her baby Brownie.

There was a picture of Tom at Fort Riley, Kansas in rumpled fatigues with no stripes on his sleeve when he went off to war at age nineteen. The year 1943 was marked next to it. Another one was of him as a corporal, after he passed the test for flight school and had just arrived for pilot training at Randolph Field outside San Antonio. The cadet would soon cut the two stripes off his sleeve and fasten a gold bar to his collar. Leeann said Tom rose two grades in the officer ranks. By the end of the war he was a captain, having earned his twin silver bars after successful night raids over Hamburg and Frankfurt targeting railroads, bridges, and oil refineries. There were no pictures of him looking like a Gregory Peck in *Twelve O' Clock High*—with an oxygen mask, aviator goggles, helmet with radio-receiver ear cups, parachutes strapped to his back and chest—flying bombing missions over Germany. The man sitting beside me at the table, in the photo taken after V-E Day, was impressive in his leather jacket and soft cap standing in front of his B-29. Like in the 1945 film *God Is My Co-Pilot*, the seat next to Tom in the Boeing airplane must have been spiritually occupied.

After the war, Tom decided to remain in the service of his country. He re-enlisted but at a price. The Army was having a Reduction in Force at that time. Uncle Sam did not need so many officers in peacetime, or pilots to drop bombs. Tom was one of the many soldiers that got riffed in 1946, downgraded if they wanted to stay in.

The Army offered him sergeant E-5 and the captain traded in his bars when he signed the papers. He was assigned to a weapons technical support outfit. Several pictures in the album were of Arms in a Class A Eisenhower jacket or fatigue shirt with three stripes and one rocker on his arms, the little T in the center of the patch visible.

"We got married in nineteen forty-nine," Leeann said. She smiled and turned to look at her husband.

I liked the shot of the skinny nineteen-year-old girl with Tech Sergeant Tom in dress uniform, this time with two rockers showing, cutting their wedding cake. They met at a barn dance one Saturday night in her town not far from Camp Roberts, California where the new E-6 noncom was stationed. A year after they were married, with a baby on the way, war in Korea broke out between North and South. This was an opportunity for Tom to move up to the officer ranks again. The former bomber pilot had no difficulty getting into helicopter training school at Camp Wolters, Texas. There was a picture of him, now a CW1, with his buddies in the graduating class. Written in the white border on bottom was December 18, 1951.

Via album photos and Leeann's gabbing, I was privy to the full story of Tom and his chopper assignments after the Korean War. First he was sent to the Air Training Department of the Field Artillery School at Fort Sill, Oklahoma to help train helicopter pilots. Then, in 1954 that unit was moved to the Army Aviation Center at Fort Rucker, Alabama, and Tom and the other instructors went along with the transfer. The Armsons packed their bags again in June 1957, for Tom's new overseas tour to help win the war of words with the Soviet Union. Coincidentally, that was the month I too packed a bag, but for boot camp at Fort Dix, New Jersey. When I was making my exit *from* Brooklyn, Tom and Leeann with the little one were making their entrance *into* Brooklyn. They checked into the Army Terminal at the water's edge and boarded the ship to Germany on the twenty-seventh, the same day I joined the Army.

"You've been in Munich almost three years now." I commented.

"Yes," Leeann answered. "We like it here. Tom just extended for one year. The Army allows an overseas tour of four years maximum."

"When will you be going home, Dave," Tom asked, speaking to me for the first time.

"I rotate back in early June." I deliberately avoided the "sir" now that the CW3 and I had off-duty social contacts.

"David is planning on starting college," Leeann said somewhat proudly, "or perhaps going back to Israel for a year first."

Tom looked as if he was about to say something, but did not. Either he was uninterested in anything I was doing or it seemed normal to him that a young Jewish boy would want to live in Israel, the country his Jewish wife must have raved about soon as she came home.

"I met a girl over there," I explained. "A soldier in the Israeli Army. She thinks all young Jews should come to Israel to help build up the country."

Leeann looked over to her husband once more. "Tom . . . David may have fallen in love with a girl wearing a uniform." She smiled again. "I fell in love with you in your uniform."

With that embarrassing tidbit of information, I looked at my watch. "It's getting late. I should be leaving." I stood up. "Thank you for showing me your album. In three weeks I hope to show you my pictures of Israel and the girl I met. I'll be back here for Passover. The slides should be developed by then."

"I look forward to seeing them," Leeann said politely. "And I know Tom does too."

I said a heartfelt good night to my new older friends. I shook hands again with Mr. Armson but the wife who often spoke for him only touched fingers with me. I think she wanted to kiss me on the cheek but held back because of her husband's presence.

The next morning, a Saturday, I got the key to the office from Ramirez and went in. With no work distractions and alone behind my desk, I typed a long letter to Yael.

The papers I was asked to prepare the day after I returned from Israel were for the summary court martial of Sergeant McCarty. Mr. Horner accused him of dereliction of duty, of not doing his job as the leader of Team 18. Apparently, it was a problem of numbers. There were missing pieces of electronic equipment in the shop, units were not repaired on time, and spare parts were in short supply. Horner claimed the official inventory of parts and equipment did not match the units on the floor and items in bins and boxes. As the NCOIC, McCarty was responsible.

I started doing the papers on that Friday and completed Horner's referral on Monday. Horner signed the charges and the papers were mailed to Böblingen, our company headquarters. Clerical personnel there would complete the paperwork and that suited me fine. It was a dirty job and I did not like doing it.

A summary court martial was the least serious of three types of legal action Mr. Horner could have initiated. If found guilty, McCarty was likely to be reduced in rank one grade, fined, and be restricted to the post for up to thirty days. The NCO was fortunate he was not accused of more serious offenses—such as theft of government property, going AWOL, intoxication while on duty, or disobeying a direct order—as a special court martial would have been convened. That could have meant a bust all the way down to private, up to one year in the stockade, and a Bad Conduct Discharge. McCarty was in no danger of being summoned before a general court martial, as that proceeding was reserved for an officer who was charged with wrongdoing and for the enlisted ranks in cases of murder, rape, grand theft, or espionage. Greater jail time and a Dishonorable Discharge would have been meted out for the hapless soldier convicted of such criminal offenses.

My SFC friend naturally was very upset about the impending court martial, even though he could not be put in the can or kicked out of the Army. He had almost fourteen years in with no blemishes on his record, not even an Article 15, a non-judicial means of punishment for violations of military discipline or regulations. McCarty enlisted a year after V-J Day, went to electronics school at Fort Gordon, was a tech sergeant before the Army did away with those ranks, and saw action in Korea. Despite his Irish heritage, McCarty had no inkling for politics. He did not jockey for power, butter-up higher ups, or seek connections with authority figures, those of the same rank or above. He earned his stripes not by kissing ass but by doing his job, avoiding trouble, assuming greater responsibility, and biding his time.

"I didn't do anything wrong," the man I respected and I liked kept saying to me with a long face and sad eyes. "Every team in the one-seven-ty-sixth has some pieces of equipment that get misplaced and has parts that are unaccounted for. That's normal in an electronics repair shop."

It was Friday, April first, after the week's work was done. I was sitting with McCarty in the front seat of his '55 Ford. He wanted to talk to someone he thought might help him.

"Then why is Horner after you?" I asked. I took notice of the trumped up charges against him as I typed the court martial referral papers.

"Horner thinks by hanging me he'll look good to his superiors . . . show them he's doing a good job by finding fault with the NCO in charge of the shop. He thinks he'll get promoted because of this . . . wants to retire soon."

McCarty's explanation of his difficulties was interesting to me as a twenty-year-old with no experience in such matters. Rather than blame himself for any mistakes or incompetence, he reproached his boss and the military system. Such an account seemed plausible but I could not understand why Horner would be so cruel or vindictive. I sympathized with the team leader as I felt the same way about my bosses in Nuremberg, the two Bs who got rid of me for no apparent reason. I didn't do anything wrong, yet I was relieved of duty, punished for I don't know what. I looked at McCarty and the patch on his sleeve, three stripes and two rockers, chevron of a rank that may be changed soon.

"Does Horner have any proof of his allegations?" I asked the sullen sergeant like a lawyer.

"He got Dickson to be a witness against me. Dickson will lie and swear that all the things Horner claims are wrong in the shop are true. The little son-of-a-bitch wants my job and a promotion too."

"Dickson would do that," I said. "I never liked him. He's only an

E-five, a specialist with no official authority, and yet tries to boss everyone around."

"In two weeks is my court martial in Boblingen . . . on Wednesday. Can you come to testify for me? Horner has to let anyone in the company go if he's a witness. I can take you in my car."

McCarty's request surprised me. I wanted to help him but I couldn't for a number of reasons. "In two weeks, Tuesday, Wednesday, and Thursday, I'll be on three-day pass," I told the accused but not yet condemned soldier. "It's Passover, an important Jewish holiday. Ramirez gave me off. I'll be at McGraw the whole time."

"Oh."

"Besides, what can I say? I don't work in the shop. I haven't been in Munich that long."

"You can testify to my good character, that you never saw me not doing my duty. You work in the Area Office. You can swear that you never heard Horner say I disobeyed his orders."

McCarty was grasping at straws if he thought I could stretch the truth and say something that would help him. "I don't think that would do much good. Even if I testified to what you asked, it doesn't mean what Horner accused you of didn't happen. And I still need to be in Munich for Passover."

"Oh," he eked out again in disappointment.

"What about the other guys in the shop," I suggested. "They would be better witnesses. They know more about what's going on."

McCarty's head turned downward. "I already asked them. They all said no. They don't want to get involved."

I sat in the car a while longer without saying much before I excused myself and went to chow. Walking to the mess hall, I thought how similar my situation with McCarty was with the one many years earlier between my mother and our former landlord whom the new landlady tried to evict from his store. Like Mama on Mermaid Avenue I was mum, had no advice for a man tormented by someone with authority over him and threatened with the loss of his livelihood.

On April eleventh, I left the Area Office early. Passover began that evening at sundown. The three-day pass Ramirez arranged for me was from 0800 on the twelfth to 0800 on the fifteenth. I cleaned up, changed to civies, signed out on a normal evening pass, walked briskly out of Henry, and took the bus and two streetcars to McGraw Kaserne. On the Munich-area's main barracks, a traditional Seder was planned for this first night of the seven-day Jewish holiday celebrating the exodus of the Israelites from Egypt. I checked into the Transient Billets in the east central part of the base, near the main gate and post office. I was assigned to a room for four with two double-decker bunks. I took the bottom bunk near the window facing another building. From the number of rolled mattresses, it looked like I would be the only one sleeping in this room without a view.

The annual Seder was held in the main room of the Community Club. It is celebrated as a Feast of Liberation, a meal to give thanks for one's freedom and to offer hope to those who are not yet free. That point weighed on my mind, as I knew Sergeant McCarty, a decent man and a good soldier, was now in bondage and I could not, or chose not, to help him.

I sat at a long table next to Leeann, with Tom and their daughter directly across from us. The four of us looked like a family, with me being a kind of Uncle David. My second Seder in Germany was very much like the first. There were plates with matzo, dishes with bitter herbs, parsley, salt water, gefilte fish, chopped liver, red and white horse radish, roasted eggs, and the tasty mixture of nuts and fruit. The rabbi in his white robe at the head of the table recited much of the service reading from a Haggadah. Those around the table, military and civilian, American and German, sipped wine from silver cups, read passages from their Haggadahs, and took turns asking the Four Questions. I was sure this was not the first time Tom went through this, but the Gentile guest at this Jewish ritual still had a puzzled look on his face every time something was said in Hebrew or someone broke a piece of matzo, dipped it in herbs or salt water, or scooped up a bit of charoset. I thought the man who said very little was going to say something when the door was opened for the Angel of Eliyahu to enter, to be greeted and welcomed by all who have faith in a God that will take care of us.

My last Seder under arms was in the company of Arms. In little more than two months I would be delivered from my three-year enlistment bondage. Ironically, I celebrated Passovers 5719 and

5720 in a country that started a world war at the end of 5699 to eliminate Seders for all time as there would be no Jews left to observe the holiday.

At the conclusion of the Seder, Leeann turned her head to face me. "Why don't you come to us on Wednesday after dinner? I'll make dessert. Bring your slides from Israel."

"Okay . . . thanks. What are you doing tomorrow for the second Seder?"

"I'm going to a friend's home at Perlacher Forest. Tom is on duty tomorrow night. What will you be doing?"

"I'll be in my room on post," I said, "reading *Exodus*."

The next day I started to read the book Leeann loaned me. In the morning, after chow, I went back to my room, stretched out on my bunk, put two pillows under my head, held *Exodus* on my chest, and turned to Book 1, Chapter One. The natural light coming in from the window was all I needed. I remained reading in that position for over three hours, then got up and went to chow again in the mess hall two buildings away. After lunch, it was back to the bunk and Leon Uris' novel. I did not put it down for the next five hours until it was time for the third Army meal of the day. After dinner, with the overhead light on, I read some more. By the time I called it quits on Tuesday, I was up to Book 2, Chapter Six.

Leeann was right about *Exodus*. It was the most interesting, not to mention most educational, book I had ever read. I especially liked the flashback chapters that covered the history of the Jews in different countries in Europe, Poland and Russia especially. I put in my brain facts and details before and after the Nazis came to power, tales and truths my mother never told me. Preparing for college was what I was doing in an Army barracks, a different kind of combat.

Wednesday was the same routine. I began reading of the Dreyfus Affair in France, which I had never heard of, and about Theodore Herzl, whom I knew little of but once saw the signpost on the street in Brooklyn named after him. In the morning another transient trooper came into my room and took one of the three empty bunks. He saw me reading, said a few words, and left. Hours later when he returned, he saw me on my back in the same exact position.

"Jesus," the stranger said. "You haven't moved an inch."

"I'm trying to finish this book. It's over six hundred pages. I only get up to go to chow and the latrine."

After dinner I walked across McGraw to Leeann's apartment. I was now at Book 3, Chapter Ten. I had absorbed knowledge of the agricultural colonies in Palestine, British Mandate, birth of Ari Ben Canaan, the novel's main character who obviously represented the young and strong Israeli fighting men, pre-war Arab riots, Adolph Hitler and the Grand Mufti, the ship *Exodus* that sailed from Cyprus packed with desperate concentration camp survivors, British blockade, and Gan Dafna kibbutz. I brought with me the Uris book and my one-eyed slide viewer that I bought in the PX in Nuremberg, the same little device I used to show Karin my pictures of Paris.

Leeann and I talked about the best-seller and its characters and scenes. We speculated about how the story would be depicted in the big-budget Hollywood movie with an all-star cast that was being filmed in Israel as we spoke. Between breaths, she held the viewer up to the floor lamp each time I inserted a new slide showing various locations and tour stops.

"I'm sorry Tom isn't here to see these," Leeann noted," he's still on duty." The viewing and talking without the non-Jewish husband in the room seemed to sharpen her sense of identity.

Thursday, the last day of my pass, I read until dinnertime, but after chow I did not return to Henry as I originally planned. I stayed a transient one more night to finish reading *Exodus*. I took Leeann up on her offer for Tom to drop me off at my Kaserne the next morning on his way to Schleissheim. Instead of peering out the windows of two streetcars and a bus, I turned pages learning about the conflict in the General Assembly of the United Nations, vote for a Jewish homeland, partitioning of Palestine, Arab revolt, and important role President Truman played in the creation of the State of Israel. Ironically, the lengthy work I devoured during Passover in 1960 ended in Book 5, Chapter Five with a scene of the Seder in 1948 in the Ben Canaan household. Leon Uris, the veteran Hollywood screenwriter, concluded his popular novel on both a sad and happy note, the vindictive killing of a loved one in the Promised Land and the Jews' exodus from two thousand years of exile into freedom.

On Friday at 0630, I waited for Tom at McGraw's main gate. He showed up on the dot in his '56 Chevy. For most of the nearly thirty-minute drive to Henry, the chief warrant officer and I chitchatted. I left his wife's copy of *Exodus* on the front seat as I said goodbye to Arms and exited the vehicle. That day I decided to call him Tom, like a family friend, and the gentle man did not object.

The first time I was informal with Leeann's husband turned out to be the last time I would ever speak to him.

When I came into my room, I was in a rush. I changed into fatigues, make it to the mess hall by 0730, and reported to the Area Office just before 0800 so as not to be late on my first day back at work after my three-day pass. I managed to accomplish all three tasks.

Ramirez said nothing about McCarty all morning. I knew his fat Spanish ass was on the fence. He did not take sides or express an opinion and failed to come to one of his team leader's defense. I got the feeling the Big Enchilada did not approve of the court martial, but he simply fed Horner's ego in this matter.

It was only after lunch that I learned what happened, when I went to the shop to check on parts and equipment. Dickson was sitting at McCarty's desk, feet on a bottom drawer pulled out, sporting three stripes and one rocker on his sleeve, the new E-6 chevron. The son-of-a-bitch snitch did get McCarty's job and did get promoted to staff sergeant. McCarty was nowhere in sight. He was given the day off to get his shit together for temporary residence in the barracks. He also needed time to get his *mind* together, I gathered, for his new role in the company, which he now undoubtedly hated.

The McCarty court martial was the talk of the barracks among my comrades in the 176th all weekend, from Good Friday to Easter Sunday. The Christian soldiers all seemed to be hanging from a cross, all except Dickson of course. No one dared mention McCarty's name to Dickson. The teammates who chickened out and refused to testify for their boss were in pain because they ought to have said to their new boss "God will punish you for being a Judas." Dickson, the corpuscular calumnious cocky cocksucker remained off post, avoiding contact with his fellow Americans who knew what he did and resented him for it. He probably was at some grimy Gasthaus drinking Bier, knocking Steins, and shouting "Prost" with unknowing Germans to rejoice his undeserved rise in rank, pay, and authority. Shoes and boots with four-inch heels the little Dick should have worn to elevate his stature, not step on a teammate with flats.

Horner and McCarty were summoned to Bōblingen for the company court martial. Three judges were appointed to hear the case, a major from the 379th Signal Battalion, the field grade officer required to head such a panel, plus two lieutenants from the 176th. The judges thus were part of the same company and battalion as the accuser and accused, officer buddies of the accuser but in a different class and coterie from the accused. Horner testified first. The CW3 laid out a litany of charges against Sergeant McCarty for so-called dereliction of duty as team leader in the electronics repair shop. Specialist Dickson was the next witness to raise his right hand with his left on the Bible. The senior repairman in the shop corroborated every distortion and exaggeration that spewed from the warrant's mouth. All McCarty could do when his turn came to testify was deny the charges, point to his clean fourteen-year record, and act as his own character witness. No other teammate stepped up to the witness chair to stand up for the shop boss who stood up for them for promotions, passes, and privileges.

Additional testimony to question or cross-examine the flimsy evidence presented against the accused was not ordered by the panel. The three judges needed no Papal conclave to render a verdict. Justice was swift and harsh. Before the gavel fell a second time on Wednesday's hearing, the major in the minor Kangaroo Court informed Sergeant E-6 McCarty he was now *Specialist E-5* McCarty, relieved of leadership duties, and restricted to the barracks for thirty days. The magnanimous judges told the busted war veteran he should consider himself fortunate they did not impose a fine to make him pay for the missing parts and equipment.

On Thursday, Specialist E-5 Dickson received orders he was now *Sergeant E-6* Dickson and the new leader of Team 18. "Take tomorrow off," a robust Ramirez told a morose McCarty later that day, "but clean out your desk first and find a stool at one of the workbenches."

The day after Easter, it was as though I was on some kind of cross myself. I wanted to "get shorty" for what he did to McCarty, level something against the stumpy shit that would get him cut down in

rank. But that would have been a futile gesture. Ii pained me that I
did not beam over to Böblingen to appear before the judges on my
friend's behalf, at least *try* to help him. On Tuesday I could have
driven with McCarty to our home base in order to testify on Wednesday, since I would not have missed the Seder on Monday evening.
Had I done so Horner would likely have relieved me of my cushy
job, not wish to look at me in his office any longer. He might have
even found some reason to court martial me. But I chose, selfishly,
not to forgo three days of off-duty time and the uninterrupted opportunity to read the book I was interested in. Helping a fellow
soldier by going against a warrant is what cost me the office job in
Nuremberg I liked. Had I been altruistic, my Jewish ass could have
been sitting on a stool in the shop on Good Friday, probably next to
the seat that was dusted off for the busted repairman, nailed to a
wooden bench, wiring and fixing pieces of equipment eight hours a
day until my rotation back to the States in seven weeks. That was
one cross I did not wish to hang from.

A few days later McCarty and I once again sat in the front seat of
his Ford. He wanted to talk and I was the only team member he
could or would confide it. I stared at the patch newly sewn on his
fatigue jacket, a blue bird with a yellow umbrella, just one specialist
rank higher than mine. We were now peers despite the difference in
age and military experience.

There was a noticeable and profound change in McCarty's de-
meanor and emotional state. The former sergeant—always relaxed
and jovial and speaking fluently—was now tense and gloomy and
for the first time was stuttering. When he spoke, he hesitated a great
deal, repeated syllables, and prolonged words. There were occasional blockages, and he was unable to get certain sounds out. Com-
municating with difficulty, the obviously nervous wreck manifested
facial contortions and awkward bodily movements. I did not draw
attention to the poor man's struggles with his speech by turning my
head every time his eyes widened or mouth stretched or chin moved
to vocalize a sound or word seemingly stuck in his throat like a
chunk of meat. He kept saying, or rather wanted to say, that he
served his "country," but he blocked on the second syllable of the
word. What I heard was a soldier's favorite barracks sobriquet to
describe the object of his sexual desire, but I thought my friend was

referring to his service to Horner, a man he despised, by voicing a *feminine* derogatory term.

I understood McCarty's fractured utterances. Understanding *why* such a nice guy should be suffering so much and for nothing at all was the problem I had. He told me how humiliated he was every day, working alongside the troops he supervised for over two years, moving his fingers mechanically over wires and resistors and capacitors but unable to concentrate on what he was doing. Dickson, the runt who ratted out a comrade, derived pleasure, McCarty strained to tell me, by ordering him around for Mickey Mouse things.

As in our car conversation two weeks earlier, I listened to the downtrodden man but again I had nothing to say that would comfort him. He was treated badly and it evidently affected his whole personality adversely. Like the biblical Job who suffered at the hands of Satan, and never knew which sin he committed, McCarty suffered by the mendacious words of a demonic warrant officer and conflicting interests of three devilish judges.

CHAPTER 16: TO SEA OR NOT TO SEA

The letter was waiting for me on my bunk when I came into my room after work that Friday, the twenty-second of April. The envelope was very different than those I received from family members and friends in the States. It was square-shaped rather than rectangular with red-and-blue stripes around the border, and had funny-looking stamps pasted in the upper-right corner. I knew it was from Israel before I saw the return address or postmark in Hebrew.

I sat on my bunk and read Yael's letter instead of rushing off to the mess hall. It was handwritten, a little difficult for me to comprehend in the unfamiliar cursive scribbled by someone who learned to read and write English as a second or third language.

21 Nissan 5720

Dear David,

Thank you for your letter. I am glad to hear you safely arrived back in Germany. I too was happy we met in Tel Aviv and I enjoyed our talk and the time we spent together. But my friend was not so happy with your friend who was not so nice to her.

Now I am back at work in my army unit. Like you I also sit at a desk and type letters and file papers. I am going out of the army in four months but I do not know yet what I will do. My parents want me to go to the university but I like to try living on a kibbutz. Yisroel needs young men and women like you and me to work on farms and grow food for our people and for people in other nations.

I understand how you feel. You are American and live in the United States with your family and you are not decided if you want to come live in Yisroel. I would like some day to visit the United States but I believe I belong in Yisroel, a nation for all Jewish people. I do not know what it would be like living in a place where Jews only are a small number. But from what you say New York has many Jews and that perhaps is different.

I hope you decide to come here when you go out from American army in June. I can show you where is the kibbutz I want to go to and you can live there and start to learn Hebrew. You do not need money. Everything is free. I have friends there already. When I go out from my army in August Ill meet you at the kibbutz. I will help you to speak Hebrew. On Shabbat, we can visit my parents in Tel Aviv. We have extra room you can sleep in. I think you will like them as they are East European as your parents are. When I know you better, maybe I will come to New York to meet your parents and family.

Today is last day of Pesach. It is a big holiday here. All work closes for first two days. I was home in Tel Aviv with my whole family for the Seder as I do every year. I hope you in Munich had a nice Seder at the army camp what you told me you will go to with your friend from the tour you were in Yisroel with. I am sure at the end you said next year in Yerushalayim, but here in Yisroel we do not have to say it. Maybe we will together be for Pesach next year in Tel Aviv.

Soon will be Independence Day in Yisroel, on 6 Iyar or 3 May on your calendar. Just twelve years ago we become a nation. There is so much work yet to be done and that is why Yisroel needs young people like me and you. In Tel Aviv there will be a parade on Ben Yehuda Street. My army unit will march down the street and I will be there too. We are very proud here in Yisroel of the soldiers who fight against the Arabs, our enemy, and those who die.

I hope you stay well and I hope you write to me again.

Fondly,
Yael

"What have you got in your pocket?" one of my roommates sitting across from me in the mess hall asked. "Looks like the foreign letter I put on your bunk."

Yael's letter was sticking out on top. I did not bend the envelope to button the left pocket of my fatigue shirt. It was against regulations not to button pockets, and more than once during my time in the Army a sergeant or officer reminded me of that. But I was now a short-timer and I could care less. The letter was next to my heart, warming me to a 19-year-old Israeli girl's proposition to come and live in her country, work with her on a kibbutz, meet her parents, and sleep over in the family's apartment.

"It's from a girl I met in Israel. She's in the army too. Wants me to come back after I get out."

"You gonna do that?" the PFC with a long tour left in Germany said.

"I don't know yet," I answered truthfully. "I have exactly two weeks, until May sixth, to apply for discharge in Germany."

"Well," my roommate quipped. "You got a lot of decidin' to do."

He was right of course. I had fourteen days to decide my immediate future.

Since that April 1958 day in radar school at Fort Monmouth, when the lieutenant I spoke to suggested I go to college when I got out, I thought of nothing but that. This past year, I put my college plans on hold when I had that pleasant four-month summer solstice shtupping a nice German girl. But the morning after we broke up, because I found out she was a Fräulein Hitler, I snapped back to the goal that possessed me. I studied hard for several months, took a breather from G.I. joints and Gerry bar-girls, prepared myself for the all-important College Boards, and took the test in January, the last opportunity for college admission in September. But now I was faced with a dilemma. Was I going to put college on hold again, not sail to the States for my discharge, and instead apply for a DD-214 here so I could fly to Israel?

That decision burdened me for the next two weeks. Should I change course once more for a girl, this time a yaldah, one who was not bad looking but whose face and body were not my ideal, simply because she was Jewish and entreated me to come to her country? What awaits me in the Promised Land with this girl? I wondered. Should I or would I marry her? I could be sweating up my clothes during the day plowing farm fields alongside her and then sweating up the sheets at night in a bunk bed on top of her. I knew I would be working without pay but I did not know if she would be loving without a wedding ring.

"To sea or not to sea," that was the question I kept asking myself.

By May sixth, I had to elect whether to truck it to Böblingen in early June, ride the train to Bremerhaven, board another troop ship, sail through the North Sea and out into the Atlantic, or sink a sea and ocean voyage, get handed a Deutschland discharge in late June, grab a taxi to Munich Airport, and hop on an airplane to Tel Aviv.

I didn't write home about this matter. I knew I had to make up my own mind. My mother would have approved of me standing under the canopy with any Jewish girl, even if it meant putting off college. My father probably would say "Do what you want . . . you always do that anyway." I was sure my sister would be supportive, saying "David, I love you no matter what you do." My grandfather no doubt would not have argued against my going to a foreign country to find my way or calling, as that is what he did when he was my age.

For two weeks my actions, or rather *inactions*, reminded me of Burt Lancaster in *From Here to Eternity*. In Honolulu the day before Pearl Harbor, the procrastinating First Sergeant tells a surprised and annoyed Deborah Kerr, wayward wife of his company commander, he did not put in the application for a commission, as they had planned weeks earlier, so he could rotate back to the States and they could eventually marry.

"I filled it out but I didn't sign it," a rueful Burt revealed to the lover he knew he disappointed, his head down to avoid looking at her. "I took it out of my desk a dozen times, but I couldn't put it in."

Had a blustering Burt put it in to satisfy a divorcing Deb, the action would have been for naught anyway, shot down at 0750 the next morning by the Japanese air attack. Well, I could have shaken hands with fellow New Yorker Lancaster in that movie. He didn't want to be an officer, kept putting off a decision, finally withheld his papers, and upset the woman he said he loved.

In her letter, Yael sounded very much like a girl with an eye toward marriage. In that regard, she could have touched fingers with Kerr. A looming betrothal, however, was not the main factor that helped me make up my mind. The deadline came and went. Like old Burt, I did not sign or put in an application. The chief clerk in the Orderly Room that Friday could have sworn he never received a request from me for a discharge in Germany. Unlike Burt on December 6, 1941, I did not know if I would disappoint the female who liked me but I never told I loved.

What led me to the final judgment to withhold my papers, to mimic what Lancaster did in a 1953 movie? My reasons so long ago were simple, easy to recall today. I didn't want to be a kibbutznik, I wanted to go home to my family, and I wanted to start college before I turned twenty-one.

Like a parent who could not abandon a child, on May 6, 1960 I could not let go of the baby I nurtured for two years, the primary life goal I was striving for.

I wrote a second letter to Yael, thanking her for writing to me but informing her that I will not be stepping off an airplane in Tel Aviv anytime soon. I told her I will write to her again when I am back with my family in Brooklyn and wished her well if she does work on a kibbutz for the good of Israel and the Jewish people after she completes her compulsory active military service.

CHAPTER 17: THE SPY WHO STAYED OUT IN THE COLD

After Pesach and the McCarty court martial, I had a chance to go to McGraw Kaserne and see Lieutenant Gibson. I thought he would be irritated with me for not contacting him weeks earlier after I returned from Israel but he wasn't.

"Don't sweat it, Streiber," he said, after I expressed reluctance to continue being a handler for him on a coreligionist. "We have two other soldiers working with us now on the Berger matter. He sought them out at Jewish services too and they came to us. Berger told them he was a spy for Israel to gain their confidence."

"Oh" was all I could say in response.

"We may be closing in on Berger soon. We think we have enough evidence now to have him arrested. We're just waiting for the right time."

"I guess you don't need me much anymore."

"That's right, Streiber. You can come in from the cold now."

"The cold?"

"That's just an expression we in counterintelligence use. The cold is when you are acting as a spy, are out there all alone and isolated, without love and companionship, and can't tell anyone about what you are doing. You can't afford to make friends when you are in the cold as you are in danger of being discovered all the time."

"That's interesting. I see."

"Apparently, Berger decided to stay out in the cold . . . to continue his spying for East Germany. He could have come to us and told us what he was doing. We would have given him a break. But, we'll be contacting the German police before long and putting him out of action."

"I see," I said again. "I'll be leaving now . . . unless you need me for something else."

"You can take off, Streiber."

"Okay." I saluted, did an about face, and left.

On the Strassenbahn back to the Hauptbahnhof, it occurred to me that the lieutenant did not thank me. Well, why should he? I was sure my handler work was not much help to him, and he knew I was an unwilling participant in his effort to snare a Jewish-American spy.

Or, perhaps the M.I.G. chief was just not the appreciative type, especially to those he pressured into spying for him.

Riding the Blue Goose bus to Henry Kaserne, I was glad this nasty business was over. I thought about how similar Horner and Gibson, two buddies in the Army, were doing their jobs. Both men were out to get someone else. Both men used military means and resources to that end. And that someone else, in both instances, was, or seemed to be, a nice guy.

The last Friday in April, I went to Jewish services at McGraw as usual, this time not planning to question Harold if I happened to see him there. My spying days in the cold were gone. .

Harold was sitting on a bench three rows in front of me. He was holding a prayer book and occasionally leaning over to say something to the young man next to him, who had a brown-paper package beside him. The young man in civies no doubt was an American soldier, judging from his clothes and haircut. Perhaps he was one of the two new recruits that Gibson boasted he collared for spying.

With the conclusion of the service, congregation members stood up and started to walk across the hall where the Oneg Shabbat was held. Harold was a few steps ahead of me. I watched him as he approached the doorway to the other room. The Oneg lasted about half an hour. Harold left with the soldier who was sitting next to him earlier. I left too and was not far behind the dynamic duo.

The two men, one middle-age and the other young, waited outside the barracks at the Strassenbahn stop. I watched them as the young one passed the package to Harold who held it under his arm. Just then two West German police officers appeared from nowhere.

"You are Harold Berger?" one of the officers said in English.

Harold was stunned. I couldn't see his face but I was sure he had a look of surprise on it. "Yes," he answered meekly.

The Polizei caught Harold red-handed, taking a package from an American soldier no doubt containing classified material. They put handcuffs on him right away. This sting operation was likely perpetrated by Lieutenant Gibson to catch a thief and spy, M.I.G.'s target for some time. The German police, I was sure, had a description and photograph of the middle-age American supplied by the intelligence chief.

"Please, come now with us. You are under arrest."

Harold was led away with his head lowered and helped into a waiting police car. I really felt sorry for him, although I knew this scene was inevitable. Congregation members watching nearby were visibly shaken seeing one of their own in police custody.

The Strassenbahn stopped and the soldier/handler boarded it. I got on too but sat far away from the young traitor.

The arrest of Harold Berger, an American who served in World War II, was headline news among the U.S. military in Munich. The article in the *Stars and Stripes* reported that it was the Bundesamt für Verfassungsschutz, the Federal Office for the Protection of the Constitution, that apprehended him.

The East German Hauptverwaltung für Aufklärung, the Main Directorate for Reconnaissance, recruited Harold during one of his visits to East Berlin. The woman he met presented herself as Jewish working for Israeli Intelligence. It wasn't long before she lured him into her bedroom and engaged him in pillow talk about obtaining information and materiel about the U.S. Military. She knew he was left-leaning and had an ideological commitment to Communism.

As an American civilian not attached to the U.S. military in West Germany, Harold can only be tried by a German court. The federal prosecutor said Mr. Berger was accused of "maintaining treasonable relations with an eastern intelligence service," which was a common charge in espionage cases. Under West German law, non-Germans living in the Federal Republic can be charged with treason if they are suspected of giving security information to agents of hostile countries. Harold allegedly supplied information to the Communist East German state security ministry.

"Because I'm Jewish, I don't agree with the idea of rearming West Germany," Harold stated in his defense of the charges. "I was in the Army during the war. I saw what the Nazis did to Jews in the concentration camps. I tried to get information for someone I believed was an Israeli intelligence agent."

Harold's first contract with Communist agents was while he was on a trip to Moscow. He met a representative of the East German domestic and foreign trade agency. Later he showed up at the trade agency in East Berlin and made contact with the East German intelligence service. The American spy made 15-20 trips to East Berlin and two to Moscow before being arrested.

"The trips were for my import-export business only," Harold insisted.

Harold was to go on trial in Federal Court in Karlsruhe. The man I liked would be the first American citizen charged with spying in a West German court.

The Berger affair filled my thoughts the early part of May, a month before my scheduled return to the States and discharge. How could an educated American and war veteran, I asked myself, be taken in by a woman he just met, agree to obtain information for her and pass it along, and be oblivious to the consequences of treason? He must have figured supplying information to the Israeli government, which was strongly opposed to the rearmament of Germany, would help prevent a possible resurgence of Naziism.

Something that was reported Harold said in his defense of spying I could not get out of my mind.

CHAPTER 18: CAMP DACHAU

I awoke early that Sunday morning, the fifteenth of May, after a restless sleep. I had wrestled all night with the thought of going there based on what Harold said. By dawn I reached a decision. Before I changed my mind, as I had done several times, I would go.

The foreboding place was only fourteen kilometers northwest of Henry Kaserne. During my four months in Munich, I could have gone there almost any day after work or on a weekend. All I had to do was take the bus that went north or just stand on Ingolstadter Strasse, put my hand up, and stick my thumb out. Busses, trucks, and automobiles swooshed by this main road all the time. But when opportunities to go arose, I always found some excuse for not going. I guess subconsciously I was afraid to go, afraid of what I might see there, afraid of my reaction to it. In little more than two weeks, I would be leaving for the States. If I waited, I might not get another chance. It was now or perhaps never.

I grabbed some breakfast at the mess hall but I did not have much of an appetite. The guys I shared a room with, awake but still in their bunks, saw me change from fatigues into civies. They all knew I was not on my way to attend mass or sing in the church choir but none asked me where I was going this early in the morning, on post or off. Had any of them wanted to know, I would not have said anything anyway.

I left the barracks planning to hitch a ride. The northbound bus only went as far as Oberschleissheim, about halfway to my destination. I thought it would be easier to hitchhike the whole way from an Army base than to take the bus and then try in a strange town to thumb the rest of the way or deal with local buses I knew nothing about. It was almost nine-thirty when I reached the main road. Few vehicles were passing by at this hour. I did not signal cars with German license plates, the wide and short white plate with black lettering, as I often overheard Americans say that Krauts usually do not pick up hitchhikers, especially foreigners. I did not drive but I suspected the road manners of Germans left much to be desired. Before signaling, I scrutinized passing vehicles for U.S. plates only.

Several automobiles and an Army truck stopped in the fifteen minutes I was thumbing. None of the drivers was going all the way so I just thanked them and remained standing in the same spot near the Kaserne. For a few moments, I ceased looking for a ride and bent down to re-tie my shoelaces.

I heard a car stop. I glanced up and saw a gray Volkswagen. The driver stretched across the seat and spoke through the open window. "How far you going, buddy?"

The young American surprised me, seemed to appear from nowhere. He was in civilian clothes and by calling me buddy he clearly identified himself as a fellow soldier. I was caught off guard and hesitated after I stood up.

"What's the matter, buddy? Don't you want a lift?"

"Yes, I want a lift," I finally answered.

"Well, where to?"

The thought of saying it still produced coldness in my stomach, even though this was the fourth or fifth time. "Dachau."

"Hop in. That's where I'm going. I can drop you off."

I got in and thanked him for picking me up. I thought it strange that another G.I. would be heading to infamous Dachau at exactly the same day and time I was.

"You at Henry?" he asked as he drove off.

I nodded. "Yes."

"What outfit?"

"The One-seventy-sixth Signal."

"Never heard of it," he said.

"We're a small unit, a team of electronics repairmen. We're attached to the Thirty-fifth Artillery. Boblingen is our company headquarters . . . near Stuttgart."

"I'm at Eastman Barracks myself."

"Where's that?" I asked. I had never heard of that base.

"It's in Dachau . . . right near the old concentration camp."

Just hearing the words concentration camp made me apprehensive, but in front of a stranger, someone likely not Jewish, or not knowing that I was Jewish, I spoke in an indifferent tone. "I didn't know we had a barracks there."

The driver turned to look at me. "Oh yeah. We have a big barracks there. Eastman used to be the garrison for the SS guards at the camp. It was also a training center for guards. Now it's part of the Twenty-fourth Infantry Division. The area stockade and laundry are in Dachau too."

"I didn't know that," I said, thinking the Army's jail for the troops in Munich was certainly in an appropriate location. "I only heard and read it was a concentration camp."

"It still is . . . in a way," the American who picked me up looked at me again and commented with a smile, "but without the people dying of disease and hunger or cold. The wood shacks are now full with refugees . . . Germans who were kicked out of Czechoslovakia and those escaping from the Russian Zone."

"I didn't know that," I said again.

"Is that where you want to go?"

"Yes," I eked out and nodded.

The postwar protector of the peace in Europe, barracked near the place I was headed to, continued driving toward this hell on earth for the unfortunates confined there in the not too distant past. This former Nazi site I had to see for myself before I went back to the States.

Dachau was the first of many concentration camps set up by the Nazis throughout Germany and the occupied territories. In March 1933, Heinrich Himmler, Chief of Police of Munich and SS Reichsführer, built this new type of restrictive facility at an abandoned munitions factory in the northeastern part of this quaint medieval city. It was for the detention of political prisoners, opponents of the Third Reich, Hitler's government that just came to power. About 4,800 Communists, Social Democrats, trade unionists, and known anti-Nazis were systematically rounded up and told they were being taken into protective custody in the interest of public security and order. In time, other targeted groups were likewise interned—Jehovah's Witnesses, Gypsies, homosexuals, repeat criminal offenders. Hitler's willing executioners sent relatively few Jews to the Dachau encampment in the early years unless they fell under one of these other categories.

In 1937, with prison labor of course, the SS constructed a large complex of buildings adjacent and to the west of the concentration camp for its headquarters, barracks, and recreation. For the thousands of SS guards stationed there, it was pleasant living in a small town. The SS Kaserne was four times the size of the prisoners' compound. It had shops, a movie theater, restaurants, a community center, post office, hospital, and swimming pool. On a street named Avenue of the SS, there were eight large white houses with attractive red roofs for the camp's high-ranking officials. The next year, after Krystallnacht, more than 10,000 Jewish men were transported to Dachau. Along with over 20,000 non-Jewish men, my brethren were suffering in dilapidated, unheated, unsanitary, and overcrowded long wooden huts, or blocks as they were called, while SS guards enjoyed creature comforts in well-equipped concrete buildings. Christian leaders were not immune from the Reich's wrath either. Church records indicated at least 3,000 priests, bishops, deacons, and preachers who defied the Nazis were imprisoned at Dachau. Hitler's debut camp operated the longest. In twelve years, upwards of 200,000 of his enemies and undesirables from thirty countries passed through the iron gate.

Camp Dachau was important for Nazi history not just because it was the first concentration camp but because it was the prototype. The basic organization and layout developed by its first Kommandant—a secure prisoner's compound separated from the command center and living quarters for the guards—was applied to all subsequent camps. Every small and large city in Germany had some of its citizens suddenly whisked away and carted off to one of these God-forsaken destinations. At Dachau, rumors about conditions and prisoner treatment were so powerful and instilled such fear that, by 1935, Bavarians were uttering warning jingles to the tune of: "Dear God, make me dumb, that I may not to Dachau come."

Although many died within the compound, Dachau was not an extermination camp, not a factory of death like Auschwitz or Treblinka. Tuberculosis, malaria, malnutrition, forced labor, exposure, lack of sanitation, and medical experimentation all took their toll on the condemned souls behind the electrified barbed-wire fence. Before 1942, there was only one two-chamber crematorium, for the disposal of inmates who died naturally, but then other ovens for cremation were constructed, along with a gas chamber, when the demand for human disposition outstripped the camp's limited capacity. In 1944, a women's section was opened. Before long babies cold and hungry were crying in the straw bunks next to mothers who had no milk or blankets for them. During the last months of the war, as Allied forces advanced into Germany, concentration camps near the front lines were evacuated and prisoners transported to Dachau, causing extreme overcrowding. Sealed railroad cars arrived almost daily, often with more people dead than alive. Typhus epidemics flared up from the strained hygienic conditions and weakened state of the prisoners.

Liberation came on April 29, 1945, the same day, coincidentally, that Himmler, after being captured by the British, committed suicide. The 31,000 prisoners freed at Dachau were a diverse population from different countries, with about one-third of them Jews. The American assault began at 0600 hours with two Seventh Army infantry divisions and a tank battalion. Foot soldiers stepped over corpses all about the grounds. Tanks rolled over bridges and German fortifications. U.S. troops came upon thirty boxcars filled with bodies in an advanced state of decomposition. Piles of the naked and the dead were lined up neatly in rows between the inmate barracks and the camp fence. A lowly Leutnant was now the Kommandant, as the cowardly Herr General ran off with over a thousand SS guards the day before. A white flag was hoisted at one of the watchtowers. A Red Cross representative persuaded the adjutant in charge not to abandon the camp, fearing the prisoners would escape and spread the typhus fever. An Obersturmführer attempted to surrender but was shot and killed in the confusion. Dozens of prisoners broke out and killed 40 guards, some with their bare hands. A private in I Company told reporters he was personally involved in the death of more than 60 Germans. By late afternoon—thanks to U.S. paratroopers, riflemen, and tanks—the German surrender was complete. Supreme Commander Eisenhower issued a communiqué and told the world that our forces "mopped up" the infamous Dachau concentration camp and that 300 SS guards were "quickly neutralized."

Five-star Ike, however, failed to mention what soon became known as the Dachau massacre. Some American troops, horrified by what they saw and evidently whipped up in a frenzy, killed over 100 Waffen SS after they had surrendered. Charges were drawn up against several soldiers, in particular a machine gunner nicknamed Birdeye who yelled "They're trying to get away" before he opened fire with his .30 caliber on Germans with their hands in the air. General Patton, recently appointed military governor of Bavaria, not known for any sympathy toward the Hun, never cross-examined witnesses and soon dismissed the charges. The mass killings were not the only unfortunate incident on that day of celebration. A U.S. lieutenant ordered four German soldiers at gunpoint into an empty boxcar and shot them dead. Another American liberator clubbed and then killed injured SS Soldaten lying on the ground but still moaning and groaning from the assault. Several G.I.s looked the other way when two released prisoners still in their striped pajamas beat a guard to death with a shovel. One of the prisoners had been castrated by the German being murdered.

Days after liberation, American troops trucked the good citizens of Dachau over the age of eighteen to the former concentration camp, to document Nazi atrocities with reliable witnesses and to begin the re-education process. Germans did not believe there was a death camp in their midst, thought it was an Allied trick. The unwilling townspeople were given a free public tour of the horrors that occurred on the other side of the electrified fence that forever ensured their city a disreputable name. Fittingly, the locals, many former Nazis, were made to dig mass graves for the piles of rotting corpses lying about, then cart and dump the lifeless bodies. Over 2,000 camp inmates died after liberation, creating additional digging and dumping work for Dachauers. The women were selected to do "women's work," care for the sick and clean dozens of boxcars where people expired after a week without food or water.

"Wir wussten nicht," they all said, claiming they did not know what went on at the campsite on the edge of town that was off limits to them.

As they marched by the crematoriums and mounds of naked dead, the postwar forced laborers took out handkerchiefs to cover their noses and wipe away tears. For years residents of the town could not help noticing carloads of people going in every day but no one coming out. What did these unrepentant Germans think when they eyed black smoke rising from the chimneys and breathed in the stench of burning flesh that permeated the countryside?

After liberation, the U.S. Army likewise used Dachau as an internment camp, but for Germans accused of war crimes, and as the locus for their trials. In 1948, the Bavarian government began housing refugees from the East, mainly ethnic Germans, in the inmate blocks. The 34 huts were renovated, subdivided into small apartments with a common laundry room and toilet. Where huts once contained 180 prisoners squished in 60 three-tiered bunks, they now housed in relative comfort 12 families who escaped from the Russian yoke. The SS Kaserne east of the prisoners' compound, 18 modern buildings with enviable housing and recreational facilities, was converted into a military base for our troops and their dependents. One building of new Eastman Barracks was named the Dachau American Elementary School. On the spot where evil-minded Germans once planned torture and killings, little Johnnies and Janies now learn the three R's.

By the time we reached Dachau, it was ten past ten. It seemed like any small German town on a sunny Sunday spring morning. People were on their way to church, children were playing on the sidewalks, flowers were in bloom. The driver proceeded through the city on Schleissheimer Strasse, then turned right onto Alte Römerstrasse. He stopped the car at Pater-Roth-Strasse, a road that came in from the left. I could see the camp up ahead.

"This is it, buddy. You still want to get out here? I have to turn to get to my barracks."

I looked to where he was pointing. "Yes," I said meekly.

I got out, turned around, lowered my head, and looked into the open window. "Thanks for the lift."

"Don't mention it. Say, if I were you," he started to say as he put the car in gear, "I wouldn't stay too long in there. You might come out wanting to kill someone."

I began walking toward the camp. My camera, with the fresh roll of color film I loaded before I left Henry, dangled from my neck. I could make out the inmate blocks, and I snapped a wide-angle shot at a distance. Soon I was at the main entrance, standing in front of a passageway that led through the center of a two-story concrete building. An iron gate filled the opening. The three words "Arbeit Macht Frei," once welded into the gate, were missing, removed after the war. This famous Nazi slogan, placed at the entrance to all the concentration camps, was a complete misnomer. Work in the camps did not make you free, it made you sick or dead. Before I walked through the gate, I took a picture of it and of the view behind me, the route prisoners followed from the rail line to the camp. It was a reluctant walk, a trudge marked by trepidation.

There was a large building to my right, with short wings at either end. This had been the camp's Administration Building, but now—with showers, a laundry, kitchen, and food storage areas—it served the domestic needs of refugees for the past dozen years. Behind this building was a long stone house, used as a jail by the Nazis, ironically our area stockade in 1960. I saw some American soldiers with a large white capital P on the back of their fatigue jackets outside doing supervised chores. If Mr. Horner and Sergeant Dickson had their way, McCarty would be one of them.

To my left were two rows of 17 long structures in noticeable dilapidation, the original holding cells for Germany's home-grown dissenters. As I moved closer, I made out they were one-story wooden huts, the kind a hearty huff and a puff might blow down. Lines of rope were attached between huts and poles in the yard, with clothes hung out to dry. Women and children were out in front. They looked at me without uttering words or showing emotion. Who was this young man? I imagined they must have wondered. Is he on a sightseeing tour? Why is he taking pictures of poor refugees with no place else to live? I looked at the sad faces with inquisitive eyes before me, but I was unable to communicate my understanding of these people's plight. At least they were better off than those forcefully trucked or railroaded here from 1933-45.

Between the Administration Building and the 34 inmate blocks was a large open space called Roll-Call Square. Here SS guards held prisoner checks and assemblies, carried out hangings and floggings, perpetrated beatings and shootings. The public nature of this courtyard was not only ideal for executions but also for one particular type of punishment, the ordering of those who disobeyed any rule to stand completely still for hours on end or be shot for scratching their nose or wiping their brow. It was not comforting to know that jailed G.I.s line up daily to be handed letters from home and work assignments on the very soil where Jewish and Christian enemies of the Reich met torture and death. I held my camera sideways and snapped a shot of the tall cross erected by Polish survivors after liberation, so sacred was this ground to camp prisoners.

The perimeter of the compound still had, fifteen years after the war, the eight-foot concrete wall. In front of it, the electrified barbed-wire fence angled on top was also there, but just on two sides, the south and west. The fencing on the north and east legs apparently had been torn down. Just inside the double perimeter was a five- or six-foot-wide ditch, filled in on the eastern side of the encampment. The ditch was now dry but once contained water. A strip of grass lay in front of the ditch. The western flank did not need a watered ditch as the narrow Würm Canal flowed alongside it. I counted seven concrete and brick guard towers around the inmate barracks, one partially demolished. SS Soldaten with rifles standing watch easily picked off anyone so much as stepping on the grass. The concrete wall stood on the north, east, and south sides of the prisoner's area. The west side, facing the SS barracks, never had a wall. Perhaps Himmler wanted his garrisoned troops to keep an eye on prisoners at all times.

I walked along the dirt road that ran between the two sections of inmate blocks. At the end, in the northeast corner of the compound, near the wall, there were two small buildings. One was formerly the disinfection hut, now a restaurant with the word GASTSTÄTTE over the doorway. This "place for guests" to eat at a former concentration camp, where tens of thousands starved to death or survived as human skeletons, probably did a thin business. Dachau was not Disneyland and not too many visitors would have a hearty appetite after stomaching the remnants of the atrocities committed here. The other building might very well have had SEXSTÄTTE over its doorway, as it was the camp brothel, a place for inmate women to satisfy the sexual needs of male guards.

In the northwest corner, opposite the disinfectory and brothel, there was the market garden, a large plot to grow fresh vegetables, for the guards but not the guarded. It seems those who did not eat well had to be deloused so as not to infect those who did eat well. And those who were repeatedly violated physically and emotionally had to endure the pain so others could be pleasured.

Having seen all there was to see within the fenced area, I walked back to the gate and exited the prisoner's compound. On my right, near the market garden but outside the fence, were two one-story buildings not far apart, one large and the other small. I moved toward them cautiously. I passed a sign that pointed to the larger building. The word KREMATORIUM was spelled out in black letters against a white background. Reading it sent shivers up and down my spine. A guard stood near the fence. People were walking around this site. A small statue signified that this was a British, French, and American memorial. Between the two buildings was another, and larger, statue on a pedestal. This one, dedicated in 1950, was the unknown concentration camp inmate, an emaciated man wearing a raincoat and trousers to conceal the bodily deterioration.

The larger building was directly in front of me and I entered it. Barrack X it was designated. The first room I saw was large. Two small windows separated the metal hooks that hung on the walls at intervals of eight or nine inches. This no doubt was the undressing room. The adjoining room was a little smaller but had no windows. There were shower heads high on the walls but there were no shower handles at waist height, no water drains on the floor, and no water pipes anywhere. I knew this fake shower room in reality was Dachau's gas chamber. When the door was shut tight and caustic vapor emanated from the wall heads with a hissing sound, those about to enter the next world were deceived no longer. Guards on the other side of the soundproof walls remained oblivious to the condemned prisoners' shrill screams and door pounding.

I knew what awaited me in the third room and hesitated before entering. There were three free-standing double ovens with doors wide open for all to see how the Nazis methodically disposed of those poor souls they had no use for in this world. I looked inside the heavy metal monsters and saw the long tray with rollers used to slide bodies in, the gas nozzles to fire up the ovens, and the receptacles on bottom to catch the ash and bones. Who could imagine what it was like psychologically for the Dachau prisoners given the task of cleaning the crematoria? They had to scoop out human remains, pile them in wheel barrows, cart them off to an open pit, and bury the residue of friends or relatives or block mates in an unmarked grave.

I left the building through the side door and went around to the back. In one corner there was a large stone plaque embedded in the ground. The inscriptions in English, French, and German read: "Here Lies the Ashes of Thousands." I wiped a tear from my eye. Thinking there was nothing more to see, I started to leave. Then I noticed the smaller building. From my reading of *Exodus*, I knew what to expect in the building I just came out of, but I was totally ignorant as to what was in this other one. What could possibly be in there? I knew it was not the place of the medical experiments because they were conducted within the prisoners' compound. One of the blocks was used by the Nazi doctors who deviated from their sworn Hippocratic Oath. They needed a lot of space for their unorthodox scientific equipment, unnecessary operating tables, and inhumane observation rooms.

I entered the smaller building and saw it had only one room. There was no place for either undressing or gassing. And it only contained one oven, noticeably smaller than the six in the other building. I was still perplexed as to the purpose of this building. Then I glanced over to my left and saw a large vat with a wire mesh basket hooked onto it. My head shifted back-and-forth from the vat and basket to the small oven, again and again. Suddenly it dawned on me what this was used for—infanticide. The vat held boiling hot water and infants were "French-fried" in the basket before being shoved into the oven and given the grace of cremation.

My legs seemed to turn to jelly. My whole body quivered. I wanted to cry out to the Lord, but stopped short of uttering his name in vain in front of the two civilian visitors in the building. How could Germans in the twentieth century, cultured people who listened to Wagner and read Nietzsche, do such a barbaric act? Who were these people who could kill innocent babies like lobsters for the dinner table? My mother may have been right about Germans after all. I left the building gasping for air. The intangible force that brought me here was powering me in reverse. I staggered toward the road that led me to this horrible Nazi hideaway.

Camp Dachau was a veritable Hotel Concentration. I remember running toward the door, I had to find my passage back to the place I was before. Part of it was such a lovely place, had such a lovely face. There was plenty of room at the Hotel Concentration. Any time of year, you can be forced to register here. But guests were not living it up at the Hotel Concentration. They never heard the freedom bell, for them it was not heaven but rather hell. Hotel Concentration was programmed to receive, you could check out any time you like but you could never leave.

I cannot remember how I got back to Henry Kaserne that Sunday. Five decades later my mind is a blank as to any bus ride. I must have thumbed a ride from the camp road with an American soldier stationed at Eastman. If so, I was in a daze for most of the fourteen kilometers, dwelling on what I observed as I walked around the camp, especially the last stopping point. Now I knew for sure what the people in my neighborhood with tattooed numbers on their forearms, including sweet little Anna and mean old Mrs. Mittler, experienced in Germany. I wondered too what Karin would have said had she seen this Nazi site, whether she still would have maintained what Hitler did was right.

On May twenty-first, six days after my trek to Dachau, the capture of Adolf Eichmann in Argentina by Israeli Mossad agents was announced to the world by Prime Minister David Ben-Gurion. The notorious Nazi war criminal, hiding out under an assumed name for fifteen years, was apprehended outside the house on Garibaldi Street in Buenos Aires where he lived with his wife and children. Colonel Eichmann was head of the Gestapo's section on Jewish affairs, the chief architect of the plan to exterminate the Jews of Europe. Facilitating and managing the logistics of mass deportations of Jews from the occupied territories to extermination camps in the East was his specialty and responsibility. Eichmann was secretly transported to Jerusalem for trial and punishment. More than the capture itself, the world was shocked to learn that the man responsible for the deaths of millions did not look sinister or act beastly. The soft-spoken, well-mannered, ordinary-looking German was the epitome of the banality of evil. SS guards the likes of a Colonel Eichmann, albeit of lower rank, must have handled the vat and basket in the smaller crematorium at Dachau.

I heard the news on the radio while I was sitting on my bunk writing what was to be my last letter home. The Eichmann affair opened old wounds, raised issues Germans preferred to forget or not discuss, brought to light events Americans and those of other nationalities believed were over and done with and long forgotten.

I could not know then, two weeks before I was calendared to leave Germany, that the war and Nazi atrocities, what I struggled so hard to comprehend during my time there, were for many people in many countries around the world about to enter a new phase of painful remembrance.

CHAPTER 19: THE LAST WEEKEND

"Nürnberg, bitte," I said, trying to pronounce the city as Germans do.

The ticket clerk at the Munich Hauptbahnhof asked me something in German that I did not fully understand, but I did recognize the word zurück. My mother used to say it when she wanted me to come back.

"Ja, und zurück." I motioned with my hand toward myself for additional language support and copied his pronunciation.

"Acht und zwanzig Mark," the clerk said, telling me how much the round-trip ticket cost.

I slid two twenty-Mark bills under the thick glass that separated me from the middle-age man. I understood him to mean twenty-eight Marks. He returned my change, a ten-Mark bill and two one-Mark silver coins.

"Weiviel Uhr." I asked for the time the next rain will leave and pointed to my watch.

The German looked to the chart on the wall by his left side. "Sieben Uhr fünfzig."

Seven hours fifty I knew he indicated, but I did not know how to ask what track the train would be leaving from. "Wo," I said, simply for where, pronouncing the *w* like a *v*, as before.

He answered in one sentence, uttering something that sounded like "glice," a word I did not recognize, and "sechs," which I knew was the number six. "Danke," passed from my unsmiling lips as I turned away from the clerk.

It was seven thirty. In the middle of the station, not far from the ticket counters, there was a big black board with white letters that hung overhead. I looked up at it and my eyes focused on the line that read Gleis 6 Nürnberg 7.50 Uhr. There was no need for me to run to Track 6 to catch my train. I had twenty minutes. I walked around the Hauptbahnhof, peeked in shop windows, and observed German people whom I would not be seeing much of anymore. This time I wandered about in a New Germany railway station, no chalky-complexioned Deutscher, Homosexueller or otherwise, followed me or approached me.

I boarded the third car of the train and found a seat by a window.

The trip to Nuremberg would take a little more than three hours. I had plenty of time to ponder my return to whence I came.

It was Friday morning, the twenty-seventh of May. I was on a three-day pass and had to report back to my company by noon on Monday. This was my last weekend overseas. I requested the time off and Ramirez gave it to me, a going-away present I gathered. It was the Memorial Day holiday and almost everyone, officers and noncoms and troopers alike, would be away. On Tuesday at 0900, I was told, I should be standing in front of the barracks with my packed duffel bag and AWOL bag, ready to be picked up and transported by truck to company headquarters. The overseas bag with my civilian clothes, which could not be taken with me on the ship, would be put in the U.S. Mail that morning to arrive in Brooklyn, New York ahead of me. By this time the following Friday in Böblingen, after three days of processing to leave Germany, I would be sitting on another train going north, but this one headed all the way to Bremerhaven.

I felt I must go back to Nuremberg before I crossed the Atlantic again. On Luitpoldstrasse some unfinished business awaited me. Like a patient in psychoanalysis, to move my life forward I first had to go backward. I missed the city of my longest assignment in the Ar-my, the place I thought of as a home away from home, the town I had such good times in. For the past four and a half months, I was beset with the thought of seeing Marianne and, most especially, of going to bed with her. In Munich, I could not get her out of my mind, and I did not meet any other Fräulein remotely as attractive as she with what effort I expended looking. I hit the Domino Bar and Havana Bar on Goethestrasse, or Gertystrasse as Americans called it, two G.I. waterholes near the Hauptbahnhof, but came up dry. I longed to walk the streets of Nuremberg once more where I came of age as a young man. This trip was not planned to go back to Zirndorf and spy on, or connect with, Karin, but that was a possibility. Before I set sail for America I yearned to fasten a bowman's knot with the sexiest girl I met in Germany on my side of the color line.

This last weekend trip, I sincerely prayed, would not turn out to be an experience for me like Ray Milland's in *The Lost Weekend*, a man obsessed with alcohol, ready to go on a binge at every turn, blacking out from his bender and ending up in a hospital ward. I was a drunkard of sorts, drunk with thoughts of one particular Fräluein lying naked next to me. But I hoped I would not spend the next three days in like manner as Milland, making the rounds at popular bars just staring into an empty glass with the girl's likeness reflected in it, or chasing hallucinatory visions of little Marianne-faced rats coming out of a hole in the wall.

I arrived at the Hauptbahnhof in Nuremberg after eleven. Like a man on a mission I exited the station quickly and walked to the left, past the medieval tower, and around the corner to Luitpoldstrasse. There was only one thought in my mind, hooking up with Marianne, the very attractive blond I met and often saw in the Flying Dutchman but could never dance or make a date with. Whether she took payment for her affections or was just a good-time girl, I knew not and cared not. This was the Bavarian babe I thirsted for and could not go home without carnal knowledge of. She was almost as captivating as the girl in the snack bar, but I was sure this pick of mine did not plow herself on the dark side of my fellow American soldiers' field of intimate relations, whether recompensed or not.

Briskly along the south side of Luitpoldstrasse I moved. The Flying Dutchman happened to be on that side and, coming from the station, it was also closer. In my search for Marianne I reasoned I would check that establishment first since I never saw her anywhere else. As I approached the Dutchman, however, I suddenly changed course and crossed the street. Some unknown force was compelling me, probably instinct or premonition or both, to try the Luitpold instead, the first G.I. joint in Germany I drank in. As I opened the door and stepped inside, I was struck by the Luitpold's emptiness and lack of gaiety, a ghost Gasthaus that time of day. No patrons eating or drinking, no music to be heard. At a table to my left, near the kitchen and bar, four people were sitting and talking, the only souls in the place, waiters and waitresses off duty it seemed.

To my utter amazement, Marianne was at that table, on the end facing me. I could see her clearly from head to toe. The hair was a bit shorter than what I remembered but that same beautiful unsmiling face was in my sight. She was wearing a tight-fitting skirt that rested, in her sitting position, above the knees. Her legs were crossed and I could see her shapely calves and inviting lower part of her thighs. She looked up at me and peered unemotionally. Her features were practically flawless, eyes and nose and mouth formed as if carved by Michelangelo. A waist jacket draped over her shoulders. Her full breasts were revealed by the thin blouse.

For a moment I thought I was hallucinating, drinking from the same bottle as Ray Milland lost for the weekend, seeing only what I wanted to see. It was difficult to believe I had such good luck and perfect timing. No sooner had I left the train station, walked a few paces, and poked my head into a bar I never saw Marianne in that I happened upon the very person I was seeking. With no wasted time and little effort, I now had my eyes on the prize. But, would I be able to *unwrap* this prize package and get more than a look inside?

I casually walked over to her, pulled up a chair from another table, and sat down across from the statuesque bar queen I traveled 170 kilometers to see and touch. I said nothing to her or to the three others, not even hello. She recognized me I could tell.

"I don't see you for long time," Marianne said without emotion. She continued looking at me but gave no indication, not even a Mona Lisa smile, that she was glad to see me.

She remembered me and I was very pleased. It saved me the embarrassment of having to remind her I was the American she often turned down for a Dutchman dance or date. That was all mox nix now anyway. "I was transferred to Munich in January," I explained simply.

"Oh," she let out, somewhat surprised by my comment. "Why you come back to Nürnberg?" Her tone was still cold and indifferent.

I looked at her with a serious face, as intensely as I could, without blinking or smiling, eyes directly into her eyes. "I came to see you," I told her straight out in plain English. It felt good telling a German girl the truth for a change.

She looked at me as intensely as I was looking at her but said nothing further. If she was moved by my undisguised compliment and come on, she did not show it. I was enamored of her but whether she found me attractive or wanted to unite with me now was an open question.

After a pause, I spoke again. "Why don't we get out of here and go someplace?" I asked boldly, far from sure what she might say. In this delicate situation, I did not mention anything about a hotel room, which I had to rent anyway whether I hooked up with her or not.

A moment later, she simply got up from the table, put her arms through the jacket, picked up her handbag, and left with me. Evidently, Marianne had no other plans for the afternoon and believed me when I said I came back purposefully to see her. No doubt she was flattered and did not find me too bad looking either. For all the times she spurned my advances, perhaps she now wanted to make it up to me.

Soon as we were on the street, I reached for the hand of my veritable valentine to clasp as we walked. Her figure was not less than Greek, but her smile was a little weak. Finally touching the flesh, if only on an extremity, of one of my two fantasy Fräuleins after more than a year of waiting, rendered me flush with romantic thoughts. With my fingers between hers, my heart beat slightly faster. This was like a dream come true but I feared at any moment my reverie might end by her pulling her hand away and taking off by herself. Simply being with her put me on cloud nine. The fact that she was probably four or five years older did not faze me. She was blond, blue-eyed, the height I liked, had marvelous facial features, possessed an enviably contoured body, and was very near the image of the German girl I had in my mind when I was transferred to this country. Short, dark-haired, wide-hipped Karin, and tall, stringy, toothy Elsa, were no comparison to the one I now engaged by the hand.

We walked around the Old Town section in Nuremberg. It was a warm spring day, no overcast in the sky, suitable for meandering and getting to know the girl I knew nothing of but had thought so much about. I brought my camera with me and I took some pictures, one with Marianne when I asked, or rather motioned, a passerby to snap the shutter for us. A while later we were standing in front of the fountain near St. Mary's Church. As I was advancing my film and adjusting the light meter setting for the next shot, I heard my name called out.

"Hey Dave . . . Dave."

It was Steve. I recognized the familiar voice when I looked up and saw him approaching us. His arms were above his head and he was waving to me just like he did on our first day in Germany at the Stuttgart station. A woman and a child were by his side.

"What a coincidence seeing you here," Steve said.

"Yes," I agreed, shaking his hand. "This is Marianne." I put my arm around her waist and gently moved her forward. "Marianne, this is Steve, my roommate when I was stationed here, and Ursula." The little girl looked up at the grownups in bewilderment amid all the greetings in English.

"What are you doing in Nurnberg?" Steve asked, pronouncing the city American style.

"I'm going home next week. I wanted to see the city again. What are you doing here? I thought you were transferred to Hanau."

"I was. But we finally got married last month. We had to come back to sign some papers . . . and pick up Heidi." Steve patted the little girl on the head and smiled.

The girl five or six years old still seemed bewildered. Steve and I stood off to the side and brought each other up to date about our Army assignments, while Marianne began talking to Ursula in German. Then I saw Marianne reach into her purse, pull out what looked like a small candy, and hand it to the child.

"Danke," the little girl said.

I watched Marianne as she took the child by the hand, walked over to a street vendor, and bought her an ice cream in a cone. Ursula stood by silently as her daughter licked her treat. I was surprised by this spontaneous show of affection by Marianne for a strange child. Given her life style of hanging out in G.I. bars and leaving with different men, I would not have thought Marianne was the maternal type.

It seemed like old times being with Steve and Ursula, but I knew it was new times. This was mid-1960, my affair with Karin was over eight months earlier, in weeks I would be getting out of the Army, Steve had almost two-and-a-half more years to serve if he does not re-enlist again, my buddy from the States and Germany at not quite twenty-one was a married man and stepfather, and I would soon be attending college classes and cracking textbooks while Steve would still be benched in a Signal Corps shop testing and repairing electronic equipment. Steve looked happy as he now had what he wanted, his own family, albeit with much responsibility. I was happy that my Army days were numbered and I was not married to a German, but sorry for the way Karin and I broke off and her not getting what she wanted, marriage to an American.

Ursula came over to where Steve and I were standing, and occasionally glanced at Heidi with Marianne. "How long you stay in Nürnberg?" she asked me.

"Until Sunday or Monday."

I thought the wife of an American would push for one of her countrywomen and ask me if I were going to see Karin, like she did after I returned from Paris, but said nothing along that line. I would have told her I'm with Marianne now had she asked. Nevertheless, I was curious as to what happened to Karin.

"Have you seen or spoken to Karin since we broke up?" I asked Ursula. I knew they were good friends and thought Karin may have contacted her after I walked out, to apologize or get back together with me perhaps. Marianne was still out of earshot.

"No. I not see Karin again. She not call me."

Steve jumped in as usual. "Don't worry good buddy. You're off the hook. Karin probably met another G.I. or a German. She could be married by now . . . even carrying a baby."

I showed no emotion at hearing this eventuality, but I felt a pang in the pit of my stomach. Yes, Karin could be married by now but I *was* worried. If she were pregnant it could be mine or someone else's. That was the news I wanted to hear, but only if I were not the daddy.

Marianne came back holding the little girl's hand. We all talked for a while longer and then said our goodbyes and auf Wiedersehens. Steve and Ursula had things to do together, and so did Marianne and I.

I asked Marianne if she wanted to get something to eat. She said no. I asked her if she wanted to go back to Luitpoldstrasse. She said no again. So we simply walked around some more until we found a bench to sit down on. Holding hands with her, I tried to make it a tender gesture, get her to warm up to me, but she kept her hand in mine irresolutely. I very much wanted to lean over and kiss her, but she showed no emotion or love interest while sitting next to me in public. In that respect, Marianne was not at all like Karin. I refrained from putting my arm around her or making any romantic move as I thought that might upset her. I could only hope the situation would change later in private. Her English was better than Karin's but ironically we talked less, and not a word about Germany after the war or German-American marriages or my being in the Army. When a priest and two nuns in full habit happened to walk by, she broached the subject of sex.

"I don't believe priest don't have woman," Marianne said, looking at the three in Catholic dress after they passed us. She went on to criticize the church and its officials, mainly for presumed sexual transgressions. I gathered she did not go to mass on a regular basis or lend her voice to the choir and had no plans to become a postulant in a local convent. An Audrey Hepburn in *The Nun's Story* she was not.

"You're probably right." I agreed with her whether I believed it or not as I wanted to be on her good side. Besides, as a Jewish boy I knew little about priests and their male habits, or whether they foraged under female habits.

"Priest like any man," she added. "He need woman."

"Bestimmt," I said, a word I learned from her Flying female friend. I could not and would not argue with her on this point, in English or fractured German, given what I myself had in mind for the evening.

We sat quietly for some minutes. I continued to hold Marianne's hand, still excited by her physical presence and physical appearance, even though there was little warmth or reciprocation in her manner. The silence was rather pleasant, though, a quiet reflection of what might come.

"Where you sleep tonight?" she suddenly asked me.

"I was going to get a hotel room later."

"I know place," she said confidently.

I turned to look at her. "Okay."

At the hotel she would take me to, I presumed we would not have any trouble from, or late night entry by, the desk clerk over my not being a groom for the room. With the matter of us sleeping together out of the way, I was confident this trip to Nuremberg would not be a lost weekend.

Marianne led me to a Pension near the Pegnitz River. We checked in after five. She spoke to the desk clerk in a familiar tone so it was apparent she had been here before. I had my AWOL bag, she carried nothing except her handbag. The room had modest accommodations—a double bed, end table and lamp, a chair, and a dresser with an attached mirror. She put her bag down on top of the dresser. I watched her as she stood in front of the mirror and prettied herself up, the first order of business for any Fräulein with an American soldier. She ran a brush and comb through her hair, then applied some makeup. I was impassioned by her seemly face and alluring figure, not to mention the stirring I felt by being alone with her in a hotel room.

"Why don't we lie down and rest for a little while?" I said obliquely looking over toward the bed. That was not too much to ask, I thought, of this Pension's frequent guest, the person who brought me here. I could not wait to get between the sheets with the deutsche doll I met almost fifteen months earlier but who always eluded my grasp.

Marianne turned her head to me, lipstick still in hand. "Nein," she countered abruptly.

The sharpness and negativity of her one-word response was unsettling. It reminded me of little Anna back in Coney Island saying the same German word to me, as a boy of eleven, when we were alone in her apartment and I had gone too far with her. Marianne put the lipstick in her handbag, picked it up, and moved toward the door. "I go now," she said forcefully.

She spoke those three words with a determination I had not known before with any female, American or German. At that moment I realized she had her own mind and was going to do whatever she wanted and I had no choice but to wait for her. I stayed in the room for a spell, disappointed that she left so soon after we unlocked the door and without giving me anything to remember her by.

Later I went out for a walk and got something to eat. I came back to an empty room, still not knowing if or when Marianne would return. She was a party girl all right, I told myself. She was probably sitting around her favorite table at the Dutchman right now, downing beers and Schnaps paid for by different men, doing what she normally does on a Friday night, not letting my unexpected presence in Nuremberg interfere with her lifestyle. Or, she could have gone out by herself because she had business to attend to, like Elsa, to earn part of her living on a weekend. Either way, I tried not to dwell on what a postwar German girl who hung out in G.I. joints would be doing that night, or with whom. I just hoped she would come back and do something with me. There was nothing for me to do in the room save look at the four walls or climb into bed alone. I did not bring a book with me and there was no radio or TV. I retired a little after eleven, my normal bedtime.

I was awakened by someone opening the door. From the light in the hallway, I made out it was Marianne. She must have picked up a spare key from the desk clerk. I switched on the lamp and looked at my watch. It was three thirty. I had the good sense not to ask where she had been or with whom, content with the fact that she did return and I would soon be getting what I came to Nuremberg for. My dream girl did not say anything as she moved into the room. She quickly undressed, threw her clothes on the chair, and slipped under the sheet next to me with only her panties on. Whether it was the first time Marianne had been to bed since I met her that morning I did not want to know.

We made love but I was not William Holden, she was not Jennifer Jones, and what passed between us was definitely not a many-splendored thing.

Marianne had a good kisser but she was not a good kisser. I brought my lips to hers, to French kiss this German girl like I enjoyed doing with Karin. I wanted Marianne's mouth open to me, her tongue thrashing about, her lips wetting mine. But disappointed I was with her brand of oral togetherness. The Fräulein with a pretty face shunned deep or extended kissing. I was fortunate to rub cheeks with her. Next I put my hand and fingers to work. First I caressed her delightful top half, softly squeezing one side and then the other, relishing the much larger cup size relative to either Karin or Elsa. But when I began tugging at Marianne's nipple, pressing two finger joints as gently as I could, she said "Nein" and pulled my hand away. I put my mouth to that nipple and got a few sucks in before she turned her chest away from me.

My disaffected bed partner lay on her left side. I ran my hand over her covered hips, down her bare leg, back up again, and around to her front. I started to separate those shapely thighs and slither under her panties to moisten her and heighten my sensuality with the same digital strokes. Suddenly she turned toward me, lifted her buttocks, and took her panties off. The party girl evidently did not like to be pawed on the bottom as well.

"Mach schnell," she commanded, now on her back with her knees up and feet flat on the mattress.

I fingered the favored frontal body part slightly but she was not yet wet. "Mach schnell," she repeated, spreading her legs more.

I moved to mount her but I was not that hard and had difficulty getting it in. It was like that first time with Karin on the grass out in the woods. I could feel I was only halfway up. I thrust and released, pushed and pulled, schneller and schneller. Marianne pumped with me, unlike Karin who often remained motionless. I usually came right away with Karin wearing a rubber but bareback with Marianne I was not shooting off.

Five, ten minutes must have passed. We were both sweating but no sticky white bullets were coming out of me. I thought Fräulein Nein would say no again and shove me off her but she kept moving rhythmically with me. Finally, I came and that was a welcome relief, more so for my emotional than anatomical satisfaction. We disjoined and without saying anything more or doing anything more went to sleep.

My first connection with attractive and sexy Marianne was a revelation. Intimate relations with her while we were stretched out naked on a double bed in a private room was less gratifying than the kissing and coupling I had with plain-looking Karin sitting on a cramped callous couch with both of us clothed and I worried that her mother or sister might bust in on us. I was not in any college class but I learned an important lesson about love and life at four in the morning that last Saturday in Germany. The perceived beauty of a female's face and figure may be bound inextricably to a man's sexual arousal and romantic sensibilities but not to the actual pleasure he might derive from later foreplay and coitus.

We both woke up late but well before checkout time. I tried to snuggle up to the lovely lady beside me and get her to go a second round, hopefully not a repeat perfunctory performance, but she was not into morning tenderness or lovemaking. I would have to be satisfied with just the one romp she granted me in the middle of the night. Marianne was unattainable. She was too much the independent type, self-absorbed rather than concerned about the man lying next to her. I could not kiss her in the way I wanted and she was far from affectionate. Asking or motioning the German girl to do me French was fruitless as she no doubt would nix oral contacts requiring greater familiarity or commitment on her part. Unlike Elsa or Karin, Marianne was not loquacious, in German or English, and I could never tell what she was thinking or how she felt about me.

After we dressed, I asked her if she wanted to eat breakfast or spend the day together but she declined. It seemed I could not take up any more of the fair Fräulein's valuable time. She did not ask me for money and I was sure she did not take any dollars or Marks from my wallet when I was not looking. Quite the contrary, she gave me something to *put* in my wallet, a small head shot of herself recently taken by a photographer.

I said "Thank you" and kissed her goodbye, more a brush of lips than an ardent mouth-to-mouth exchange. She whisked out of the room before I could get my AWOL bag packed. I never saw Marianne again. Her 1960 picture, resting appropriately behind my ass during waking hours, to be viewed or shown to others, was more than enough in the years that followed to remember, or brag about, the best-looking girl I laid in Germany. As picture-perfect as she was, she was not the Fräulein who pleased me the most. That opinion I would keep to myself.

At the Hauptbahnhof on Saturday afternoon, I hung around for a while before I boarded any train. "To see or not to see," that was the question I asked myself this time.

I could not decide whether to take the train to Zirndorf and try to see Karin, or simply go to another track and head back to Munich. Now that I accomplished what I came to Nuremberg for, there was nothing keeping me here. But I had two more days left on this last weekend in Germany, a final opportunity to tie up a loose end, my broken relationship with Karin, before leaving for the States. I did not know if she married or if she is with child or if that child was mine. I thought I might stand in a hidden spot across the street from Karin's house and wait, hours if necessary, to get a glimpse of her. If she was with another guy, or had a protruding belly, that would be good to know. If I did not see her, then I could take the bus and two streetcars to Merrell Barracks, say hello to my former teammates, flop on an empty bunk for the night, and try again on Sunday. I wanted to learn what happened to Karin, but I did not want to be seen by her or be caught stalking her or make a fool of myself.

About an hour later, I was on the train to Munich.

CHAPTER 20: A FAREWELL TO ARMS

By the time I arrived at the barracks, it was after six thirty and I had missed chow. I went directly to my room, emptied my AWOL bag, and put the things in my foot and wall lockers. Then I high-tailed it over to the snack bar for my favorite non-mess-hall meal—two hamburgers, French fries, a coke, and a slice of pie. After eating, it was still early and I decided to take in a movie. It could be my final flick at Henry, I thought. On Sunday I planned to go into Munich for the last time, Monday was Memorial Day and I had to pack three bags, one with my civies to parcel-post home, and on Tuesday I set out to Böblingen.

Playing at the post theater that Saturday night, coincidentally, less than three weeks before I would be leaving the military, was *A Farewell to Arms*, Hollywood's second take on Ernest Hemingway's autobiographical novel. I very much enjoyed this movie, a tragic story of young lovers torn apart by war. Rock Hudson is the American conscientious objector who enlists in the Italian Army in 1916 to drive an ambulance. He meets and falls in love with Jennifer Jones, a Red Cross nurse reluctant to get involved with a man again after the death of her lover from war injuries. Rocky is injured and sent to the hospital, but he does not bury his heart with his wounded knee. Jenny is eager to nurse him back to health, succumbs to his masculine charms, and in a darkened room out of sight of the head nurse takes care of the horny hunk who can move all of his body parts except the knee. Soon Jenny is with bambino and Rocky is dispatched to the front again and punching his way through the German lines. After a fierce battle and barely making it back to his Italian base, the foreign lieutenant is wrongly accused of desertion and suspected of spying. A twenty-second military trial and a death sentence to be carried out immediately is all it takes for him to decide to knock over a lamp, flee from the firing squad, and jump into the river. Fed up with war and killing, every woman's reel dream is now a real deserter and bids farewell to arms. The two lovers manage to escape by rowboat across a lake to neutral Switzerland, but do not marry and do not live happily ever after.

The Swiss miss has complications from the pregnancy and is hospitalized. The nurse-turned-patient pushes out a stillborn baby and dies on a bed with a pallid face and a tearful Rock beside her. I liked the scene at the end, where the father/husband who never was wanders away from the hospital in a daze and walks down the center of a a wide tree-lined boulevard alone in the early morning light to start a new life. Like Hemingway and Hudson, it was time for me to leave a war-torn country, board a boat to a new land, cross a large body of water, shed my uniform, wave goodbye to the Army, and put down my arms. Like Ernest himself but unlike the soldier he created from his Great War experience, I did not have to desert, hide, or risk a firing squad to begin a new chapter.

"Streiber . . . Streiber . . . wake up."

A spec four was standing over me when I opened my eyes, shaking me on the shoulder. I recognized him right away as the CQ that usually covered the Orderly Room on weekends.

"You have a phone call," he said. "Some lady wants to talk to you. Says it's urgent."

"What?" I was still a little groggy and not fully awake.

"Get up. I put her on hold. She needs to talk to you now."

"Okay . . . okay . . . I'll be right down."

"Make it snappy," the CQ commanded as he walked away from my bunk.

It was Sunday morning about nine. I overslept and missed chow as I sometimes did on Sundays, as I was very tired from my two-day trip to Nuremberg and the late movie when I came back. Who could be calling me? That was my first thought as I threw back the sheet and blanket. Could it be Marianne whom I kissed goodbye to only twenty-two hours earlier? On Friday I mentioned the name of my Kaserne to her. Maybe she wants me to return to Nuremberg? Racing through my mind were images of a more affectionate Fräulein with a dynamite face and body. But after I slipped into my fatigue trousers and shower clogs and hurried downstairs to the orderly room, I became worried. Was it Mama on the telephone at three in the morning in New York? Zeyde at his age could have died, or God forbid someone else in the family. I'd have to fly home right away, leave most of my things behind for someone else to pack and ship.

I picked up the receiver lying sideways on the CQ's desk. "Hello."

"David?" I heard the woman on the other end say in a weak voice and start to cry as she spoke. I couldn't tell who it was but I knew it was not Marianne or Mama. She soon became hysterical and I hardly understood what she was saying. Then, another woman came on the line and introduced herself as Leeann's friend from Perlacher Forest. I listened as I was told the bad news.

"Leeann can't talk much. Tom was killed Friday in a helicopter crash. The memorial service is today at twelve o'clock . . . in the chapel near the Community Club. Leeann would like you to attend. She said you knew Tom. Can you be there?"

Now it was *I* who was practically speechless. A man, a handsome one at that, with a loving wife and child, in the prime of life, an impressive military career mostly behind him and a comfortable retirement ahead of him, suddenly struck down. Strange, my transit to and from this country is connected to air traffic deaths of people I knew and/or liked. Days before I am to leave Germany I learn my friend's husband is killed in a flying accident, just as days before I was to travel to Germany I hear that the singer I admired, Buddy Holly, met his demise the same way.

"Oh, how awful," I finally said without answering her question, still stunned by the news.

"Can you be there?" she asked again.

"At McGraw Kaserne?" I inquired to be sure.

"Yes."

I looked at the clock on the Orderly Room wall. "Yes . . . I can make it in time."

"Good. We'll see you then," she said. "Twelve o'clock."

She hung up before I could ask what happened or how Leeann was.

CW3 Thomas C. Armson was killed on 27 May 60 at 1348 hours near the Hohenfels training area northeast of Munich. Two reporters from the *Stars and Stripes* he was transporting to the site of ongoing field maneuver exercises died with him. The Army's preliminary investigation determined that Mr. Armson lowered his Sikorsky H-34 in a narrow corridor between two high mountain ranges and crashed when high winds and downdrafts caused the piston-powered, single-engine helicopter to stall and fail to regain sufficient altitude. The chopper's four blades kept spinning but the whirlybird went down rapidly instead of up slowly. To Tom's family, it came as no consolation to later learn that the Sikorsky Company was in the process of modifying the H-34 with the addition of flight stabilization systems.

There were about fifty people in the chapel at McGraw Kaserne when I entered fifteen minutes before the Presbyterian service began. I took a seat toward the rear. Almost half the congregants were men in uniform, sergeants and warrant officers, Tom's buddies at Schleissheim Army Airfield. The others were in civilian clothes, men and women, friends of Leeann's and their spouses in and out of the military. A somber atmosphere filled the vaulted chamber, an organist played a funeral dirge. I saw Leeann and her daughter sitting in the first row. A closed coffin, draped with an American flag, rested on a bier in the center up front. The pastor in a black robe stood at the pulpit and recounted the life of Tom Armson as a devoted husband, loving father, dedicated soldier, and veteran of two wars. He spoke about the men in Tom's unit who cared for and respected him, how tragic his untimely and unnecessary death was, and how sorely he will be missed by family and friends. I could hear Leeann sobbing, I could see the daughter's head on her mother's shoulder.

The pastor opened his Bible. "The Lord is my shepherd," he began reading, and then recited the entire Twenty-third Psalm in the Book of David.

I understood why this was for Christians a favorite hymn in the Old Testament. No one wrote more poetically and faithfully than the Hebrew King a thousand years before Christ about man's preparation for entering the next world—restoring one's soul, being guided in straight paths, walking through the valley of the shadow of death, fearing no evil, expecting goodness and mercy to follow all the days of one's life, and dwelling in the house of the Lord forever. Tom was forced into the world to come before his time, in a final farewell to arms, without saying goodbye to his comrades and loved ones. The shadow of death no longer hovers over the man soon to be entombed as it does the living. He now dwells with the Lord for all eternity while we mortals can only hope to enter that house one day.

As I sat and listened to the Christian service, I thought about the only other funeral I attended, that of my grandmother's six years earlier. It was a very different experience—with an open casket, service in Hebrew, sermon in Yiddish, and many adults crying, not just Zeyde. I also thought about the Seder night when I was sitting across the table from Tom breaking matzo with him, looking at the face of a man who would be effaced from this earth in less than seven weeks. The wheel of misfortune was spinning and in short order would stop at his number. Now I was sitting in a church pew across the street, observing the unopened casket containing the mangled body of the man who fell from the sky. CW3 Armson in 1960 joined ranks with General Patton in 1945. Both Army officers confronted death many times during two wars but survived only to die in a freak accident in peacetime.

On the day before Memorial Day, a day of remembrance for our war dead, I bid farewell to Arms, a man I only saw on three different occasions but who I knew was a decent human being and did not deserve to go the way of all flesh so violently or so swiftly. After the service, I followed a small crowd of people back to Leeann's apartment. She hugged me tightly when she saw me, still choked with emotion. The widow Armson and I now had something else in common. Both of us will be packing our bags soon, going back to the States, and starting a new life. Leeann handed me another piece of paper with a handwritten address on it.

The next day, I was getting ready to go home with a tied-up duffel bag. Tom too was going home, but in a zipped-up body bag. He was buried with full military honors in Leavenworth National Cemetery in Kansas, his home state, known locally as the Old Soldier's Home. Tom was not one of the old soldiers dug in there but this would be his home henceforth.

I spent three days in Böblingen at Panzer Kaserne processing out of Germany. My bunk was on the third floor of the company headquarters building, in the same room for transients that I slept in when I first came to the 176th Signal and was awaiting my team assignment. I still found it hard to believe that in this man's Army of strict rules and regulations, and intransigent noncoms and officers, a nineteen-year-old private first class was able to weasel out of going to Fulda and wangle his way to Nuremberg, the hands down much better location Fräulein-wise and attachment company-wise. Lieutenant

Finston, a possible current or former Landsmann, was a life-saver that day fifteen months earlier.

The First Sergeant gave me a sheet that I had to "clear post" with. It was a long list of places on Panzer that I had to go to and have someone in charge put his initials next to, to sign off on me. I had to traipse around the barracks I long ago passed through for less than two weeks and get checked out. On the list was the EM club, library, PX, gymnasium, service club, craft shops, movie theater, and more. For two days I felt like a fool asking the soldier on duty I never met before to clear me, sign that I did not owe any dues, leave sports equipment behind, fail to return borrowed books, or maintain a continuing connection to the post in some way. Before I could depart the company I also had to pick up my medical, dental, and personnel records to take with me on the boat home, as well as turn in my field gear, rifle, and helmet. At the gymnasium on my last full day at Panzer, it was difficult to find someone authorized to sign. I went back there twice, all to no avail, so I made up the initials HJ and scribbled it myself.

"Who signed this," the company clerk asked me, after I handed him the completed form and he looked it over. His finger was on the line item I falsified. He obviously took the cockamamie post clearing process more seriously than I did.

"Some guy at the gym," I said.

"Who?"

"I don't know. I never even went in there to work out or play sports."

The spec four was a different clerk than the one I recall going to when I wanted to speak to Finston about changing my assignment, but he had that same arrogant manner and disrespect for the troops he was supposed to serve. That must have been why the C.O. picked him for the job. He looked at me suspiciously. "You don't know who HJ is?"

I shook my head. "No." That at least was no lie.

"Okay," he said, letting the matter drop. "Tomorrow I'll take you off the morning report."

On Friday June third, I and two other soldiers going home were taken by truck to the Stuttgart Hauptbahnhof to catch the train to Bremerhaven. Unlike the PFC who came up to me the day I arrived at this station, and clued me in about Germany, I did not tap on the shoulder an American in uniform who looked lost, buy him a piece of cake, and offer him free advice on carnal contacts with Fräuleins on both sides of the color line.

The westerly boat trip home in late spring took seven days, two days off the time it took to cross the Atlantic in an easterly direction in winter. This time I was not the Chaplain's assistant or anyone else's. With some diversionary tactics I managed to avoid being selected at random for any shitty details. I couldn't help noticing that the white sergeants in charge often picked the black privates to mop the floors, clean the latrines, and do the KP that was necessary.

We docked at the Brooklyn Army Terminal late Friday night, the tenth of June. I went on deck early the next morning, eager to see the borough of New York I was born in and to call home the first chance I got. Several troopers stood in a corner looking out over the bay. One was holding a portable radio with the volume turned up. The first song I heard back in the New World was a tune new to me, Sam Cooke's *Wonderful World*. The lyrics referring to academic subjects—biology, trigonometry, history, French—in the context of love caught my attention. Soon I would be a college student grappling with those subjects and looking for romance like any twenty-year-old male. A wonderful world, I hoped, awaited me as a civilian in Coney Island.

Coming off the boat we were scurried into a waiting military bus and taken to Fort Dix. All we were told that Saturday was to put our gear in the barracks, secure it in wall lockers, pick up our weekend pass, change into Class A's if we wanted to leave the post, and return by 0600 Monday, at which time we would begin our processing out of the Army. Inside of an hour I had telephoned home and was on the New Jersey Transit bus to New York.

CHAPTER 21: WELCOME HOME

"David . . . David, you're home," my sister called out to me, jumping up and down like a ten-year-old girl would do.

She was standing in front of our building and saw me get off the Mermaid Avenue bus that stopped across the street at the corner of West 23rd. I hurried to meet her before she stepped off the curb. She reached for me and I lifted her up and kissed her. Her arms tightened around my neck. Just then Mama and Zeyde came out the door and rushed over to me.

"Dovidl . . . Dovidl," my mother cried out. "Borukh hashem . . . thank God." She had tears in her eyes. She pinched me twice on my arm. "Is that you . . . really you?"

Zeyde hugged me. "Dovid . . . Mama told me you called. I don't go out. I vait for you."

I kissed Mama and Zeyde. "I'm so happy to be home, so happy to see all of you. Where's Papa?"

"Upstairs by the window he is," my mother said.

I looked up and saw my father smile and wave to me. I smiled and waved back. Just then I noticed the cardboard sign above the doorway to our building, blocking out the number 2214. **Welcome Home David** it read.

The four of us hugging and kissing, standing in the middle of Mermaid Avenue on a Saturday in late afternoon, attracted the attention of neighbors sitting in their folding chairs near the curb. All eyes were on me in my Class A khaki uniform, someone the busy-bodies had not seen in a year and a half or longer. Mrs. Mittler was not among them and I was grateful for that. The last thing I wanted was for Frau Hitler to come up to me and ask me how I liked Germany, or start talking to me in German. This was like the day I left home, and the day at the Brooklyn Army Terminal, the same people. Later that evening, it would be déjà vu again too.

Just then, Richie crossed the street from his building. This time he was not out of breath and not in his Eisenhower jacket or fatigue shirt or any other remnant of his Army uniform. "Hey, Davey, good to see you," he said, as he extended his hand to me.

I greeted Richie and we chitchatted for a minute or so. I thought he was going to ask me if I got married in Germany but he said nothing of the kind. My sister was standing next to me with her arms around my waist and head to my chest.

Richie stepped back a little. "I gotta run, Davey. We'll go out tonight. I'll come and get you around ten or eleven." Before I could say yes or no, he turned and hurried away. Evidently, my good friend assumed I took his advice and there was no Nazi Schatzie in my life.

Before too long we all went upstairs to the apartment. In my room there was something new, a desk. It looked like a piece of second -hand furniture, but that made no difference. It was just what I need- ed for my new role as student. A large brown envelope from Brook- lyn College sat on top. Papa had gotten the desk for me, stripped it, and put on a coat of varnish. I thanked him for it but I noticed he had somewhat of a sullen look on his face.

I had a wonderful welcome-home party that evening, made pos- sible by the much larger apartment we now had and Zeyde and Papa going down to the grocery to pick up more food and bottles of soda. Aunts, uncles, and cousins came over, some quickly since they lived in Coney Island, others a while later coming from Flatbush. One uncle and his wife traveled the long distance from the Bronx and I very much appreciated that. My overseas bag with civilian clothes arrived the day before and I changed into something more com- fortable. I was the center of attention, bombarded with questions for hours. What did you do in Germany? What did you see in Paris and Rome? What was Israel like? What are your plans now?

By nine o'clock my relatives had gone to their own homes and I could finally relax. What a day it had been. Up early in the morn- ing, getting my gear together, making my way off the ship amid thousands of troopers, being bussed to Fort Dix, bussed back again to New York, taking the subway to Coney Island, hurrying to catch the Mermaid Avenue bus instead of walking seven and a half blocks, hugging and kissing immediate family, shaking hands with a friend, partying with my extended family members, answering questions.

By ten o'clock I had showered and shaved and was sitting at my new desk reading a magazine, waiting for my late night date to show up. At a quarter to eleven I heard someone coming up the stairs to our apartment, familiar footsteps as it were. As he usually did, Richie entered my room without knocking. This time he did not have to plead with me to go out. I was sure he had a welcome-home present planned for me.

"I'm going out with Richie for a little while," I said to my parents in the rear of the apartment. Mama was in the kitchen, Papa was lying down in the bedroom with his clothes on, still looking a little worried about something.

"Boys, don't stay out too long," she warned us, as if I had an early morning call to head back to the barracks or stand reveille on Mermaid Avenue.

"Mama, it's okay. I'll be going back to Fort Dix tomorrow night. I can sleep late."

I let Richie lead the way and didn't ask where he was taking me. It came as no surprise that we did not go to Nathan's for a hot dog and did not go to the Clam Bar for a beer. My lifelong pal and procurer over sixteen months earlier led me along Mermaid a block and a half to 21st Street. We turned left and walked on the right side of the street to a now-familiar basement apartment, garbage cans still out in front.

The puertorriqueña answered the door. She looked at Richie, then at me, and after a moment's hesitation, smiled. "Oh, hello. Bienvenido a casa, G.I.," she said in her linguistic mix.

She recognized me and welcomed me home and I was pleased. Richie pushed the door back and walked in and I followed. The girl was in a snug T-shirt and skimpy shorts, looking sexy as hell. Unlike the last time, we did not wake her up. I took it she was ready for me now and, by her recognition and smile, even keen on satisfying me. My eyes zeroed in on her good-size tits and erotic folds around the crotch.

"Take care of my friend here," Richie said at once. "I'll see you tomorrow."

"Reechee, why you no come yesterday and geeve me what I need?"

"I don't have it," he answered firmly. "I'll be back tomorrow."

What they were talking about I had no idea and dared not ask. It was none of my business. My business was in the bedroom with the girl. Richie took off, she took my hand, walked me to the other room, and closed the door.

The puertorriqueña may not have gotten what she needed that night, and seemed a little high-strung, but she nevertheless gave me what *I* needed. I got head, nice and juicy, and I got tail, nice and tight. She treated me as the handsome americano she said I was the first time I bedded down with her, happy to make amor with me a second time. The Spanish lovemaking bestowed on my body in a grimy Coney Island apartment was far more satisfying than the indifferent affection a cold-blooded and attractive German showed me in a Munich hotel two weeks earlier. I shot off like a rocket, I could hardly contain myself.

I watched her as she slipped back into her panties, my eyes finding those flopping tits I so enjoyed touching and sucking. She put a bathrobe on to see me to the door. I turned to say goodbye and this time she reached up and kissed *me* on the lips. We were lovers after all, it seemed, and perhaps for the foreseeable future too.

"Thank you very much," I said.

"De nada."

"Can I come and see you again?"

She nodded. "Sí . . . and tell Reechee he come."

Whether she wanted to see Richie for a roll in the sack or something else, I didn't want to know. As for me, she and I both knew the purpose for which I will be calling late at night. "Goodbye," I said again. "Hasta la vista."

I went straight home, this time by the longer route, via Neptune Avenue and 23rd Street. It was not yet midnight and I did not wish to run into anyone I knew on 21st near Mermaid. I moved slowly, my body without any tension, and I heard nothing above the calm of the evening. On the bay side of the island, there were no rocks for ocean waves to break against and no life buoys with clanging bells. I was alone, yes, but I was *home* and did not feel abandoned.

On my overseas tour of duty, I had come full circle. The last girl to fit me in before I shipped out to Germany was the first to favor me after I stepped back into the States.

Eleven days before my official termination date, I was discharged. It was the policy of the Army to process soldiers out as soon as they return from overseas, not keep them any longer and have to pay them for additional days. I and the other troopers in my transient company were told a certificate would be mailed to us at our home address when we completed our reserve duty, but for now we would receive papers with the relevant information of our service. We were advised we could apply for unemployment benefits immediately, as the government considers discharge from the military tantamount to being "laid off" from a job.

"You can be proud you served your country," the sergeant in charge of processing said to us that last day. "You can look anybody in the eye and say 'I served my country . . . have *you*'."

That simple statement struck a chord with me. For most of my three years in the Army, I believed I made a mistake by enlisting and yearned for the day when I would be out. Now that the day has arrived, I felt rather good about my service, like the sergeant noted. Much to my surprise, in view of my previous negativity, I even began to feel *nostalgic* about my time in uniform, my tour in Germany especially. That feeling would stay with me for more than half a century.

On Wednesday the fifteenth, I was handed my final papers along with my final pay. In more than temperature and cloud formations, it was a warm and sunny day for me, the start of a new life. At Fort Dix, I had also come full circle. The first Army base I set foot on turned out to be the last I would march on.

A week before the beginning of summer, I bid *my* farewell to arms.

EPILOGUE: GONE BUT NOT FORGOTTEN

In June 1960 I left Fort Dix, New Jersey with papers in hand that read "Honorable Discharge," a stamp of approval by the U.S. Army that would stay with me for the rest of my life. The DD-214 was indicative of the good, or at least faithful, service I performed for Uncle Sam in peacetime, including the occupation of a conquered nation. My record, though not outstanding, was free of Article 15 punishments, courts martial, or trouble with higher authority worthy of a dishonorable or bad conduct discharge. In three years under arms I earned a badge of honor that I could wear always. It was proof of fulfillment of my military obligation and I had a right to list it on college forms for academic credit, applications for employment, and requests for veterans' benefits.

Back home that summer, it was a time of transition for me. My Army life was over, and I tried to forget it. My priority now was to adjust to a new life as a college student. But as I soon came to realize, it was far easier to put my uniforms in mothballs than put Germany out of my mind and erase the seasoned young life I experienced there.

My transition from soldier to student paralleled the presidential election that year. The country was on the verge of a big change too, about to place a new man in the White House regardless of which party was victorious. In July, the young senator from Massachusetts won the Democratic nomination. I watched him on television and listened to his acceptance speech. John Kennedy spoke about the United States being on the edge of a New Frontier, the frontier of the 1960s, the frontier of unknown opportunities and perils in the areas of foreign policy, space exploration, and domestic poverty. I and millions of other people my age were moved by Kennedy's words, vision, optimism, and caution.

The idea of a new frontier appealed to me greatly as it characterized my life at the time. I was a twenty-year-old ex-G.I. ready to enlist in a different army, one comprised of young men and women fighting with books instead of rifles in order to gain valuable ground and reach sought-after targets. Come September, I would be on a New York City college campus, marching across an unknown territory. Like the country I served, I would be facing new opportunities and perils. College enrollment, however, was not the only post-discharge frontier I had to cross. My family and my neighborhood were standing on the edge of a strange border too.

My father, a man who lived through the Great Depression, needed a new deal. His shop in Lower Manhattan closed and relocated to Hong Kong. The textile printers' union had no other factory to assign him to. After twenty-two years of working in the same industry, at age forty-nine and without a high school diploma, Papa had few prospects for another job. He collected unemployment but that would run out in twenty-six weeks. I feared I might have to forgo college and work to help support the family, but my maternal uncle in the Bronx saved us from falling off the brink. He was a baker, learned the trade from Zeyde, and spoke to his union representative about a job for my father. Less than two weeks before I had to enroll in school, Papa was hired as a bakery helper. The starting pay was low, but it was steady work and the breadwinner of the family brought home brown bags filled with bread and cake every day.

Coney Island, I could not help noticing, was more nonwhite than what I recalled before I left for Germany. The city was moving poor black families in the area slated for redevelopment between Ocean Parkway and West 8th Street to Coney's bungalow colony in the West 20s and 30s, a few blocks from our door. And the island of Puerto Rico must have been going through an economic depression, as more and more of its residentes were hopping on airplanes bound for Nueva York. Our corner of the borough was getting a disproportionate share of the newcomers, who often piled into apartments vacated by Jewish and Italian families. Coney residents saw this invasion by two different racial groups as a direct threat to their way of life, but hoped the community would stabilize. The Luna Park Houses, now near completion, were cold and cheerless brown-brick structures shorn of any adornments. They resembled the low-income project north of Neptune between 31st and 33rd Streets, and were not much of an improvement in Coney's character.

The most important frontier I had to cross was the change of mind set. My Army days were gone but not forgotten. I may have left Germany but Germany did not leave me. Overseas I was in a soldiers' field of sexual indulgence and peacetime play. As a civilian in New York, I could not get four Fräuleins out of my head. Karin,

Marianne, Elsa, and the girl in the snack bar represented different facets of my romantic life and still haunted me. I learned about love, the physical kind, with a German girl I cared for but could not marry, with another I craved for more than a year only to be disappointed in our one encounter, with a third who turned me off but opened up to me every time I needed her, and with a colorblind cutie whose name I never got and whose pants I never got into but who rattled my erotic passions. I wondered what kind of girl I would meet in New York or pick up on campus that would lay down for me the way the three in Germany did. The Coney chiquita two blocks away was merely a stopgap, a Spanish combo of a Marianne and an Elsa that could take care of me mañana and mañana.

Germany and the Nazis were still with me in New York, in terms of my reading if nothing else. Newspapers reported that the government of Israel was preparing to try Adolph Eichmann for crimes against the Jewish people, war crimes, crimes against humanity, and membership in a criminal organization. I and the whole world would soon learn more about Hitler's Germany and the architect of the Final Solution than what came out at the Nurenberg trials fifteen years earlier. And I got my hands on another book about Germans and the war that was on the best-seller list, The Last of the Just. *It was a story of a Jew, a righteous soul who bore the world's pains, murdered at Auschwitz. I devoured that novel like I did* Exodus *a few months before.*

Even Hollywood brought Germany home to me that summer, in the form of the Elvis Presley movie G.I. Blues. *I went to see it at a neighborhood theater but I was greatly disappointed by its portrayal of American soldiers in postwar Germany. Obviously scripted to capitalize on Elvis' real-life service in the Army, and filmed on location at his actual Kaserne, the musical-comedy had absolutely nothing to do with a typical soldier's experiences in the Germany Elvis and I just returned from. On screen there were no black soldiers in Elvis' company, no conflicts between Germans and Americans, no derogatory comments about blacks mouthed by white soldiers, no segregated G.I. bars, no focus on Fräuleins who crossed the color line, no references to the war, no mention of the Nazis near destruction of European Jewry. I exited the movie theater stunned by the vacuous presentation of a life that so affected my sensibilities, determined one day to write the true story of Sergeant Presley's and Specialist Streiber's Germany.*

On September 6, 1960, the day after Labor Day, I went to Brooklyn College to register for my tuition-free classes. For more than two years, since that chance meeting with the lieutenant at Fort Monmouth, this was the day I had been striving for. In my wallet, I was packing almost a hundred dollars to pay fees and buy books. For fifteen cents I took the Surf Avenue bus at the corner of 22nd Street to the last stop, walked across Avenue U, and transferred to the Nostrand Avenue bus. I got off at the intersection of Flatbush Avenue and headed toward Avenue H.

The two bus rides were my ticket out of Coney Island.

ABOUT THE AUTHOR

Raymond M. Weinstein was born in Brooklyn, New York in 1939. After graduating from Abraham Lincoln High School in 1957, he enlisted in the U.S. Army. He completed the radar repair course at Fort Monmouth, New Jersey, was assigned to Ford Ord, California, and in January 1959 was transferred to Germany. Following his discharge in June 1960, the author enrolled in Baruch College of the City University of New York, where he received a B.B.A. in business statistics in 1963. He also earned an M.A. in sociology in 1966 and a Ph.D. in sociology in 1968 from the University of California at Los Angeles. He taught sociology at Wilkes University in Wilkes-Barre, Pennsylvania, John Jay College of Criminal Justice, CUNY, and the University of South Carolina at Aiken, where he retired as Distinguished Professor Emeritus of Sociology in 2012.

During his teaching career, the author published more than four dozen academic works—mainly articles in professional journals but also chapters in books and entries for encyclopedias. His writings covered various topics such as mental illness, psychiatric patients, illicit drug use, social service organizations, total institutions, urban communities, Coney Island, Disneyland, amusement parks, and Elvis Presley.

The novel.draws heavily on the author's experiences as an American soldier, especially his final five-month tour of duty in Munich, Germany. He is now working on a sequel, a novel dealing with the main character's life in the 1960s as a college and university student living back home in Coney Island—a Brooklyn neighborhood suffering from white flight, the influx of racial minorities, and the severe deterioration of both its residential section and amusement area. Further sequels dealing with the main character in later years are planned.

The author currently lives in White Plains, New York.

The Author
March 1959
East Block, Merrell Barracks

The Author
July 2010
East Block, Federal Agency for Migration and Refugees
Formerly Merrell Barracks

ACKNOWLEDGEMENTS

In this work of fiction about American soldiers in postwar Germany, social and historical data covering the Nazi era as well as the period from 1945-1960 are included. The author wishes to thank Gerhard Jochem and Susanne Rieger, historical researchers in Nuremberg and Munich, for their cooperation and assistance over several years that greatly aided him in writing accurately about their country in those times. Help with important details was also received from others in Nuremberg, notably Eckart Dietzfelbinger in the Documentation Center at the former Nazi Party Rally Grounds and freelance writer Peter Heigl.

For bits and pieces of data about other cities and sites in Germany, the author is indebted to Stefanie Mühlfelder at the Tourist Information Office in Zirndorf, Hermann Träger at the German Railway Museum, Angela Stilwell at the Munich City Museum, Andreas R. Bräunling at the Dachau City Archives, and Dirk Riedel at the Dachau Concentration Camp Memorial Site.

Thanks are extended to Karl L. Stenger, Associate Professor of German at the University of South Carolina at Aiken, for the correct usage and spelling of German words and terms utilized throughout the book. The author also wishes to acknowledge the following professors and colleagues in the English and Foreign Languages Departments at USC-A, in alphabetical order, for giving him the benefit of their expertise from time to time: Timothy Ashton, J. Donald Blount, William N. Claxon, Stephen L. Gardner, Andrew Geyer, Stanley F. (Shimke) Levine, Tom Mack, Layech Malfoudy, Daniel J. Miller, Lynne Austin Rhodes, and Katie K. Smith.

For particular historical material on Nazi Germany and the United States, the author is indebted to Valdis O. Lumans and James O. Farmer, Jr., his colleagues in the USC-A History Department. For facts about the military of decades past, the assistance of Delores E. Oplinger at the U.S. Army Signal Corps Museum at Fort Gordon in Augusta, Georgia, and Michael Plumley at the Fort Hamilton Post Library in Brooklyn, New York, is greatly appreciated.

The author's primary task of drawing a true picture of what it was like to be an American soldier in Germany in 1959-1960 could not have been accomplished without the exchange of telephone calls and e-mails with his former Army buddies and civilian friends in Nuremberg and Munich at that time, who selflessly shared their recollections of events, people, and military matters of fifty years earlier. Heartfelt gratitude goes out to Michael H. Friedman, Billy B. Capers, Arlene Gottlieb Dryer, Herbert R. Jacobson, and Joel Prives. The memories of Richard A. Gray, Ivor W. Jeffreys, and Thomas Spahr, who were stationed a few years later than the author at his Nuremberg barracks, likewise proved valuable. Ex-G.I.s in Munich about the same time as the author, found via internet websites, willingly aided in descriptions of that city and its U.S. Army posts. Maurice C. Evans, Ralph Falconi, Don Hiett, Ted Hovey, Wayne Perkins, Don Russell, and Stephen A. Wilson deserve acknowledgment here.

Honorable mention should also be given to long-time friends of the author—John B. Manbeck, William H. Marsh, Alexandra Moravec Ocampo, Sheldon Salsberg, Allan H. Sklar, Mary S. Smith-McCarty, and Donna K. West—who over the years assisted him in sorting out his thoughts for this and previous books.

Last but not least, the author's two sons, Rodney J. Weinstein and Marshall S. Weinstein, are singled out for special thanks. They helped their father immensely with the technical/computer elements of book-publishing, listened patiently to his ideas on character and plot, commented intelligently on thematic parts of the novels, and brought into focus the younger generation's point of view on topics and events that took place long before their time.